ROUTLEDGE ·

GENERAL EDITOR

ALEXANDER POPE
Selected Poetry and Prose

ROUTLEDGE · ENGLISH · TEXTS
GENERAL EDITOR · JOHN DRAKAKIS

WILLIAM BLAKE: *Selected Poetry and Prose* ed. David Punter
EMILY BRONTË: *Wuthering Heights* ed. Heather Glen
JOHN CLARE: *Selected Poetry and Prose* ed. Merryn and Raymond Williams
JOSEPH CONRAD: *Selected Literary Criticism and The Shadow-Line* ed. Allan Ingram
CHARLES DICKENS: *Hard Times* ed. Terry Eagleton
JOHN DONNE: *Selected Poetry and Prose* ed. T. W. and R. J. Craik
HENRY FIELDING: *Joseph Andrews* ed. Stephen Copley
BEN JONSON: *The Alchemist* ed. Peter Bement
ANDREW MARVELL: *Selected Poetry and Prose* ed. Robert Wilcher
JOHN MILTON: *Selected Poetry and Prose* ed. Tony Davies
WILFRED OWEN: *Selected Poetry and Prose* ed. Jennifer Breen
ALEXANDER POPE: *Selected Poetry and Prose* ed. Robin Sowerby

Forthcoming

Robert Browning — *Selected Poetry* ed. Aidan Day
Geoffrey Chaucer — *The Wife of Bath's Prologue and Tale and The Clerk's Prologue and Tale* ed. Marion Wynne-Davies
Joseph Conrad — *Heart of Darkness* ed. John Batchelor
George Eliot — *The Mill on The Floss* ed. Sally Shuttleworth
Thomas Hardy — *The Mayor of Casterbridge* ed. J. Bullen
Gerard Manley Hopkins — *Selected Poetry and Prose* ed. R. J. Watt
James Joyce — *Dubliners* ed. Stan Smith
D. H. Lawrence — *Selected Poetry and Prose* ed. John Lucas
Christopher Marlowe — *Dr Faustus* ed. John Drakakis
Mary Shelley — *Frankenstein* ed. Patrick Lyons
Percy Bysshe Shelley — *Selected Poetry and Prose* ed. Alasdair Macrae
Edmund Spenser — *The Faerie Queen Book 1 and Selected Poems* ed. Elizabeth Watson
Virginia Woolf — *To the Lighthouse* ed. Sandra Kemp
William Wordsworth — *Selected Poetry* ed. Philip Hobsbaum
W. B. Yeats — *Selected Poetry and Prose* ed. Graham Martin

ALEXANDER POPE

Selected Poetry and Prose

Edited by
Robin Sowerby

ROUTLEDGE · LONDON AND NEW YORK

First published in 1988 by
Routledge
11 New Fetter Lane,
London EC4P 4EE

Published in the USA by
Routledge
in association with Routledge,
Chapman & Hall, Inc.
29 West 35th Street,
New York NY 10001

Printed in Great Britain by
Richard Clay Ltd, Bungay, Suffolk

British Library Cataloguing in
Publication Data

Pope, Alexander
Alexander Pope: selected poetry
and prose.
I. Title II. Sowerby, Robin—
(Routledge English texts).
828'.509   PR3622

ISBN 0-415-00665-1

Library of Congress
Cataloging in
Publication Data

Pope, Alexander, 1688–1744.
  Selected poetry and prose.

  (Routledge English texts)
  Bibliography: p.
  I. Sowerby, Robin. II. Title. III. Series.
PR3622.S6 1988   821'.5   87–24891
ISBN 0–415–00665–1 (pbk.)

Contents

Introduction

As yet a child, nor yet a fool to fame,
I lisped in numbers, for the numbers came.
(*An Epistle to Dr Arbuthnot*, 127–8)

He considered poetry as the business of his life; and, however he might seem to lament his occupation, he followed it with constancy; to make verses was his first labour and to mend them was his last.[1]

Alexander Pope, born in 1688, the only son of moderately well-to-do Catholic parents (his father was a linen merchant) had a London childhood in comfortable circumstances. His family moved to Binfield in Windsor Forest when he was about 12. He was educated partly by priests in the home, then at a Catholic school in Twyford near Winchester, and subsequently under the tutelage of a former fellow of University College Oxford who had set up a school near Marylebone. His youthful literary endeavours were encouraged by his father and fostered by influential friends. His first publications (*The Pastorals* in 1709, *An Essay on Criticism* in 1711 and the first version of *The Rape of the Lock* in 1712) brought him immediate fame and success. In this period he made a number of enduring friendships with leading literary figures like the satirist Jonathan Swift, John Gay, author of *The Beggar's Opera*, Thomas Parnell, a poet who later gave him scholarly help with his Homer, and Dr John Arbuthnot, man of letters and the Queen's physician. Together they were members of an association calling itself the Scriblerus Club designed in Pope's words to ridicule 'all the false tastes in learning under the character of a man of capacity enough [Martinus Scriblerus] that dipped into every art and science but injudiciously in each'.[2] Later Pope's *Dunciad* (1728) and Swift's *Gulliver's Travels* (1726) doubtless owe much to this earlier association.

The great preoccupation of Pope's life from 1714 when he started translating the *Iliad* to 1726 when the final volumes of the *Odyssey* were published was his translation of Homer. On the proceeds of subscriptions to the project (advance payments made to the poet and his publisher by those who wished to see Homer in modern English and had faith in Pope's ability to prove adequate to the task) he became financially secure and therefore independent of aristocratic patronage and free to shape the course of his literary career.

In addition to the rewards of recognition and success both tangible and intangible, Pope had to endure critical attack from the beginning. In the preface to an edition of his *Works* in 1717, he declared: 'The life of a wit is a warfare upon earth', and in the early eighteenth century that warfare was often prosecuted with a ferocity that may surprise and shock us in the twentieth. The malignant spirit of many of the attacks against Pope is illustrated by Dr Johnson in a quotation from John Dennis, no mere literary hack but a leading critic of the day, who later attacked *The Rape of the Lock* but who is here writing about *An Essay on Criticism*:

Let the person of a gentleman of his parts be never so contemptible, his inward man is ten times more ridiculous; it being impossible that his outward form, though it be that of a downright monkey, should differ so much from human shape as his unthinking immaterial part does from human understanding.[3]

As a boy Pope had contracted a form of tuberculosis which resulted in curvature of the spine and stunted growth so that he was never more than 4 feet 6 inches tall. This condition worsened with age and entailed physical pain and dependence upon others. In the 'Epistle to Dr Arbuthnot' he speaks of 'this long disease, my life' (l. 132). His adversaries readily seized upon his weakness and physical abnormality (in the same poem he also refers to 'The libelled person and the pictured shape' (l. 353)) and much play was made with the letters of his name, A.P..E. He had the support of friends, but was always a controversial figure in the literary life of his times. Even the Homer translation involved him in controversy when he quarrelled with the more genial figure of Joseph Addison over the latter's promotion of a rival (and inferior) version of the first book of the *Iliad* published by his protégé Thomas Tickell. His private response was to compose the portrait of 'Atticus' later included in *An Epistle to Dr Arbuthnot* (1735). He did not intend publication at the time, but the portrait circulated among friends, one of whom, Francis Atterbury, the Bishop of Rochester, encouraged him to employ further the talent it showed for sharp satire. But it was not until Lewis Theobald in his edition of Shakespeare of 1726 pointed out the deficiencies of Pope's own Shakespearian venture published in the previous year that Pope, possibly to forestall further criticism, entered the warfare of the wits with a vengeance that delighted his supporters and dismayed his enemies. *The Dunciad* with Theobald as its hero was published anonymously in 1728 but Pope's authorship was soon suspected. Thereafter he was increasingly drawn to controversial satire, though not exclusively since *An Essay on Man* (1733–4) also belongs to this period. Nevertheless there is a marked change in Pope's literary career after the Homer translation towards the moral, the didactic, and the satiric.

As a result of his literary earnings, in the year after his father died he moved into an elegant country house at Twickenham in 1718, then well outside the city of London, where he lived with his mother until her death in 1733 and then on his own, for he never married, until his death in 1744.

Here he planted the vines and the quincunx which his verses mention; and being under the necessity of making a subterraneous passage to a garden on the other side of the road, he

3

adorned it with fossil bodies, and dignified it with the title of a grotto; a place of silence and retreat, from which he endeavoured to persuade his friends and himself that cares and passions could be excluded.[4]

He cultivated his own garden with diligence and, detached at Twickenham from the life of business and the court yet near enough the centre to be in touch, he lived out his version of the good life dedicated to friendship, conversation, and books that is recommended in many of his poems, notably the verse epistles and of these particularly *The Imitations of Horace*. A collection of letters in prose extending to four large volumes, some of which he published in his own lifetime, provides a record of the style and values of the man and of his various interests and social relationships. His poetry was always his main preoccupation: he continued composing and revising to the end and was working on a final edition of his poems in the last months of his life. It is reported that three weeks before he died he was sorting out presentation copies of the first volume for his friends with the comment:

Here am I, like Socrates, distributing my morality among my friends just as I am dying.[5]

At the time, and more so in retrospect, the year of Pope's birth, 1688, was a momentous one in British constitutional history. For the second time in a century an English monarch was deposed. The execution of Charles I in 1649 came after a prolonged civil war and resulted in the rule of Oliver Cromwell followed by the restoration of the Stuart monarchy in 1660. It must have seemed to those who opposed the absolutism of Charles I that little had been gained after two decades of upheaval, for, although Charles II was invited back by Parliament with whom he negotiated terms, the powers of the monarchy were little restricted. Charles II ruled with greater political sensitivity than his father but the Stuart monarchy came to grief over a question that proved beyond his powers to solve. Charles himself had no legitimate children so that his natural heir on the hereditary principle was his younger brother the Catholic James, Duke of York. The religion of James was seen to be a threat to the established church and to the traditional independence of Britain. Forces in Parliament, predominantly Dissenters (Protestants who separated themselves from the communion of the established Church of England) and low Anglicans proposed to exclude James from the throne. They were opposed by those supporting the royal prerogative (including naturally the King), who were generally high Anglicans. It was at this time that the terms Whig and Tory were first used in opposition as abusive terms to describe supporters and opponents of the Exclusion Bill. To some extent this division echoed the religious and political polarization of the earlier civil war. The King and the anti-exclusionists prevailed, and James succeeded on Charles's death in 1685. His conduct as King, however, confirmed the fears of his opponents and alarmed his supporters, who felt that the established constitution of Church and state was in danger. Whigs and Tories joined forces in 1688 to invite over the Dutch Prince William of Orange, husband of James's daughter Mary who had been brought up on the instructions of Charles II in the Protestant faith. James's army deserted in large numbers and he took refuge in Catholic France at the court of Louis XIV, who continued to uphold his claim to the throne. Parliament offered the throne jointly to William and Mary on conditions set out in a Bill of Rights. The hereditary principle was replaced by a parliamentary succession and the sovereign was required to be Protestant. A number of provisions in the bill shifted power away from the monarch and towards Parliament. Thenceforward the government of the kingdom was more of a partnership between the monarch and the Parliament largely controlled by the nobility. The absolutist tendencies of the Stuart monarchs before 1688 were checked and thereafter England had a more mixed constitution in marked contrast to the absolute monarchy holding sway in France. Nevertheless the monarch continued to exercise great power, and the royal prerogative in appointments and dismissals remained effective throughout the eighteenth century. The Toleration Act of 1689 allowed freedom of worship for Dissenters (though not for Catholics) so that in the so-called 'Glorious Revolution' of 1688–9 a constitutional settlement was achieved without bloodshed that was broadly acceptable to a majority in the kingdom.

Supporters of the exiled James, known as Jacobites from the

Latin version of his name Jacobus, were thereafter always a small minority including many Roman Catholics, some Tory Anglicans who questioned the legitimacy of the succession in 1688 and later, largely for dynastic reasons, many Scots. As Catholics, Pope's family might have felt excluded from the settlement of 1689, for Catholics experienced a variety of restrictions relating to property and residence, education, politics and professional life. Technically they were required to live ten miles from the centre of London. The universities were not open to them, nor could they hold public office. Nevertheless their minority status did not hinder their economic activity even though they were subject to special taxes. Pope's father was a successful businessman. The poet himself retained the religion of his upbringing. In his letters and his poems his Catholicism is not much in evidence, and it is apparent that his religious beliefs were tolerant and enlightened. Nevertheless his religion must have set him apart to some extent from the mainstream of English life. In practice, there was increasing toleration of Catholics doctrinally and at the same time continuing suspicion of them politically in view of the perceived threat from the king over the water. In 1689 James landed in Ireland and was defeated by William at the Battle of the Boyne. In 1708 there was an abortive French invasion. In 1715 came the first Jacobite uprising in Scotland in support of James's son James Edward whose claim was recognized by the French King and who was known subsequently as the Old Pretender, and in the year after Pope died came the final uprising in 1745 in favour of Charles Edward, grandson of James II and called the Young Pretender.

When Pope began his literary career, the childless William and Mary had been succeeded by Mary's younger sister Anne. England was heavily involved in foreign campaigns prosecuted by the Duke of Marlborough, who had succeeded William III as leader of the grand alliance of English and Dutch forces against the power of France. Party rivalry in this period was intense and centred upon Tory resistance to religious toleration promoted by the Whigs and upon Tory attempts to bring to an end the long foreign campaign, which was a drain upon the resources of the gentry. Whig views on foreign policy were promoted by Joseph Addison in *The Spectator* and by Richard Steele in *The Tatler*. The Tory view was promoted in pamphlet form by Jonathan Swift. The Tories were in power when the peace of Utrecht celebrated in 'Windsor Forest' was signed in 1713. Tories and Whigs were not formally organized into parties and the terms are only loosely connected with easily defined values and interests. In this period the Tories are usually identified with the established Anglican Church and the squire-archy and the Whigs with the interests of Dissenters, with the landowning aristocracy, and with the commercial interests of the rising middle classes.

An issue that divided Whigs and some Tories concerned the succession to Queen Anne, none of whose offspring had survived childhood. Even before she came to the throne, Parliament had decreed in 1701 that the succession should go to her nearest Protestant relative, Sophia, the Electress of Hanover, the granddaughter of James I. The Tories reopened the issue in the last year of her reign when illness made her demise likely, making overtures to James Edward, the son of James II, which foundered when he refused to give up his Catholicism. Nevertheless when the Queen died the Tory cause was greatly damaged. One of their leaders, Robert Harley, Earl of Oxford, was imprisoned in the Tower and another, Henry St John, Viscount Bolingbroke, fled the country for France where he became James's Secretary of State. He forfeited his estates and his peerage. Pope had known them both from association in the Scriblerus Club and there seems to be an allusion to their fate at the close of the 'imitation of Horace' addressed to Bolingbroke in 1737 and included in this selection. The new King George, the son of Sophia who had just predeceased Anne, naturally chose his ministers from among the Whigs who had staunchly supported his succession and who remained in the ascendancy for the next fifty years. Many Tories had supported the Hanoverian succession but they were seriously weakened by association with their Jacobite brethren particularly in the wake of the Jacobite uprising in Scotland in 1715.

The Whig ministry was soon dominated by the personality and policy of Sir Robert Walpole, who held the offices of First Lord of the Treasury and Chancellor of the Exchequer continuously from 1721 to 1742. He aimed through continuing Whig supremacy to secure the Hanoverian succession against any aspirations to the contrary among Tory Jacobites. The twin pillars of the policy by which he gained several electoral victories were economic success with low taxation and a peaceful foreign policy. He gained the confidence of George I (1714–27) and of his son who succeeded him, and was able to use their power of royal patronage to party advantage. Never before had so much power been concentrated in any of the monarch's ministers, and this great power itself was often the main target of attack on the part of his critics. To opponents his extensive network of patronage was corrupt, and his peaceable foreign policy an expediency which appeased Britain's commercial rivals. The unpopularity of individual financial measures could be exploited by the opposition, but in general Walpole's economic management was successful. Many historians look back upon his rule as a time of political stability and growing national prosperity. One of his main opponents was Pope's friend Bolingbroke who had been pardoned in 1723 and allowed to return to England. In the early 1730s Bolingbroke sought to build up a new Country party made up of former Tories and Whig opponents of Walpole, with the aim of protecting the independence of Parliament against what they regarded as the corruption of Walpole's government. In the later 1730s a new opposition group of self-styled 'patriots' gathered around George II's son Frederick, the Prince of Wales, for which Bolingbroke wrote his most famous work, *The Idea of a Patriot King*. But none of his political aspirations came to anything, and when Walpole was eventually removed it was because in the eyes of his own supporters he had outlived his usefulness. The Whigs then regrouped under new leadership.

Pope had always had friends and social contacts across the main religious and political divisions, though his own inclinations were undoubtedly Tory, as his early association with the Scriblerians and his continuing friendship with Bolingbroke might indicate. To what extent he may from time to time have had Jacobite leanings it is difficult to say. In 'Windsor Forest' he happily identified himself with the ruling powers in the land and praised the peace of Utrecht recently negotiated by the

Tories and disapproved of by some of the Whigs. After 1714, he was no longer a political 'insider', but since as a Catholic he was not eligible for office he could never have contemplated the kind of career in which literature went hand in hand with government service as in the case of the Whig Addison or the Tory Swift. Hence the events of 1714 were not the personal blow to Pope that they were to his Protestant friend Swift. In an age when most literary men had some clear political affiliation and when poets were courted by politicians, perhaps because of his religion and his health, Pope remained more detached than most. In this of course he was aided by the financial independence he achieved through his Homer translation. He was never a party man and never addressed political issues as directly as, for example, John Dryden, who as poet laureate at the court of Charles II had written many poems in support of the government, notably *Absalom and Achitophel* in 1686. Pope always prided himself upon his independence, and in his poems his expression is often teasingly elusive:

> My head and heart thus flowing through my quill,
> Verse-man or prose-man, term me which you will,
> Papist or Protestant, or both between,
> Like good Erasmus, in an honest mean,
> In moderation placing all my glory,
> While Tories call me Whig, and Whigs a Tory.
>
> ('To Mr Fortescue', ll. 63–8)

Nevertheless part of that independence was not merely detachment but conscious opposition to Walpole and all his works. *The Imitations of Horace* are not exclusively political poems, but one of the more marked ways in which they differ from their originals, in which Horace represents himself in broad sympathy with the ruling order, stems from Pope's oppositional stance.

INTRODUCTION TO THE POEMS

The best introduction to the literary career of Pope is one of his own earliest works, *An Essay on Criticism*, published in 1711 when he was only 23, in which the young poet sought to clarify for himself and his times both the principles necessary for the formation of good judgement and the spirit in which the critic should set about his task. In the course of it, he renews in contemporary terms traditional humanist ideas about art and its relation to the nature of things that were part of the common European inheritance from the classical world. Here is the most positive and attractive representation of that broad-based humanism in the light of which he later attacked false learning, improper study, short views, narrow interests, and bad taste, in *The Moral Essays, An Epistle to Dr Arbuthnot* and *The Dunciad*. If we survey his literary life as a whole, it serves almost as a manifesto, though it was doubtless not quite intended as such at the time.

In its form, organization, and style the *Essay* emulates the achievement of the Roman Augustan poet Horace as poet and critic in his verse epistles on the subject of art and literature, notably his *Ars Poetica*. Pope's characterization of Horace in the *Essay* may virtually be applied to himself:

> Horace still charms with graceful negligence,
> And without method talks us into sense,
> Will, like a friend, familiarly convey
> The truest notions in the easiest way.
> He, who supreme in judgement, as in wit,
> Might boldly censure, as he boldly writ,
> Yet judged with coolness, though he sung with fire;
> His precepts teach but what his works inspire.

(ll. 653–60)

Both poets have in common a particular conception of good sense, ease of expression and address, the rare art of being attractively didactic (for the *Essay* is a work of exuberant wit), and a paradoxical blend of coolness and fire in which critical authority is allied to poetic talent so that the poem becomes the embodiment of the critical attitudes it advocates.

But if the *Essay* is to serve as a useful introduction, we must attempt to follow Pope's own principle:

> A perfect judge will read each work of wit
> With the same spirit that its author writ.

(ll. 233–4)

In some accounts of Pope, the *Essay* is used to deduce a rather formidable set of period attitudes labelled 'neo-classical' often on the assumption that it only has real value as a period piece. With this assumption may also be found the feeling that the characteristic attitudes of the period stressing imitation of the ancients and adherence to the rules were narrow and limiting. Allied to this feeling is the prejudice that no critic before Coleridge in the nineteenth century can have much of value to say about literature because of the limiting terms in which the discussion is conducted. The world has moved on since Pope. But with a little historical perspective, we can see not only that the *Essay* transcends the narrower limitations of its time, but also that it embodies a critical ideal that can still challenge us today.

The *Essay* was written at a time when the so-called 'Querelle des anciens et des modernes' which had caused much intellectual ferment in France was reverberating in England. One extreme felt that the moderns could not possibly compete with the established masterpieces of the ancients; modern culture was inevitably overshadowed; the other that the unenlightened ancients had been superseded by the moderns writing in an age when man had come of age through exploration of the natural sciences. Ancient or modern is not of course merely an argument in this period but one for all time. In the twentieth century our ancients are no longer the classics of Greece and Rome but the classics of our own literature of which Pope is one. The years spent on the Homer translation and *The Imitations of Horace* testify to the veneration of the ancients ('Hail, bards triumphant!', l. 189) expressed in the *Essay*. But as a modern poet who was confident of his own talent and ability he approached the great authors of the past not in a spirit of abject humility but as a potential equal who hoped to rival their success. At its creative best, the Renaissance impulse did not of course aim at reproduction of the ancients (such an aim was a snare and delusion since the world has indeed moved on from antiquity) but rather sought inspiration from the great ancients that might aid fresh creative endeavour in the present. There is all the difference in the world between imitation that is servile and imitation (and translation too) that is creative. It is not therefore surprising to find that Pope in the *Essay* avoids extremes and is neither ancient nor modern. The comprehensiveness of his mind precluded allegiance to the narrower dogmas of his day:

> Some foreign writers, some our own despise;
> The ancients only, or the moderns prize.
> Thus wit, like faith, by each man is applied
> To one small sect, and all are damned beside . . . .
> Regard not then if wit be old or new,
> But blame the false, and value still the true.
>
> (ll. 394–7, 406–7)

These lines are eloquent testimony to his catholic taste and to the searching independent spirit that informs the *Essay* and the literary career to which it is a prelude.

If we are to judge the spirit of the work, then we must have a sympathetic understanding of the terms in which Pope discusses literature, both in the more general sense and also literally in giving back to words like 'wit' and 'judgement' (which may roughly be translated as the creative and the critical faculty respectively) the richer meaning they had in his time. In passing it may be noted that Pope allows no simple distinction between them for judgement is necessary to the poet just as true taste in the critic is an inner light derived from heaven. But even when it is acknowledged that Pope's terms have a wider range than the same words today, there remains a further stumbling block in the way of sympathetic appreciation of the account of poetry contained in the *Essay*. Pope followed Aristotle and Horace in maintaining the clear distinction of the ancient rhetorical tradition between sense, *res* (matter), and style, *verba* (words), using the old metaphor in which language is the dress of thought. In pre-Romantic criticism sense and style, or content and form, are brought together in the central concept of decorum or propriety:

> For different styles with different subjects sort,
> As several garbs, with country, town, and court.
>
> (ll. 322–3)

As imitation of the ancients can be either servile or creative so the concept of decorum can be mechanically or imaginatively applied. In Pope's case, we owe the different strengths of *The Dunciad* and *The Rape of the Lock*, as well as the Homer translation, to his discriminating sense of the linguistic requirements of an heroic poem. As to the larger question of form and content, for practical reasons the distinction continues to be made, and it is very difficult to continue the discussion of literature for long without falling into it even if it is recognized, as doubtless Aristotle, Horace, and Pope recognized, that ultimately the distinction is invalid.

However, the main thrust of the argument about criticism in the *Essay* emerges clearly enough. Pope asserts what was for him a principle by which he sought to guide his whole life, that criticism and poetry should serve human ends in the widest sense. The critic must certainly be learned ('A little learning is a dangerous thing', l. 215) but learning is not enough ('So by false learning is good sense defaced', l. 25). Memorable is the ridicule of the impertinent critic:

> The bookful blockhead, ignorantly read,
> With loads of learned lumber in his head.

(ll. 612–13)

It is the way in which learning is applied that is stressed. For true judgement involves the whole man ('Nor in the critic let the man be lost', l. 523) just as it must concern itself with the whole work in its total effect. The true critic must 'survey the whole' (l. 235), judging the parts by the end they serve; those who judge (and write for) artistic effect alone whether it be conceit (imagery, particularly like that of the metaphysical poets, ll. 289ff), style (ll. 305ff), or numbers (versification, ll. 337ff) concentrate upon the means at the expense of the end and so fall short of the comprehensiveness required for true judgement whether in critic or poet. This comprehensiveness, which is so striking an ideal in the *Essay*, is not to be achieved without rigorous self-examination for the true critic (and artist) must seek to transcend prejudice, party spirit, idiosyncrasy, envy, and above all pride and self-conceit. The character of the good critic (ll. 629–44) is therefore the character of the good man ('Good nature and good sense must ever join', l. 524). Pope constantly keeps before us the relation between poetry, criticism, and moral sense. True wit, true judgement, and true taste do not merely belong to a realm we might label the aesthetic; they are only possible when literary endeavours are fully integrated with the rest of life. The *Essay* offers a useful introduction to Pope, but its real value is the value it had for its first audience; it challenges us as readers, and every reader is a potential critic, to examine both the grounds of our taste, and the criteria we apply in making our judgements.

The central proposition in which the broad-based humanism of the *Essay* is grounded is a declaration of faith, almost a hymn to the divine and unchanging light of nature, in language that suggests the first cause:

> First follow Nature, and your judgement frame
> By her just standard, which is still the same:
> Unerring Nature, still divinely bright,
> One clear, unchanged, and universal light,
> Life, force, and beauty, must to all impart,
> At once the source, and end, and test of Art.

(ll. 68–73)

Here is Pope's belief in the underlying order that gives dignity, beauty, and meaning to the cosmos. Included in this metaphysical conception is a statement about the nature of man. Within the grand scheme of things, man has his appointed place, and man stands in the same relation to nature irrespective of considerations of time and place, or culture and society. The proposition

> Nature and Homer were, he found, the same

(l. 135)

entails a belief that, however different archaic Greece and eighteenth- or twentieth-century Britain may be, these differences are the accidents of time and place, for what Homer had achieved in his poems is the representation of humanity in its timeless aspects. Homer enables us to see clearly how man stands in relation to nature, to things as they are. The equation of Homer with nature may be said to embrace both content and form; what is natural is both the object represented, that is human passions and actions, and the manner of representation, that is narrative method and style. Let us take, for example, the

14

main plot of the *Iliad* revolving around the anger of Achilles. Homer does not waste time telling us about inessential aspects of Achilles' life and character that do not have a bearing upon his anger, nor does he tell us about the siege of Troy from the beginning. He begins in the middle of things concentrating attention only upon those particulars which relate to his central theme. This selectivity, Homer's *method*, enables us to see Achilles' behaviour in a clear light because we are given a central core without distracting and inessential particulars. Of course much of the *Iliad* may seem to have little direct bearing upon the main action, but in the final analysis the episodes are subordinate to the irreducible plot. Achilles is powerfully individualized so that it is not being suggested that Homer has created bloodless archetypes. But he has arranged his main plot around the anger in such a way as to give us a pattern of behaviour that in its causes and effects represents a probable if not inevitable sequence. Underneath all that is particular and individual, the anger is typical in its causes and consequences, and it is Homer's method or art that enables us to see this. Homer the artist has therefore accomplished in his poems all that Aristotle the philosopher and critic held to be the end of art; he has imposed form and order on the undifferentiated matter and random chaos of life thus enabling us to see through the particular to the universal.

It is in this light that the famous lines defining true wit are to be understood:

> True wit is Nature to advantage dressed;
> What oft was thought, but ne'er so well expressed;
> Something, whose truth convinced at sight we find,
> That gives us back the image of our mind.
>
> (ll. 297–300)

To dress Nature to advantage is to express the universal whose truth we respond to because it is bound up with our essential humanity. The famous first couplet is not of course end-stopped, and its sense is extended and clarified in the couplet that follows. When the sentence is completed and related to the ideas of the *Essay*, it is apparent that by 'what oft was thought, but ne'er so well expressed' Pope means to suggest rather more

15

than that poetry is the elegant and polished expression of commonplace notions. It is unfortunate that the line can lend itself to such a banal interpretation. What he means by a truth that convinces at sight may perhaps be illustrated by the famous remarks of Johnson on Gray's *Elegy*:

> The *Churchyard* abounds with images which find a mirror in every mind, and with sentiments to which every bosom returns an echo. The four stanzas beginning 'Yet even these bones' are to me original: I have never seen the notions in any other place; yet he that reads them here, persuades himself that he has always felt them.[6]

It is also in the light of this Aristotelian view that Pope's account of language and expression must be understood:

> False eloquence, like the prismatic glass,
> Its gaudy colours spreads on every place;
> The face of Nature we no more survey,
> All glares alike, without distinction gay:
> But true expression, like the unchanging sun,
> Clears and improves whate'er it shines upon,
> It gilds all objects, but it alters none.
>
> (ll. 311–17)

This has sometimes been understood to mean that artistic expression offers an improved version of reality, a gilded world that comforts us because it is what we might wish our own to be. But true expression does not alter objects; they are simply seen in a clearer light; it is our perception through the superior clarity of the artist's vision that is improved. The root idea is that it is the sacred function of art to throw the universal into a clear radiant light, and the sacred duty of the artist to render and express his vision with emphatic clarity. In *An Essay on Man* the poet's re-creating vision restores to man as far as this is possible in a fallen world the image of his humanity as God intended it (see p. 156). In *The Dunciad*, the effect of Dullness is

> To blot out order, and extinguish light.
>
> (IV, 14)

Dullness undoes creation:

Light dies before thy uncreating word.

(IV, 654)

In Pope's exalted conception of its nature and function, art brings man into new or renewed awareness of the profoundest truths.

The central proposition about nature is immediately followed by an injunction to the would-be critic to have due regard to the rules of art. In the modern world in which we have long been accustomed to the breakdown in traditional art forms in the interests of artistic freedom and experiment, a belief in the validity of rules or guidelines sanctioned by tradition is perhaps difficult to comprehend and may even seem faintly absurd. To the Romantics and the nineteenth century when there was greater emphasis upon the creative imagination in theories of art it also seemed to betoken an unduly mechanical attitude for poetry of the highest seriousness was felt in Arnold's phrase to be 'conceived in the soul', having little to do with abstract rules. Yet a preoccupation with the rules of art is an ancient one and not merely an aberration of this particular period. In other arts it is perhaps easier to understand the emphasis upon basic groundrules of the craft. In antiquity the ideal proportion between height and breadth in a building or between limbs and torso in the representation of the human form was arrived at in the first instance by precise measurement. In the Renaissance great artists like Leonardo da Vinci and Dürer made mathematical studies of proportion and consciously set out to establish the rules that constituted their findings. The rules are not regarded as a human invention but exist and are given in the nature of things rather as the laws of physics describe the underlying pattern of the natural world:

> Those rules of old discovered, not devised,
> Are Nature still, but Nature methodised.

(ll. 88–9)

The method that Homer discovered according to Aristotle 'by natural genius or knowledge of his art' is described by the Greek critic in his *Poetics*, and the principles there identified, such as beginning in the middle of things, concentration of time and events, unity of action, consistency of characterization, subordination of the episodes to the main plot, all came in the course of time to acquire the force of *rules*, though in fact Aristotle was not writing prescriptively but offering a philosopher's reasoned analysis of the principles underlying the masterpieces of Greek art.

The *Poetics* is a fragmentary work, mostly about tragedy but with incidental remarks about epic and other genres. Aristotle identifies the object and end of tragedy, and breaks the form into its constituent parts, analysing the means by which the end is achieved in the best sort of tragedy. He therefore himself bequeathed a method which by the time of Pope had long been systematically extended by Italian and French critics to other classical genres such as comedy or pastoral and even to non-classical genres such as tragicomedy or romance. Rules might concern the use of particular metres for particular genres, the need to keep the genres distinct and separate, to adopt an appropriate style (grand for epic or humble for pastoral), to observe proportion in structure (five acts for drama), to observe the three unities in drama (Aristotle in fact only talks about unity of action), to keep consistency in characterization, and to use spectacle and divine intervention sparingly, rigorously to subordinate the parts to the whole thereby keeping the end in view all the time, and so on. At the root of all this of course is the Renaissance admiration for the classics of Greece and Rome which were thought to have established standards of excellence in the various genres which might be emulated in the vernacular. These inspired literary masterpieces are seen to embody principles of organization and design which had enabled the poet to render the essential truth of things in the most appropriate form:

> Learn hence for ancient rules a just esteem;
> To copy Nature is to copy them.

(ll. 139–40)

The just esteem for ancient rules is balanced in Pope by a vigorous defence of the poet's right boldly to deviate from the common track and essentially to make his own rules, for rules are but a means to an end, not an end in themselves, and there is a grace beyond the reach of art (ll. 141–57).

The freedom and flexibility Pope reserved for the poet in respect of the rules reflect a freedom and flexibility he felt in relation to the masterpieces of the past from which they were principally drawn. The past was of value to Pope as it might serve the cause of true civilization in the present. Even in those poems which may seem on the face of it to be most reliant upon ancient form because they are written in genres that do not have a currency after the eighteenth century, Pope's design springs from contemporary concern. He unites the style and conventions of epic with the incongruous subject-matter of *The Rape of the Lock* not of course to mock epic, but to bring to bear upon the trivial social behaviour of the fashionable world the serious perspective afforded by epic and Homer's very different society of heroes. Yet, though this incongruity between present and past is central to the design and effect of the poem, we are also made subtly aware of occult resemblances between things apparently unlike, between polite society and the world of epic. To give one example, when Umbriel undertakes his journey to the gloomy Cave of Spleen bearing in his hand a branch of healing spleenwort, we are reminded of journeys to the underworld in classical epic. In Virgil's *Aeneid*, Aeneas entering Hades with the Golden Bough meets in spirit form all the monsters and miseries that have plagued him in the upper world. Umbriel has a parallel encounter with the miseries that afflict the polite world of Belinda: Pain, Megrim, Ill-Nature, and Affectation. Instead of classical monsters, the cave is inhabited by horrors appropriate to the female world:

> Here sighs a jar, and there a goose-pie talks:
> Men prove with child, as powerful fancy works,
> And maids turned bottles call aloud for corks.

> (IV, 52–4)

The comic miniaturization may perhaps be regarded as a parody, but startling is Pope's own note on the goose-pie: 'alludes to a real fact; a lady of distinction imagined herself in this condition'. The sexual implications of the final line have often been commented upon. The passage is not wholly nonsensical; it glances at dangers and frustrations attendant upon the social life of the *beau monde*. In fact the Cave of Spleen might be said to be translation of the classical underworld in terms appropriate to the polite society illustrated in the poem. From these dissimilar images drawn from the literature of the past and the society of the present, Pope's wit creates a new combination integrating past and present.

The integration of past and present is what he aims for in the translation of Homer. On the one hand, he used every means at his disposal to avail himself of the learning of his day and arrive at the best historical understanding of the poems following his own advice in the *Essay*:

> Know well each ancient's proper character:
> His fable, subject, scope in every page;
> Religion, country, genius of his age.
>
> (ll. 119–21)

Had the moderns of Pope's day made such an effort to acquire this historical understanding:

> None e'er had thought his comprehensive mind
> To modern customs, modern rules confined;
> Who for all ages writ and all mankind.
>
> (cancelled from the *Essay* after l. 124)

Deliberate modernizing he therefore despised. On the other hand the ancient poem has to be reconciled with the modern world and modern expression. This is the eternal problem of translation which must always be a compromise between the original and the translator, for there can be no such thing as an absolute translation. In years to come translations of our own day, which may now seem nearer to the original than Pope's, will appear equally of their time while lacking in most cases the creativity to transcend it. Pope made a virtue of necessity and aimed at fidelity not to Homer's words but to his spirit and to all that is implied in the equation of Homer with nature. While never intending to impose modern sense upon Homer, he nevertheless used a modern form, the heroic couplet, to render the classical hexameter, and would not have been in sympathy with the desire for an ideal reproduction of Homer's metrical effect expressed by Matthew Arnold in his *Lectures on translating Homer*. He was equally wary of archaizing:

20

Some by old words to fame have made pretence,
Ancients in phrase, mere moderns in their sense.

(ll. 324–5)

He aimed as always to integrate ancient and modern, rendering ancient sense as faithfully as modern expression might allow.

Of all the ancient inheritance no form was more valued by Pope than the epic deemed in the Renaissance, despite the clear preference of Aristotle in his *Poetics* for tragedy, to be the highest and noblest of genres. Right at the end of his life, he was still contemplating the idea of a national epic on the subject of Brutus (a son of the Trojan Priam), who according to legend had brought civilization from Troy to Britain, rather as the Trojan Aeneas had brought civilization to Italy (the subject of Virgil's *Aeneid*). A fragment written in 1743 survives:

> The patient chief, who labouring long, arrived
> On Britain's shore and brought with favouring gods
> Arts, arms and honour to her ancient sons:
> Daughter of Memory! from elder time
> Recall; and me, with Britain's glory fired,
> Me, far from meaner care or meaner song,
> Snatch to thy holy hill of spotless bay,
> My country's poet, to record her fame.

The Brutus fragment suggests that Pope's epic aspirations were not satisfied by translation, or by *The Rape of the Lock* and *The Dunciad*, but the same preoccupation with national life that it reveals ('arts, arms and honour') was successfully expressed in other interrelated genres, in the epistles, the moral essays, the satires, and *The Imitations of Horace*.

It is at this point that we may consider the meaning and propriety of the term 'Augustan' when it is frequently applied to Pope and his age. As a period term in Roman civilization it covers the rule of Rome's first emperor from the time when, after he had defeated Mark Antony at the battle of Actium in 31 BC, he renounced the power he had held as the triumvir Octavian and adopted the name Augustus from 27 BC to his death in AD 14. Abroad, Augustus consolidated the conquests of his predecessors by a programme of urbanization and a series of treaties with neighbouring states by which he secured the Roman frontiers; at home, he revised the old republican constitution, investing supreme power in himself as Imperator, commander of the armed forces, though disguising his power under republican forms, for his rule was ratified in the traditional way by the Senate and the popular assembly. After nearly a century of wars and civil strife, including two major civil wars, he gradually brought peace, order, and stability to Rome and her dominions. He initiated moral reforms in which he attempted to breathe new life into the old religion and instituted a grand programme of public building so that it was said of him that he found Rome brick and left it marble. He fostered the arts through the patronage of his friend Maecenas. The foremost poets of the age, Virgil and Horace, though they had been on the opposing side in the civil war, accepted the patronage of Maecenas, identified themselves with the new order, and gave expression in their poems on public themes to the new mood of self-confidence generated by the Augustan peace. Their poems are sometimes called Augustan to denote their relation to the political order and to suggest the conditions under which they were produced. But the term goes further than this to suggest a quality in the art of the poems, for the works of Virgil and Horace have been seen to have a formal polish and a refinement of expression that set them apart from the literature of the previous age, and a poise and balance that set them apart from the literature that followed. These qualities of polish, refinement, urbanity, and poise have been considered to be the hallmarks of Augustan literature, representing the high-water mark of Roman culture and civilization. It is the indubitable fact of the supreme literary achievement of Virgil and Horace that has sustained and propagated an Augustan myth wherein Latin comes to perfection of expression in the golden age of the rule of Augustus (the phrase 'golden Latin' referring to this period being a commonplace of Roman literary history), made possible by the interlocking relationship of poetry, patronage, and political power, for Virgil and Horace achieve greatness not in spite of Augustus but because of him.

This myth, embodying an ideal for some, masking reality for others, exerted a powerful fascination upon the nation states of modern Europe seeking in their cultural aspirations to emulate Greece and Rome. In his youth in Queen Anne's reign Pope had celebrated the peace of Utrecht in 'Windsor Forest', a poem inspired by the *Georgics* in which Virgil celebrated man's fruitful cultivation of the natural world in the Italian countryside made possible after peace had been restored to the political order by Augustus. But after 1714 he no longer identified himself with the ruling powers in the land, becoming with the passing of time increasingly alienated from the government and its aims, and the financial independence he achieved through his Homer translation allowed him to be independent of patron and court. In his imitation of the verse epistle addressed by Horace to Augustus (with whom the Roman poet is reported to have had cordial relations), he brilliantly uses the Augustan parallel for satirical effect since the Hanoverian King George Augustus to whom he addresses Horace's lines, in the power of Whig politicians and no lover of poetry (in his reign Colley Cibber, later to be the hero of Pope's new *Dunciad*, was created poet laureate), was no Caesar and no Augustus:

> While you, great patron of mankind, sustain
> The balanced world, and open all the main;
> Your country, chief, in arms abroad defend,
> At home, with morals, arts, and laws amend;
> How shall the Muse from such a monarch steal
> An hour, and not defraud the public weal?
> 'The first epistle of the second book of Horace imitated'
> (ll. 1–6)

Although his relation to the Horatian original is ironic at the opening here and at the end where he again addresses the august majesty of the king, in the main body of the epistle he is concerned with two arguments that seek to set a value upon poetry and to vindicate the literature of his time. The first concerns the role of poetry in the *civitas*; in its highest form poetry is useful to the state, *utilis urbi*:

> Yet let me show a poet's of some weight,
> And (though no soldier) useful to the state.
>
> (ll. 203–4)

23

The argument continues by asserting that the great genres like epic and drama in which the Greeks excelled have a moral civilizing function. There is no doubt that Pope strongly identified himself with Horace in their common endeavour in the humbler genre of the moral essay to fulfil the civilizing office of the poet as the standard-bearer and guardian of cultural values. The second thrust of the epistle is the vindication of the Augustan aesthetic (and moral) values of refinement, urbanity, and polish:

> Wit grew polite, and numbers learned to flow.
> Waller was smooth; but Dryden taught to join
> The varying verse, the full-resounding line,
> The long majestic march, and energy divine.
> Though still some traces of our rustic vein
> And splayfoot verse remained, and will remain.
> Late, very late, correctness grew our care,
> When the tired nation breathed from civil war.

(ll. 266–73)

This part of the Augustan equation is also made in all seriousness.

It may seem ironic that neither Horace nor Pope wrote in either of the great genres, tragedy or epic. Augustus himself, it may be inferred, believed that Horace had an epic subject for we find the poet repeatedly declining to sing Caesar's achievements, alleging lack of proper talent so to do. The Augustan aspiration for a national epic may be though to have been fulfilled in Rome by Virgil's *Aeneid*. But for Pope, feeling as he did about the state of Britain, the contemporary world offered no subject about which he felt a deep conviction, so that he only toyed with the Brutus legend late in life and the great Augustan poem of his dreams never materialized. The nearest he came to it is perhaps the epic satire of *The Dunciad*.

THE TEXT

Pope's poems were published in many editions in his lifetime; there are over fifteen, for example, of *An Essay on Criticism* (first published in 1711), and even four of a late poem like the

'Imitation of Horace' addressed to Bolingbroke *c.* 1737. Pope published his *Works* in 1717 and took up the task again in 1735. Temperamentally he was a perfectionist, as an artist his method was perpetually to refine his first thoughts (see *Critical commentary*, pp. 218–23), and as a professional man of letters he had an intense concern for his reputation. All these factors led him to take an active interest in successive editions of his poems, which he constantly revised.

Sometimes the changes are major. *The Rape of the Lock* was expanded from two to five cantos between the first and second editions, and the speech of Clarissa in canto V was not added until 1717. The 'Epistle to a lady' was considerably expanded in later editions. *The Dunciad* was radically rewritten with a new hero and the addition of a fourth book in 1743.

In most other poems there are some changes, and even though the general reader might consider the majority of them to be minor, since these later revisions have usually been incorporated into the text, it should be borne in mind that the dates of composition and publication given after each poem cannot be taken as absolute.

In his own arrangement of the poems, Pope did not follow a strict chronological plan, but grouped together, for example, the *Epistles to Several Persons* (later to be called *The Moral Essays*) and *The Imitations of Horace* without regard to dates of publication. Editors have generally followed his example here. The order of the poems in this selection is the traditional one, roughly but not strictly chronological. Readers assessing the shape of Pope's career should note that, although all the extracts from *The Dunciad* are placed at the end of this volume since they are taken from the substantially revised edition of 1743, the first *Dunciad* appeared in 1728 not long after the completion of the Homer translation.

In his last years and in declining health Pope fell under the influence of William Warburton, who prevailed upon him to make changes in some of his texts and whom Pope made his literary executor. After the poet's death, Warburton published an influential edition of his *Works* in 1751. The influence of Warburton on the text of Pope has only recently been unscrambled by the editors of the Twickenham edition, which must be regarded as the standard modern edition of the poems. The Twickenham editors generally retain the typography, spelling, and punctuation of the eighteenth century, which have been modernized in the text of this selection. Though occasionally capitals and contractions have been retained in the interests of emphasis and rhythm, for the most part the text conforms to modern usage. The standard modern texts of Pope for reference are:

The Twickenham Edition of the Poems of Alexander Pope, general editor John Butt, in ten volumes, London and New Haven: Methuen, 1938–68, with index (volume XI edited by Maynard Mack, 1969). Available in a single volume edited by John Butt, London: Methuen, 1963, University paperback, 1965.

The Prose Works of Alexander Pope, volume one 1711–20 edited by Norman Ault, Oxford: Blackwell, 1936, and volume two 1725–44 edited by Rosemary Cowler, Oxford: Blackwell, 1986.

The Correspondence of Alexander Pope, edited by George Sherburn, in five volumes, Oxford: Clarendon Press, 1956.

Other useful texts are given in the bibliography.

NOTES TO THE INTRODUCTION

1 From Samuel Johnson, *The Life of Pope*. The standard scholarly edition is *Lives of the English Poets by Samuel Johnson*, edited by George Birkbeck Hill, 3 vols, London: 1905. For convenience references in these notes are to the Everyman edition in two volumes, London and New York: Dent, 1925, here to vol. 2, p. 211.

2 Pope's own comment to Joseph Spence in *Anecdotes . . . of Books and Men by Joseph Spence*, edited by James M. Osborn, Oxford: Clarendon Press, 1966.

3 Johnson, *Life*, p. 151.

4 Ibid. p. 172. The verses mentioned occur in the Horatian imitation 'To Mr Fortescue', line 130, included in this selection.

5 *Spence*, p. 318, cited by F. W. Bateson in Volume III, ii of

The Twickenham Edition of the Poems of Alexander Pope, general editor John Butt, in ten volumes, London and New Haven: Methuen, 1938–68. Poems referred to in the introduction and the commentary which are not included in the selection may be consulted there, or in the one-volume Twickenham edition edited by John Butt, London: Methuen, 1963, University paperback, 1965.

6 Johnson, *Life of Gray*, Everyman edition, vol. 2, p. 392.

ALEXANDER POPE
Selected Poetry and Prose

ODE ON SOLITUDE

Happy the man, whose wish and care
  A few paternal acres bound,
Content to breathe his native air
      In his own ground.

Whose herds with milk, whose fields with bread,
  Whose flocks supply him with attire,
Whose trees in summer yield him shade,
      In winter fire.

Blest, who can unconcernedly find
  Hours, days, and years slide soft away,   10
In health of body, peace of mind,
      Quiet by day.

Sound sleep by night; study and ease,
  Together mixed; sweet recreation:
And innocence, which most does please,
      With meditation.

Thus let me live, unseen, unknown,
  Thus unlamented let me die,
Steal from the world, and not a stone
      Tell where I lie.   20

Composed c. 1700   *First published 1717*

from BOETIUS, DE CONS. PHILOS.

O thou, whose all-creating hands sustain
The radiant heavens, and earth, and ambient main!
Eternal Reason! whose presiding soul
Informs great nature and directs the whole!
Who wert, ere time his rapid race begun,
And bad'st the years in long procession run:
Who fixed thy self amidst the rolling frame,
Gavest all things to be changed, yet ever art the same!
Oh teach the mind to ætherial heights to rise,
And view familiar, in its native skies,   10
The source of good; thy splendour to descry,

---

* Numbers in square brackets refer to pages on which notes may be found.

And on thy self, undazzled, fix her eye.
Oh quicken this dull mass of mortal clay;
Shine through the soul, and drive its clouds away!
For thou art Light. In thee the righteous find
Calm rest, and soft serenity of mind;
Thee they regard alone; to thee they tend;
At once our great original and end,
At once our means, our end, our guide, our way,
Our utmost bound, and our eternal stay! 20

Composed c. 1710   First published 1717

ADRIANI MORIENTIS AD ANIMAM,
OR
THE HEATHEN TO HIS DEPARTING SOUL

Ah fleeting Spirit! wandering fire,
    That long hast warmed my tender breast,
Must thou no more this frame inspire?
    No more a pleasing, cheerful guest?

Whither, ah whither art thou flying!
    To what dark, undiscovered shore?
Thou seem'st all trembling, shivering, dying,
    And wit and humour are no more!

Composed c. 1712   First published 1730

THE DYING CHRISTIAN TO HIS SOUL

Ode

    Vital spark of heavenly flame!
    Quit, oh quit this mortal frame;
    Trembling, hoping, lingering, flying,
    Oh the pain, the bliss of dying!
    Cease, fond Nature, cease thy strife,
And let me languish into life.

Hark! they whisper; angels say,
Sister Spirit, come away!
What is this absorbs me quite?
Steals my senses, shuts my sight,   10
    Drowns my spirits, draws my breath?
Tell me, my soul, can this be death?

The world recedes; it disappears!
Heaven opens on my eyes! my ears
    With sounds seraphic ring:
Lend, lend your wings! I mount! I fly!
O grave! where is thy victory!
    O death! where is thy sting?

Composed 1712   First published 1736

TO HENRY CROMWELL, 19 OCTOBER 1709
[WITH ARGUS]

Now I talk of my dog, that I may not treat of a worse
subject which my spleen tempts me to, I will give you
some account of him; a thing not wholly unprecedented,
since Montaigne (to whom I am but a dog in comparison)
has done the very same thing of his cat . . . . You are to
know then, that as 'tis likeness that begets affection, so my
favourite dog is a little one, a lean one, and none of the
finest shaped. He is not much a spaniel in his fawning,
but has (what might be worth many a man's while to
imitate from him) a dumb surly sort of kindness, that   10
rather shows itself when he thinks me ill-used by others
than when we walk quietly and peaceably by ourselves. If
it be the chief point of friendship to comply with a
friend's motions and inclinations, he possesses this in an
eminent degree; he lies down when I sit, and walks where
I walk, which is more than many good friends can
pretend to, witness our walk a year ago in St James's
Park – histories are more full of the fidelity of dogs than
of friends, but . . . I will only say for the honour of dogs
that the two most ancient and estimable books (viz: the   20

Scripture and Homer) have shown a particular regard to these animals. That of Toby is the more remarkable, because there was no manner of reason to take notice of the dog besides the great humanity of the author. And Homer's account of Ulysses's dog Argus, is the most pathetic imaginable, all the circumstances considered, and an excellent proof of the old bard's good-nature. Ulysses had left him at Ithaca when he embarked for Troy, and found him on his return after twenty years (which by the way is not unnatural, as some critics have said, since I remember the dam of my dog who was twenty-two years old when she died: may the omen of longevity prove fortunate to her successor!). You shall have it in verse. 30

Argus

When wise Ulysses, from his native coast
Long kept by wars, and long by tempests tossed,
Arrived at last, poor, old, disguised, alone,
To all his friends and even his queen unknown;
Changed as he was with age, and toils, and cares,
Furrowed his reverend face, and white his hairs,
In his own palace forced to ask his bread,
Scorned by those slaves his former bounty fed,
Forgot of all his own domestic crew;
The faithful dog alone his rightful master knew! 10
Unfed, unhoused, neglected, on the clay,
Like an old servant, now cashiered, he lay;
And though even then expiring on the plain
Touched with resentment of ungrateful man,
And longing to behold his ancient lord again.
Him when he saw he rose and crawled to meet
('Twas all he could), and fawned, and kissed his feet,
Seized with dumb joy—then falling by his side,
Owned his returning lord, looked up, and died!

TO HENRY CROMWELL, 25 NOVEMBER 1710
[ON VERSIFICATION]

Your mention in this and your last letter of the defect in numbers of several of our poets puts me upon communicating a few thoughts, or rather doubts, of mine on that head, some of which 'tis likely I may have hinted to you formerly in conversation; but I will here put together all the little niceties I can recollect in the compass of my observation.

1. As to the hiatus, it is certainly to be avoided as often as possible; but, on the other hand, since the reason of it is only for the sake of the numbers, so, if to avoid it we incur another fault against their smoothness, methinks the very end of that nicety is destroyed. As when we say (for instance)

> But th' old have interest ever in their view

to avoid the hiatus in 'The old have interest,' does not the ear in this place tell us that the hiatus is smoother, less constrained, and so preferable to the caesura?

2. I would except against all expletives in verse, as 'do' before verbs plural, or even too frequent use of 'did' and 'does', to change the termination of the rhyme, all these being against the usual manner of speech and mere fillers-up of unnecessary syllables.

3. Monosyllable-lines, unless very artifully managed, are stiff, languishing, and hard.

4. The repeating the same rhymes within four or six lines of each other, which tire the ear with too much of the like sound.

5. The too frequent use of alexandrines, which are never graceful but when there is some majesty added to the verse by them, or when there cannot be found a word in them but what is absolutely needful.

6. Every nice ear must (I believe) have observed that in any smooth English verse of ten syllables there is natural-ly a pause either at the fourth, fifth, or sixth syllable, as, for example, Waller:

> At the fifth: Where'er thy Navy ‖ spreads her canvas wings.
> At the fourth: Homage to thee ‖ and peace to all she brings.
> At the sixth: Like tracks of leverets ‖ in morning snow.

35

Now I fancy that to preserve an exact harmony and variety none of these pauses should be continued above three lines together without the interposition of another; else it will be apt to weary the ear with one continued tone; at least it does mine.

7. It is not enough that nothing offends the ear, that the verse be (as the French call it) *coulante*; but a good poet will adapt the very sounds, as well as words, to the things he treats of. So that there is (if one may express it so) a Style of Sound: as in describing a gliding stream the numbers should run easy and flowing, in describing a rough torrent or deluge, sonorous and swelling, and so of the rest. This is evident everywhere in Homer and Virgil, and nowhere else that I know of to any observable degree.... This, I think, is what very few observe in practice and is undoubtedly of wonderful force in imprinting the image on the reader. We have one excellent example of this in our language, Mr Dryden's ode on St Cecilia's Day entitled 'Alexander's Feast, or the Power of Music'.

AN ESSAY ON CRITICISM

'Tis hard to say, if greater want of skill
Appear in writing or in judging ill;
But, of the two, less dangerous is the offence
To tire our patience, than mislead our sense:
Some few in that, but numbers err in this,
Ten censure wrong for one who writes amiss;
A fool might once himself alone expose,
Now one in verse makes many more in prose.
 'Tis with our judgements as our watches, none
Go just alike, yet each believes his own.
In poets as true genius is but rare,
True taste as seldom is the critic's share,
Both must alike from Heaven derive their light,
These born to judge, as well as those to write.
Let such teach others who themselves excel,
And censure freely who have written well.

36

Authors are partial to their wit, 'tis true,
But are not critics to their judgement too?
　Yet, if we look more closely, we shall find
Most have the seeds of judgement in their mind:　　20
Nature affords at least a glimmering light;
The lines, though touched but faintly, are drawn right.
But as the slightest sketch, if justly traced,
Is by ill colouring but the more disgraced,
So by false learning is good sense defaced;
Some are bewildered in the maze of schools,
And some made coxcombs Nature meant but fools.
In search of wit these lose their common sense,
And then turn critics in their own defence:
Each burns alike, who can, or cannot write,　　30
Or with a rival's, or an eunuch's spite.
All fools have still an itching to deride,
And fain would be upon the laughing side.
If Maevius scribble in Apollo's spite,
There are who judge still worse than he can write.
　Some have at first for wits, then poets passed,
Turned critics next, and proved plain fools at last;
Some neither can for wits nor critics pass,
As heavy mules are neither horse nor ass.
Those half-learned witlings, numerous in our isle,　　40
As half-formed insects on the banks of Nile;
Unfinished things, one knows not what to call,
Their generation's so equivocal:
To tell them would a hundred tongues require,
Or one vain wit's, that might a hundred tire.
　But you who seek to give and merit fame,
And justly bear a critic's noble name,
Be sure yourself and your own reach to know,
How far your genius, taste, and learning go;
Launch not beyond your depth, but be discreet,　　50
And mark that point where sense and dullness meet.
　Nature to all things fixed the limits fit,
And wisely curbed proud man's pretending wit.
As on the land while here the ocean gains,
In other parts it leaves wide sandy plains;

Thus in the soul while memory prevails,
The solid power of understanding fails;
Where beams of warm imagination play,
The memory's soft figures melt away.
One science only will one genius fit: 60
So vast is art, so narrow human wit:
Not only bounded to peculiar arts,
But oft in those, confined to single parts.
Like kings we lose the conquests gained before,
By vain ambition still to make them more:
Each might his several province well command,
Would all but stoop to what they understand.
    First follow Nature, and your judgement frame
By her just standard, which is still the same:
Unerring Nature, still divinely bright,   70
One clear, unchanged, and universal light,
Life, force, and beauty, must to all impart,
At once the source, and end, and test of Art.
Art from that fund each just supply provides,
Works without show, and without pomp presides:
In some fair body thus the informing soul
With spirits feeds, with vigour fills the whole,
Each motion guides, and every nerve sustains;
Itself unseen, but in the effects remains.
Some, to whom Heaven in wit has been profuse,   80
Want as much more to turn it to its use;
For wit and judgement often are at strife,
Though meant each other's aid, like man and wife.
'Tis more to guide, than spur the Muse's steed;
Restrain his fury, than provoke his speed:
The winged courser, like a generous horse,
Shows most true mettle when you check his course.
    Those rules of old discovered, not devised,
Are Nature still, but Nature methodized:
Nature, like liberty, is but restrained   90
By the same laws which first herself ordained.
    Hear how learned Greece her useful rules indites,
When to repress, and when indulge our flights:
High on Parnassus' top her sons she showed,

38

And pointed out those arduous paths they trod;
Held from afar, aloft, the immortal prize,
And urged the rest by equal steps to rise:
Just precepts thus from great examples given,
She drew from them what they derived from Heaven.
The generous critic fanned the poet's fire,   100
And taught the world with reason to admire.
Then criticism the Muse's handmaid proved,
To dress her charms, and make her more beloved:
But following wits from that intention strayed,
Who could not win the mistress, wooed the maid;
Against the poets their own arms they turned,
Sure to hate most the men from whom they learned.
So modern 'pothecaries, taught the art
By doctor's bills to play the doctor's part,
Bold in the practice of mistaken rules,   110
Prescribe, apply, and call their masters fools.
Some on the leaves of ancient authors prey,
Nor time nor moths e'er spoiled so much as they:
Some drily plain, without invention's aid,
Write dull receipts how poems may be made:
These leave the sense, their learning to display,
And those explain the meaning quite away.
   You then whose judgement the right course would steer,
Know well each ancient's proper character:
His fable, subject, scope in every page;   120
Religion, country, genius of his age:
Without all these at once before your eyes,
Cavil you may, but never criticize.
Be Homer's works your study and delight,
Read them by day, and meditate by night;
Thence form your judgement, thence your maxims bring,
And trace the Muses upward to their spring;
Still with itself compared, his text peruse;
And let your comment be the Mantuan Muse.
   When first young Maro in his boundless mind   130
A work to outlast immortal Rome designed,
Perhaps he seemed above the critic's law,
And but from Nature's fountains scorned to draw:

But when to examine every part he came,
Nature and Homer were, he found, the same.
Convinced, amazed, he checks the bold design;
And rules as strict his laboured work confine,
As if the Stagyrite o'erlooked each line.
Learn hence for ancient rules a just esteem;
To copy Nature is to copy them.   140
   Some beauties yet no precepts can declare,
For there's a happiness as well as care.
Music resembles poetry, in each
Are nameless graces which no methods teach,
And which a master-hand alone can reach.
If, where the rules not far enough extend,
(Since rules were made but to promote their end)
Some lucky licence answers to the full
The intent proposed, that licence is a rule.
Thus Pegasus, a nearer way to take,   150
May boldly deviate from the common track.
Great wits sometimes may gloriously offend,
And rise to faults true critics dare not mend;
From vulgar bounds with brave disorder part,
And snatch a grace beyond the reach of art,
Which, without passing through the judgement, gains
The heart, and all its end at once attains.
In prospects thus, some objects please our eyes,
Which out of Nature's common order rise,
The shapeless rock, or hanging precipice.   160
But though the ancients thus their rules invade,
(As kings dispense with laws themselves have made)
Moderns, beware! or if you must offend
Against the precept, ne'er transgress its end;
Let it be seldom, and compelled by need;
And have, at least, their precedent to plead.
The critic else proceeds without remorse,
Seizes your fame, and puts his laws in force.
   I know there are, to whose presumptuous thoughts
Those freer beauties, even in them, seem faults.   170
Some figures monstrous and misshaped appear,
Considered singly, or beheld too near,

40

Which, but proportioned to their light, or place,
Due distance reconciles to form and grace.
A prudent chief not always must display
His powers, in equal ranks, and fair array,
But with the occasion and the place comply,
Conceal his force, nay seem sometimes to fly.
Those oft are stratagems which errors seem,
Nor is it Homer nods, but we that dream.   180
   Still green with bays each ancient altar stands,
Above the reach of sacrilegious hands;
Secure from flames, from envy's fiercer rage,
Destructive war, and all-involving age.
See from each clime the learned their incense bring!
Hear in all tongues consenting paeans ring!
In praise so just let every voice be joined,
And fill the general chorus of mankind!
Hail, bards triumphant! born in happier days;
Immortal heirs of universal praise!   190
Whose honours with increase of ages grow,
As streams roll down, enlarging as they flow!
Nations unborn your mighty names shall sound,
And worlds applaud that must not yet be found!
O may some spark of your celestial fire,
The last, the meanest of your sons inspire,
(That on weak wings, from far, pursues your flights;
Glows while he reads, but trembles as he writes)
To teach vain wits a science little known,
To admire superior sense, and doubt their own!   200

   Of all the causes which conspire to blind
Man's erring judgement, and misguide the mind,
What the weak head with strongest bias rules,
Is pride, the never-failing vice of fools.
Whatever Nature has in worth denied,
She gives in large recruits of needless pride;
For as in bodies, thus in souls, we find
What wants in blood and spirits, swelled with wind:
Pride, where wit fails, steps in to our defence,
And fills up all the mighty void of sense!   210

41

If once right reason drives that cloud away,
Truth breaks upon us with resistless day.
Trust not yourself; but your defects to know,
Make use of every friend – and every foe.

A little learning is a dangerous thing;
Drink deep, or taste not the Pierian spring:
There shallow draughts intoxicate the brain,
And drinking largely sobers us again.
Fired at first sight with what the Muse imparts,
In fearless youth we tempt the heights of arts,   220
While from the bounded level of our mind,
Short views we take, nor see the lengths behind;
But more advanced, behold with strange surprise
New distant scenes of endless science rise!
So pleased at first the towering Alps we try,
Mount o'er the vales, and seem to tread the sky;
The eternal snows appear already passed,
And the first clouds and mountains seem the last:
But, those attained, we tremble to survey
The growing labours of the lengthened way,   230
The increasing prospect tires our wandering eyes,
Hills peep o'er hills, and Alps on Alps arise!

A perfect judge will read each work of wit
With the same spirit that its author writ:
Survey the whole, nor seek slight faults to find
Where Nature moves, and rapture warms the mind;
Nor lose, for that malignant dull delight,
The generous pleasure to be charmed with wit.
But in such lays as neither ebb nor flow,
Correctly cold, and regularly low,   240
That shunning faults, one quiet tenor keep;
We cannot blame indeed – but we may sleep.
In wit, as Nature, what affects our hearts
Is not the exactness of peculiar parts;
'Tis not a lip, or eye, we beauty call,
But the joint force and full result of all.
Thus when we view some well-proportioned dome,
(The world's just wonder, and even thine, O Rome!)
No single parts unequally surprise,

42

All comes united to the admiring eyes;   250
No monstrous height, or breadth, or length appear;
The whole at once is bold and regular.
  Whoever thinks a faultless piece to see,
Thinks what ne'er was, nor is, nor e'er shall be.
In every work regard the writer's end,
Since none can compass more than they intend;
And if the means be just, the conduct true,
Applause, in spite of trivial faults, is due.
As men of breeding, sometimes men of wit,
To avoid great errors, must the less commit: 260
Neglect the rules each verbal critic lays,
For not to know some trifles, is a praise.
Most critics, fond of some subservient art,
Still make the whole depend upon a part:
They talk of principles, but notions prize,
And all to one loved folly sacrifice.
  Once on a time, La Mancha's knight, they say
A certain bard encountering on the way,
Discoursed in terms as just, with looks as sage,
As e'er could Dennis, of the Grecian stage;   270
Concluding all were desperate sots and fools,
Who durst depart from Aristotle's rules.
Our author, happy in a judge so nice,
Produced his play, and begged the knight's advice;
Made him observe the subject and the plot,
The manners, passions, unities, what not?
All which, exact to rule, were brought about,
Were but a combat in the lists left out.
'What! leave the combat out?' exclaims the knight;
Yes, or we must renounce the Stagyrite.   280
'Not so, by Heaven,' (he answers in a rage)
'Knights, squires, and steeds, must enter on the stage.'
So vast a throng the stage can ne'er contain.
'Then build a new, or act it in a plain.'
  Thus critics of less judgement than caprice,
Curious, not knowing, not exact, but nice,
Form short ideas; and offend in arts
(As most in manners) by a love to parts.

43

Some to conceit alone their taste confine,
And glittering thoughts struck out at every line;   290
Pleased with a work where nothing's just or fit;
One glaring chaos and wild heap of wit.
Poets, like painters, thus, unskilled to trace
The naked Nature and the living grace,
With gold and jewels cover every part,
And hide with ornaments their want of art.
True wit is Nature to advantage dressed;
What oft was thought, but ne'er so well expressed;
Something, whose truth convinced at sight we find,
That gives us back the image of our mind: 300
As shades more sweetly recommend the light,
So modest plainness sets off sprightly wit:
For works may have more wit than does them good,
As bodies perish through excess of blood.
    Others for language all their care express,
And value books, as women men, for dress:
Their praise is still, – The style is excellent;
The sense, they humbly take upon content.
Words are like leaves; and where they most abound,
Much fruit of sense beneath is rarely found.   310
False eloquence, like the prismatic glass,
Its gaudy colours spreads on every place;
The face of Nature we no more survey,
All glares alike, without distinction gay:
But true expression, like the unchanging sun,
Clears and improves whate'er it shines upon,
It gilds all objects, but it alters none.
Expression is the dress of thought, and still
Appears more decent, as more suitable;
A vile conceit in pompous words expressed   320
Is like a clown in regal purple dressed:
For different styles with different subjects sort,
As several garbs, with country, town, and court.
Some by old words to fame have made pretence,
Ancients in phrase, mere moderns in their sense!
Such laboured nothings, in so strange a style,
Amaze the unlearned, and make the learnèd smile.

Unlucky as Fungoso in the play,
These sparks with awkward vanity display
What the fine gentleman wore yesterday   330
And but so mimic ancient wits at best,
As apes our grandsires, in their doublets dressed.
In words, as fashions, the same rule will hold;
Alike fantastic, if too new, or old:
Be not the first by whom the new are tried,
Nor yet the last to lay the old aside.
    But most by numbers judge a poet's song:
And smooth or rough, with them, is right or wrong:
In the bright muse, though thousand charms conspire,
Her voice is all these tuneful fools admire,   340
Who haunt Parnassus but to please their ear,
Not mend their minds; as some to church repair,
Not for the doctrine, but the music there.
These equal syllables alone require,
Tho' oft the ear the open vowels tire;
While expletives their feeble aid do join;
And ten low words oft creep in one dull line:
While they ring round the same unvaried chimes,
With sure returns of still expected rhymes;
Where'er you find 'the cooling western breeze,'   350
In the next line, it 'whispers through the trees':
If 'crystal streams with pleasing murmurs creep':
The reader's threatened (not in vain) with 'sleep'.
Then, at the last and only couplet fraught
With some unmeaning thing they call a thought,
A needless Alexandrine ends the song,
That, like a wounded snake, drags its slow length along.
Leave such to tune their own dull rhymes, and know
What's roundly smooth, or languishingly slow;
And praise the easy vigour of a line,   360
Where Denham's strength, and Waller's sweetness join.
True ease in writing comes from art, not chance,
As those move easiest who have learned to dance.
'Tis not enough no harshness gives offence,
The sound must seem an echo to the sense.
Soft is the strain when Zephyr gently blows,

And the smooth stream in smoother numbers flows;
But when loud surges lash the sounding shore,
The hoarse, rough verse should like the torrent roar.
When Ajax strives some rock's vast weight to throw,   370
The line too labours, and the words move slow:
Not so, when swift Camilla scours the plain,
Flies o'er the unbending corn, and skims along the main.
Hear how Timotheus' varied lays surprise,
And bid alternate passions fall and rise!
While, at each change, the son of Libyan Jove
Now burns with glory, and then melts with love;
Now his fierce eyes with sparkling fury glow,
Now sighs steal out, and tears begin to flow:
Persians and Greeks like turns of Nature found,   380
And the world's victor stood subdued by sound!
The power of music all our hearts allow,
And what Timotheus was, is Dryden now.

   Avoid extremes; and shun the fault of such,
Who still are pleased too little or too much.
At every trifle scorn to take offence,
That always shows great pride, or little sense;
Those heads, as stomachs, are not sure the best,
Which nauseate all, and nothing can digest.
Yet let not each gay turn thy rapture move,   390
For fools admire, but men of sense approve;
As things seem large which we through mists descry,
Dullness is ever apt to magnify.

   Some foreign writers, some our own despise;
The ancients only, or the moderns prize:
Thus wit, like faith, by each man is applied
To one small sect, and all are damned beside.
Meanly they seek the blessing to confine,
And force that sun but on a part to shine,
Which not alone the southern wit sublimes,   400
But ripens spirits in cold northern climes;
Which from the first has shone on ages past,
Enlights the present, and shall warm the last;
Though each may feel increases and decays,
And see now clearer and now darker days.

Regard not then if wit be old or new,
But blame the false, and value still the true.
 Some ne'er advance a judgement of their own,
But catch the spreading notion of the town;
They reason and conclude by precedent,   410
And own stale nonsense which they ne'er invent.
Some judge of authors' names, not works, and then
Nor praise nor blame the writings, but the men.
Of all this servile herd, the worst is he
That in proud dullness joins with quality,
A constant critic at the great man's board,
To fetch and carry nonsense for my lord.
What woeful stuff this madrigal would be,
In some starved hackney sonneteer, or me?
But let a lord once own the happy lines,   420
How the wit brightens! how the style refines!
Before his sacred name flies every fault,
And each exalted stanza teems with thought!
 The vulgar thus through imitation err;
As oft the learned by being singular;
So much they scorn the crowd, that if the throng
By chance go right, they purposely go wrong:
So schismatics the plain believers quit,
And are but damned for having too much wit.
Some praise at morning what they blame at night;   430
But always think the last opinion right.
A Muse by these is like a mistress used,
This hour she's idolized, the next abused;
While their weak heads, like towns unfortified,
'Twixt sense and nonsense daily change their side.
Ask them the cause; they're wiser still, they say;
And still tomorrow's wiser than today.
We think our fathers fools, so wise we grow;
Our wiser sons, no doubt, will think us so.
Once school-divines this zealous isle o'erspread;   440
Who knew most sentences, was deepest read:
Faith, Gospel, all seemed made to be disputed,
And none had sense enough to be confuted:
Scotists and Thomists, now in peace remain,

Amidst their kindred cobwebs in Duck-lane.
If Faith itself has different dresses worn,
What wonder modes in wit should take their turn?
Oft leaving what is natural and fit,
The current folly proves the ready wit;
And authors think their reputation safe,   450
Which lives as long as fools are pleased to laugh.

  Some valuing those of their own side or mind,
Still make themselves the measure of mankind:
Fondly we think we honour merit then,
When we but praise ourselves in other men.
Parties in wit attend on those of state,
And public faction doubles private hate.
Pride, malice, folly, against Dryden rose,
In various shapes of parsons, critics, beaus;
But sense survived when merry jests were past;   460
For rising merit will buoy up at last.
Might he return, and bless once more our eyes,
New Blackmores and new Milbourns must arise:
Nay, should great Homer lift his awful head,
Zoilus again would start up from the dead.
Envy will merit, as its shade, pursue;
But like a shadow, proves the substance true:
For envied wit, like Sol eclipsed, makes known
The opposing body's grossness, not its own.
When first that sun too powerful beams displays,   470
It draws up vapours which obscure its rays;
But even those clouds at last adorn its way,
Reflect new glories, and augment the day.

  Be thou the first true merit to befriend;
His praise is lost, who stays till all commend.
Short is the date, alas! of modern rhymes,
And 'tis but just to let them live betimes.
No longer now that golden age appears,
When patriarch-wits survived a thousand years:
Now length of fame (our second life) is lost,   480
And bare threescore is all even that can boast;
Our sons their fathers' failing language see,
And such as Chaucer is, shall Dryden be.

48

So when the faithful pencil has designed
Some bright idea of the master's mind,
Where a new world leaps out at his command,
And ready Nature waits upon his hand;
When the ripe colours soften and unite,
And sweetly melt into just shade and light;
When mellowing years their full perfection give,   490
And each bold figure just begins to live,
The treacherous colours the fair art betray,
And all the bright creation fades away!

   Unhappy wit, like most mistaken things,
Atones not for that envy which it brings.
In youth alone its empty praise we boast,
But soon the short-lived vanity is lost!
Like some fair flower the early spring supplies,
That gaily blooms, but even in blooming dies.
What is this wit, which must our cares employ?   500
The owner's wife, that other men enjoy;
Then most our trouble still when most admired,
And still the more we give, the more required;
Whose fame with pains we guard, but lose with ease,
Sure some to vex, but never all to please;
'Tis what the vicious fear, the virtuous shun,
By fools 'tis hated, and by knaves undone!

   If wit so much from ignorance undergo,
Ah, let not learning too commence its foe!
Of old, those met rewards who could excel,   510
And such were praised who but endeavoured well:
Though triumphs were to generals only due,
Crowns were reserved to grace the soldiers too.
Now, they who reach Parnassus' lofty crown,
Employ their pains to spurn some others down;
And while self-love each jealous writer rules,
Contending wits become the sport of fools:
But still the worst with most regret commend,
For each ill author is as bad a friend.
To what base ends, and by what abject ways,   520
Are mortals urged through sacred lust of praise!
Ah ne'er so dire a thirst of glory boast,

49

Nor in the critic let the man be lost.
Good nature and good sense must ever join;
To err is human, to forgive, divine.
   But if in noble minds some dregs remain,
Not yet purged off, of spleen and sour disdain;
Discharge that rage on more provoking crimes,
Nor fear a dearth in these flagitious times.
No pardon vile obscenity should find,   530
Though wit and art conspire to move your mind;
But dullness with obscenity must prove
As shameful sure as impotence in love.
In the fat age of pleasure, wealth, and ease,
Sprung the rank weed, and thrived with large increase:
When love was all an easy monarch's care;
Seldom at council, never in a war:
Jilts ruled the stare, and statesmen farces writ;
Nay wits had pensions, and young lords had wit:
The fair sat panting at a courtier's play,   540
And not a mask went unimproved away:
The modest fan was lifted up no more,
And virgins smiled at what they blushed before.
The following licence of a foreign reign
Did all the dregs of bold Socinus drain;
Then unbelieving priests reformed the nation,
And taught more pleasant methods of salvation;
Where Heaven's free subjects might their rights dispute,
Lest God Himself should seem too absolute.
Pulpits their sacred satire learned to spare,   550
And vice admired to find a flatterer there!
Encouraged thus, wit's Titans braved the skies,
And the press groaned with licensed blasphemies.
These monsters, critics! with your darts engage,
Here point your thunder, and exhaust your rage!
Yet shun their fault, who, scandalously nice,
Will needs mistake an author into vice;
All seems infected that the infected spy,
As all looks yellow to the jaundiced eye.

Learn then what morals critics ought to show,   560
For 'tis but half a judge's task, to know.

50

'Tis not enough, taste, judgement, learning, join;
In all you speak, let truth and candour shine:
That not alone what to your sense is due
All may allow; but seek your friendship too.

Be silent always, when you doubt your sense;
And speak, though sure, with seeming diffidence:
Some positive, persisting fops we know,
Who, if once wrong, will needs be always so;
But you, with pleasure own your errors past,   570
And make each day a critique on the last.

'Tis not enough your counsel still be true;
Blunt truths more mischief than nice falsehoods do;
Men must be taught as if you taught them not,
And things unknown proposed as things forgot.
Without good-breeding, truth is disapproved;
That only makes superior sense beloved.

Be niggards of advice on no pretence;
For the worst avarice is that of sense.
With mean complaisance ne'er betray your trust,   580
Nor be so civil as to prove unjust.
Fear not the anger of the wise to raise;
Those best can bear reproof who merit praise.

'Twere well might critics still this freedom take,
But Appius reddens at each word you speak,
And stares, tremendous, with a threatening eye,
Like some fierce tyrant in old tapestry.
Fear most to tax an Honourable fool,
Whose right it is, uncensured, to be dull;
Such, without wit, are poets when they please,   590
As without learning they can take degrees.
Leave dangerous truths to unsuccessful satires,
And flattery to fulsome dedicators,
Whom, when they praise, the world believes no more,
Than when they promise to give scribbling o'er.
'Tis best sometimes your censure to restrain,
And charitably let the dull be vain:
Your silence there is better than your spite,
For who can rail so long as they can write?
Still humming on, their drowsy course they keep,   600
And lashed so long, like tops, are lashed asleep.

51

False steps but help them to renew the race,
As, after stumbling, jades will mend their pace.
What crowds of these, impenitently bold,
In sounds and jingling syllables grown old,
Still run on poets in a raging vein,
Even to the dregs and squeezings of the brain,
Strain out the last dull dropping of their sense,
And rhyme with all the rage of impotence!
   Such shameless bards we have; and yet 'tis true   610
There are as mad, abandoned critics too.
The bookful blockhead, ignorantly read,
With loads of learned lumber in his head,
With his own tongue still edifies his ears,
And always listening to himself appears.
All books he reads, and all he reads assails,
From Dryden's *Fables* down to Durfey's *Tales*:
With him, most authors steal their works, or buy;
Garth did not write his own *Dispensary*.
Name a new play, and he's the poet's friend,   620
Nay showed his faults – but when would poets mend?
No place so sacred from such fops is barred,
Nor is Paul's church more safe than Paul's church-yard:
Nay, fly to altars; there they'll talk you dead;
For fools rush in where angels fear to tread,
Distrustful sense with modest caution speaks,
It still looks home, and short excursions makes;
But rattling nonsense in full volleys breaks,
And never shocked, and never turned aside,
Bursts out, resistless, with a thundering tide.   630
   But where's the man who counsel can bestow,
Still pleased to teach, and yet not proud to know?
Unbiased, or by favour, or by spite;
Not dully prepossessed, nor blindly right;
Though learned, well-bred; and though well-bred, sincere;
Modestly bold, and humanly severe:
Who to a friend his faults can freely show,
And gladly praise the merit of a foe?
Blessed with a taste exact, yet unconfined;
A knowledge both of books and human kind;   640

52

Generous converse; a soul exempt from pride;
And love to praise, with reason on his side?
  Such once were critics; such the happy few,
Athens and Rome in better ages knew.
The mighty Stagyrite first left the shore,
Spread all his sails, and durst the deeps explore;
He steered securely, and discovered far,
Led by the light of the Maeonian star.
Poets, a race long unconfined, and free,
Still fond and proud of savage liberty,   650
Received his laws; and stood convinced 'twas fit,
Who conquered Nature, should preside o'er Wit.
  Horace still charms with graceful negligence,
And without method talks us into sense,
Will, like a friend, familiarly convey
The truest notions in the easiest way.
He, who supreme in judgement, as in wit,
Might boldly censure, as he boldly writ,
Yet judged with coolness, though he sung with fire;
His precepts teach but what his works inspire.   660
Our critics take a contrary extreme,
They judge with fury, but they write with phlegm:
Nor suffers Horace more in wrong translations
By wits, than critics in as wrong quotations.
  See Dionysius Homer's thoughts refine,
And call new beauties forth from every line!
  Fancy and art in gay Petronius please,
The scholar's learning with the courtier's ease.
  In grave Quintilian's copious work, we find
The justest rules and clearest method joined: 670
Thus useful arms in magazines we place,
All ranged in order, and disposed with grace,
But less to please the eye, than arm the hand,
Still fit for use, and ready at command.
  Thee, bold Longinus! all the Nine inspire,
And bless their critic with a poet's fire.
An ardent judge, who, zealous in his trust,
With warmth gives sentence, yet is always just:
Whose own example strengthens all his laws:

And is himself that great sublime he draws. 680
   Thus long succeeding critics justly reigned,
Licence repressed, and useful laws ordained.
Learning and Rome alike in empire grew;
And arts still followed where her eagles flew;
From the same foes, at last, both felt their doom,
And the same age saw Learning fall, and Rome.
With Tyranny, then Superstition joined,
As that the body, this enslaved the mind;
Much was believed, but little understood,
And to be dull was construed to be good; 690
A second deluge learning thus o'errun,
And the monks finished what the Goths begun.
   At length Erasmus, that great injured name,
(The glory of the priesthood, and the shame!)
Stemmed the wild torrent of a barbarous age,
And drove those holy Vandals off the stage.
   But see! each Muse, in Leo's golden days,
Starts from her trance, and trims her withered bays;
Rome's ancient genius, o'er its ruins spread,
Shakes off the dust, and rears his reverend head. 700
Then sculpture and her sister-arts revive;
Stones leaped to form, and rocks began to live;
With sweeter notes each rising temple rung;
A Raphael painted, and a Vida sung!
Immortal Vida! on whose honoured brow
The poet's bays and critic's ivy grow:
Cremona now shall ever boast thy name,
As next in place to Mantua, next in fame!
   But soon by impious arms from Latium chased,
Their ancient bounds the banished Muses passed; 710
Thence Arts o'er all the northern world advance,
But critic-learning flourished most in France;
The rules, a nation born to serve, obeys;
And Boileau still in right of Horace sways.
But we, brave Britons, foreign laws despised,
And kept unconquered, and uncivilized;
Fierce for the liberties of wit, and bold,
We still defied the Romans, as of old.

54

Yet some there were, among the sounder few
Of those who less presumed, and better knew,   720
Who durst assert the juster ancient cause,
And here restored wit's fundamental laws.
Such was the Muse, whose rules and practice tell,
'Nature's chief masterpiece is writing well,'
Such was Roscommon, not more learned than good,
With manners generous as his noble blood;
To him the wit of Greece and Rome was known,
And every author's merit, but his own.
Such late was Walsh – the Muse's judge and friend,
Who justly knew to blame or to commend: 730
To failings mild, but zealous for desert;
The clearest head, and the sincerest heart.
This humble praise, lamented shade! receive,
This praise at least a grateful Muse may give:
The Muse, whose early voice you taught to sing,
Prescribed her heights, and pruned her tender wing,
(Her guide now lost) no more attempts to rise,
But in low numbers short excursions tries:
Content, if hence the unlearned their wants may view,
The learned reflect on what before they knew;   740
Careless of censure, nor too fond of fame;
Still pleased to praise, yet not afraid to blame;
Averse alike to flatter, or offend;
Not free from faults, nor yet too vain to mend.

Composed c. 1709   First published 1711

EPISTLE TO MISS BLOUNT
WITH THE WORKS OF VOITURE

In these gay thoughts the Loves and Graces shine,
And all the writer lives in every line;
His easy art may happy nature seem,
Trifles themselves are elegant in him.
Sure to charm all was his peculiar fate,
Who without flattery pleased the fair and great;
Still with esteem no less conversed than read;

With wit well-natured, and with books well-bred;
His heart, his mistress and his friend did share,
His time, the Muse, the witty and the fair.   10
Thus wisely careless, innocently gay,
Cheerful, he played the trifle, Life, away;
Till fate scarce felt his gentle breath suppressed,
As smiling infants sport themselves to rest.
Even rival wits did Voiture's death deplore,
And the gay mourned who never mourned before;
The truest hearts for Voiture heaved with sighs,
Voiture was wept by all the brightest eyes:
The Smiles and Loves had died in Voiture's death,
But that for ever in his lines they breathe.   20

    Let the strict life of graver mortals be
A long, exact, and serious comedy;
In every scene some moral let it teach,
And, if it can, at once both please and preach.
Let mine, an innocent gay farce appear,
And more diverting still than regular,
Have humour, wit, a native ease and grace,
Though not too strictly bound to time and place:
Critics in wit, or life, are hard to please,
Few write to those, and none can live to these.   30

    Too much your sex is by their forms confined,
Severe to all, but most to womankind;
Custom, grown blind with age, must be your guide;
Your pleasure is a vice, but not your pride;
By nature yielding, stubborn but for fame;
Made slaves by honour, and made fools by shame.
Marriage may all those petty tyrants chase,
But sets up one, a greater, in their place:
Well might you wish for change by those accursed,
But the last tyrant ever proves the worst.   40
Still in constraint your suffering sex remains,
Or bound in formal or in real chains:
Whole years neglected, for some months adored,
The fawning servant turns a haughty lord.
Ah quit not the free innocence of life,
For the dull glory of a virtuous wife!
Nor let false shows nor empty titles please:

Aim not at joy, but rest content with ease.
  The gods, to curse Pamela with her prayers,
Gave the gilt coach and dappled Flanders mares,   50
The shining robes, rich jewels, beds of state,
And, to complete her bliss, a fool for mate.
She glares in balls, front-boxes, and the Ring,
A vain, unquiet, glittering, wretched thing!
Pride, pomp, and state but reach her outward part;
She sighs, and is no duchess at her heart.
  But Madam, if the Fates withstand, and you
Are destined Hymen's willing victim too;
Trust not too much your now resistless charms,
Those, age or sickness soon or late disarms: 60
Good humour only teaches charms to last,
Still makes new conquests, and maintains the past:
Love, raised on beauty, will like that decay,
Our hearts may bear its slender chain a day;
As flowery bands in wantonness are worn,
A morning's pleasure, and at evening torn:
This binds in ties more easy, yet more strong,
The willing heart, and only holds it long.
  Thus Voiture's early care still shone the same,
And Monthausier was only changed in name;   70
By this, even now they live, even now they charm,
Their wit still sparkling, and their flames still warm.
  Now crowned with myrtle, on the Elysian coast,
Amid those lovers, joys his gentle ghost:
Pleased, while with smiles his happy lines you view,
And finds a fairer Rambouillet in you.
The brightest eyes of France inspired his Muse;
The brightest eyes of Britain now peruse;
And dead, as living, 'tis our author's pride
Still to charm those who charm the world beside.   80

Composed c. 1710   *First published 1712*

from WINDSOR FOREST

Thy forests, Windsor! and thy green retreats,
At once the monarch's and the Muse's seats,
Invite my lays. Be present, sylvan maids!

Unlock your springs, and open all your shades.
Granville commands; your aid, O Muses, bring!
What Muse for Granville can refuse to sing?
  The groves of Eden, vanished now so long,
Live in description, and look green in song:
These, were my breast inspired with equal flame,
Like them in beauty, should be like in fame.   10
Here hills and vales, the woodland and the plain,
Here earth and water seem to strive again;
Not chaos-like together crushed and bruised,
But, as the world harmoniously confused:
Where order in variety we see,
And where, though all things differ, all agree.
Here waving groves a chequered scene display,
And part admit, and part exclude the day;
As some coy nymph her lover's warm address
Nor quite indulges, nor can quite repress.   20
There, interspersed in lawns and opening glades,
Thin trees arise that shun each other's shades.
Here in full light the russet plains extend:
There, wrapt in clouds the bluish hills ascend.
Even the wild heath displays her purple dyes,
And 'midst the desert, fruitful fields arise,
That crowned with tufted trees and springing corn,
Like verdant isles the sable waste adorn.
Let India boast her plants, nor envy we
The weeping amber, or the balmy tree,   30
While by our oaks the precious loads are borne,
And realms commanded which those trees adorn.
Not proud Olympus yields a nobler sight,
Though gods assembled grace his towering height,
Than what more humble mountains offer here,
Where, in their blessings, all those gods appear,
See Pan with flocks, with fruits Pomona crowned,
Here blushing Flora paints the enamelled ground,
Here Ceres' gifts in waving prospect stand,
And nodding tempt the joyful reaper's hand;   40
Rich Industry sits smiling on the plains,
And peace and plenty tell, a Stuart reigns.

                    .   .   .

Succeeding monarchs hear the subjects' cries,
Nor saw displeased the peaceful cottage rise.
Then gathering flocks on unknown mountains fed,
O'er sandy wilds were yellow harvests spread.
The forests wondered at the unusual grain,
And secret transport touched the conscious swain.
Fair Liberty, Britannia's goddess, rears
Her cheerful head, and leads the golden years.   50

   Ye vigorous swains! while youth ferments your blood,
And purer spirits swell the sprightly flood,
Now range the hills, the gameful woods beset,
Wind the shrill horn, or spread the waving net.
When milder autumn summer's heat succeeds,
And in the new-shorn field the partridge feeds,
Before his lord the ready spaniel bounds,
Panting with hope, he tries the furrowed grounds;
But when the tainted gales the game betray,
Couched close he lies, and meditates the prey: 60
Secure they trust the unfaithful field beset,
Till hovering o'er them sweeps the swelling net.
Thus (if small things we may with great compare)
When Albion sends her eager sons to war,
Some thoughtless town, with ease and plenty blest,
Near, and more near, the closing lines invest;
Sudden they seize the amazed, defenceless prize,
And high in air Britannia's standard flies.

   See! from the brake the whirring pheasant springs,
And mounts exulting on triumphant wings: 70
Short is his joy; he feels the fiery wound,
Flutters in blood, and panting beats the ground,
Ah! what avail his glossy, varying dyes,
His purple crest, and scarlet-circled eyes,
The vivid green his shining plumes unfold,
His painted wings and breast that flames with gold?

   Happy the man whom this bright court approves,
His sovereign favours, and his country loves;
Happy next him, who to these shades retires,
Whom Nature charms, and whom the Muse inspires;   80
Whom humbler joys of home-felt quiet please,

Successive study, exercise, and ease.
He gathers health from herbs the forest yields,
And of their fragrant physic spoils the fields:
With chemic art exalts the mineral powers,
And draws the aromatic souls of flowers:
Now marks the course of rolling orbs on high;
O'er figured worlds now travels with his eye;
Of ancient writ unlocks the learnèd store,
Consults the dead, and lives past ages o'er: 90
Or wandering thoughtful in the silent wood,
Attends the duties of the wise and good,
To observe a mean, be to himself a friend,
To follow Nature, and regard his end;
Or looks on heaven with more than mortal eyes,
Bids his free soul expatiate in the skies,
Amid her kindred stars familiar roam,
Survey the region, and confess her home!
Such was the life great Scipio once admired,
Thus Atticus, and Trumbull thus retired.   100

Ye sacred Nine! that all my soul possess,
Whose raptures fire me, and whose visions bless,
Bear me, oh bear me to sequestered scenes,
The bowery mazes, and surrounding greens:
To Thames's banks which fragrant breezes fill,
Or where ye Muses sport on Cooper's Hill.
(On *Cooper's Hill* eternal wreaths shall grow,
While lasts the mountain, or while Thames shall flow.)
I seem through consecrated walks to rove,
I hear soft music die along the grove: 110
Led by the sound, I roam from shade to shade,
By godlike poets venerable made:
Here his first lays majestic Denham sung;
There the last numbers flowed from Cowley's tongue.
O early lost! what tears the river shed,
When the sad pomp along his banks was led!
His drooping swans on every note expire,
And on his willows hung each Muse's lyre.

My humble Muse, in unambitious strains,

Paints the green forests and the flowery plains.   120
Where Peace descending bids her olives spring,
And scatters blessings from her dove-like wing.
Even I more sweetly pass my careless days,
Pleased in the silent shade with empty praise;
Enough for me, that to the listening swains
First in these fields I sung the sylvan strains.

Composed 1704–13   First published 1713

[ON SICKNESS] (essay from *The Guardian*)

Dear Sir,
You formerly observed to me, that nothing made a more
ridiculous figure in a man's life, than the disparity we
often find in him sick and well. Thus one of an unfortunate constitution is perpetually exhibiting a miserable
example of the weakness of his mind, or of his body, in
their turns. I have had frequent opportunities of late to
consider my self in these different views, and hope I have
received some advantage by it. If what Mr Waller says be
true, that   10

> The soul's dark cottage, battered and decayed,
> Lets in new light through chinks that time has made:

then surely sickness, contributing no less than old age to
the shaking down this scaffolding of the body, may discover the enclosed structure more plainly. Sickness is a
sort of early old age; it teaches us a diffidence in our
earthly state, and inspires us with the thoughts of a future,
better than a thousand volumes of philosophers and di-
vines. It gives so warning a concussion to those props of
our vanity, our strength and youth, that we think of   20
fortifying our selves within, when there is so little de-
pendance on our outworks. Youth, at the very best, is
but a betrayer of human life in a gentler and smoother
manner than age: 'tis like a stream that nourishes a plant
upon its bank, and causes it to flourish and blossom to the
sight, but at the same time is undermining it at the root in

secret. My youth has dealt more fairly and openly with me; it has afforded several prospects of my danger, and given me an advantage not very common to young men, that the attractions of the world have not dazzled me very 30 much; and I began where most people end, with a full conviction of the emptiness of all sorts of ambition, and the unsatisfactory nature of all human pleasures.

When a smart fit of sickness tells me this scurvy tenement of my body will fall in a little time, I am even as unconcerned as was that honest Hibernian, who (being in bed in the great storm some years ago, and told the house would tumble over his head) made answer, 'What care I for the house? I am only a lodger.'

I fancy 'tis the best time to die when one is in the best 40 humour, and so excessively weak as I now am, I may say with conscience, that I'm not at all uneasy at the thought that many men, whom I never had any esteem for, are likely to enjoy this world after me. When I reflect what an inconsiderable little atom every single man is, with respect to the whole creation, methinks 'tis a shame to be concerned at the removal of such a trivial animal as I am. The morning after my exit, the sun will rise as bright as ever, the flowers smell as sweet, the plants spring as green, the world will proceed in its old course, people 50 will laugh as heartily, and marry as fast, as they were used to do. 'The memory of man' (as it is elegantly expressed in the Wisdom of Solomon) 'passeth away as the remembrance of a guest that tarrieth but one day.' There are reasons enough, in the fourth chapter of the same book, to make any young man contented with the prospect of death. 'For honourable age is not that which standeth in length of time, or is measured by number of years. But wisdom is the grey hair to men, and an unspotted life is old age.' He was taken away speedily, lest 60 that 'wickedness should alter his understanding, or deceit beguile his soul'.

I am, *Yours*

Published 1713

THE RAPE OF THE LOCK

An heroi-comical poem

To Mrs Arabella Fermor

Madam,

It will be in vain to deny that I have some regard for this piece, since I dedicate it to you. Yet you may bear me witness, it was intended only to divert a few young ladies, who have good sense and good humour enough to laugh not only at their sex's little unguarded follies, but at their own. But as it was communicated with the air of a secret, it soon found its way into the world. An imperfect copy having been offered to a bookseller, you had the good nature for my sake to consent to the publication of one 10 more correct: this I was forced to before I had executed half my design, for the machinery was entirely wanting to complete it.

The machinery, Madam, is a term invented by the critics to signify that part which the deities, angels, or daemons are made to act in a poem: for the ancient poets are in one respect like many modern ladies: let an action be never so trivial in itself, they always make it appear of the utmost importance. These machines I determined to raise on a very new and odd foundation, the Rosicrucian 20 doctrine of spirits.

I know how disagreeable it is to make use of hard words before a lady; but 'tis so much the concern of a poet to have his works understood, and particularly by your sex, that you must give me leave to explain two or three difficult terms.

The Rosicrucians are a people I must bring you acquainted with. The best account I know of them is in a French book called *Le Comte de Gabalis*, which, both in its title and size, is so like a novel that many of the fair sex 30 have read it for one by mistake. According to these gentlemen, the four elements are inhabited by spirits which they call sylphs, gnomes, nymphs and salamanders. The gnomes, or daemons of earth, delight in mischief;

63

but the sylphs, whose habitation is in the air, are the best-conditioned creatures imaginable. For they say any mortals may enjoy the most intimate familiarities with these gentle spirits, upon a condition very easy to all true adepts, an inviolate preservation of chastity.

As to the following cantos, all the passages of them are as fabulous as the vision at the beginning, or the transformation at the end (except the loss of your hair, which I always mention with reverence). The human persons are as fictitious as the airy ones; and the character of Belinda, as it is now managed, resembles you in nothing but in beauty.

If this poem had as many graces as there are in your person, or in your mind, yet I could never hope it should pass through the world half so uncensured as you have done. But let its fortune be what it will, mine is happy enough, to have given me this occasion of assuring you that I am, with the truest esteem, Madam, your most obedient, humble servant,

A. Pope.

Canto I

What dire offence from amorous causes springs,
What mighty contests rise from trivial things,
I sing – This verse to Caryll, Muse! is due;
This, even Belinda may vouchsafe to view;
Slight is the subject, but not so the praise,
If she inspire, and he approve my lays.
   Say what strange motive, goddess! could compel
A well-bred lord to assault a gentle belle?
O say what stranger cause, yet unexplored,
Could make a gentle belle reject a lord?
In tasks so bold, can little men engage,
And in soft bosoms dwells such mighty rage?
   Sol through white curtains shot a timorous ray,
And oped those eyes that must eclipse the day:
Now lap-dogs give themselves the rousing shake,
And sleepless lovers, just at twelve, awake:

64

Thrice rung the bell, the slipper knocked the ground,
And the pressed watch returned a silver sound.
Belinda still her downy pillow pressed,
Her guardian sylph prolonged the balmy rest: 20
'Twas he had summoned to her silent bed
The morning-dream that hovered o'er her head.
A youth more glittering than a birth-night beau,
(That even in slumber caused her cheek to glow)
Seemed to her ear his winning lips to lay,
And thus in whispers said, or seemed to say:
   'Fairest of mortals, thou distinguished care
Of thousand bright inhabitants of air!
If e'er one vision touched thy infant thought,
Of all the nurse and all the priest have taught,   30
Of airy elves by moonlight shadows seen,
The silver token, and the circled green,
Or virgins visited by angel powers,
With golden crowns and wreaths of heavenly flowers;
Hear and believe! thy own importance know,
Nor bound thy narrow views to things below.
Some secret truths, from learned pride concealed,
To maids alone and children are revealed:
What though no credit doubting wits may give?
The fair and innocent shall still believe.   40
Know, then, unnumbered spirits round thee fly,
The light militia of the lower sky:
These, though unseen, are ever on the wing,
Hang o'er the box, and hover round the Ring.
Think what an equipage thou hast in air,
And view with scorn two pages and a chair.
As now your own, our beings were of old,
And once enclosed in woman's beauteous mould;
Thence, by a soft transition, we repair
From earthly vehicles to these of air.   50
Think not, when woman's transient breath is fled,
That all her vanities at once are dead;
Succeeding vanities she still regards,
And though she plays no more, o'erlooks the cards.
Her joy in gilded chariots, when alive,

And love of ombre, after death survive.
For when the fair in all their pride expire,
To their first elements their souls retire:
The sprites of fiery termagants in flame
Mount up, and take a salamander's name.   60
Soft yielding minds to water glide away,
And sip, with nymphs, their elemental tea.
The graver prude sinks downward to a gnome,
In search of mischief still on earth to roam.
The light coquettes in sylphs aloft repair,
And sport and flutter in the fields of air.
    'Know further yet; whoever fair and chaste
Rejects mankind, is by some sylph embraced:
For spirits, freed from mortal laws, with ease
Assume what sexes and what shapes they please.   70
What guards the purity of melting maids,
In courtly balls, and midnight masquerades,
Safe from the treacherous friend, the daring spark,
The glance by day, the whisper in the dark,
When kind occasion prompts their warm desires,
When music softens, and when dancing fires?
'Tis but their sylph, the wise celestials know,
Though honour is the word with men below.
    'Some nymphs there are, too conscious of their face,
For life predestined to the gnomes' embrace.   80
These swell their prospects and exalt their pride,
When offers are disdained and love denied:
Then gay ideas crowd the vacant brain,
While peers, and dukes, and all their sweeping train,
And garters, stars, and coronets appear,
And in soft sounds, "Your Grace" salutes their ear.
'Tis these that early taint the female soul,
Instruct the eyes of young coquettes to roll,
Teach infant cheeks a bidden blush to know,
And little hearts to flutter at a beau.   90
    'Oft when the world imagine women stray,
The sylphs through mystic mazes guide their way,
Through all the giddy circle they pursue,
And old impertinence expel by new.

66

What tender maid but must a victim fall
To one man's treat, but for another's ball?
When Florio speaks, what virgin could withstand,
If gentle Damon did not squeeze her hand?
With varying vanities, from every part,
They shift the moving toy-shop of their heart;   100
Where wigs with wigs, with sword-knots sword-knots strive,
Beaux banish beaux, and coaches coaches drive.
This erring mortals levity may call,
Oh, blind to truth! the sylphs contrive it all.

'Of these am I, who thy protection claim,
A watchful sprite, and Ariel is my name.
Late, as I ranged the crystal wilds of air,
In the clear mirror of thy ruling star
I saw, alas! some dread event impend,
Ere to the main this morning sun descend   110
But heaven reveals not what, or how, or where:
Warned by the sylph, oh, pious maid, beware!
This to disclose is all thy guardian can:
Beware of all, but most beware of man!'

He said; when Shock, who thought she slept too long,
Leaped up, and waked his mistress with his tongue.
'Twas then, Belinda, if report say true,
Thy eyes first opened on a billet-doux;
Wounds, charms, and ardours, were no sooner read,
But all the vision vanished from thy head.   120
And now, unveiled, the toilet stands displayed,
Each silver vase in mystic order laid.
First, robed in white, the nymph intent adores,
With head uncovered, the cosmetic powers.
A heavenly image in the glass appears,
To that she bends, to that her eyes she rears;
The inferior priestess, at her altar's side,
Trembling, begins the sacred rites of pride.
Unnumbered treasures ope at once, and here
The various offerings of the world appear;   130
From each she nicely culls with curious toil,
And decks the goddess with the glittering spoil.
This casket India's glowing gems unlocks,

And all Arabia breathes from yonder box.
The tortoise here and elephant unite,
Transformed to combs, the speckled and the white.
Here files of pins extend their shining rows,
Puffs, powders, patches, Bibles, billet-doux.
Now awful beauty puts on all its arms;
The fair each moment rises in her charms,   140
Repairs her smiles, awakens every grace,
And calls forth all the wonders of her face:
Sees by degrees a purer blush arise,
And keener lightnings quicken in her eyes.
The busy sylphs surround their darling care,
These set the head, and those divide the hair,
Some fold the sleeve, while others plait the gown;
And Betty's praised for labours not her own.

Canto II

Not with more glories, in the ethereal plain,
The sun first rises o'er the purpled main,
Than, issuing forth, the rival of his beams
Launched on the bosom of the silver Thames.
Fair nymphs and well-dressed youths around her shone,
But every eye was fixed on her alone.
On her white breast a sparkling cross she wore,
Which Jews might kiss, and infidels adore.
Her lively looks a sprightly mind disclose,
Quick as her eyes, and as unfixed as those: 10
Favours to none, to all she smiles extends;
Oft she rejects, but never once offends.
Bright as the sun, her eyes the gazers strike,
And, like the sun, they shine on all alike.
Yet graceful ease, and sweetness void of pride,
Might hide her faults, if belles had faults to hide:
If to her share some female errors fall,
Look on her face, and you'll forget them all.
   This nymph, to the destruction of mankind,
Nourished two locks, which graceful hung behind   20
In equal curls, and well conspired to deck

68

With shining ringlets the smooth ivory neck.
Love in these labyrinths his slaves detains,
And mighty hearts are held in slender chains.
With hairy springes we the birds betray,
Slight lines of hair surprise the finny prey,
Fair tresses man's imperial race ensnare,
And beauty draws us with a single hair.

The adventurous baron the bright locks admired;
He saw, he wished, and to the prize aspired.   30
Resolved to win, he meditates the way,
By force to ravish, or by fraud betray;
For when success a lover's toil attends,
Few ask, if fraud or force attained his ends.

For this, ere Phoebus rose, he had implored
Propitious Heaven, and every power adored: *sacred rite image*
But chiefly Love – to Love an altar built,
Of twelve vast French romances, neatly gilt.
There lay three garters, half a pair of gloves;
And all the trophies of his former loves: 40
With tender billet-doux he lights the pyre,
And breathes three amorous sighs to raise the fire.
Then prostrate falls, and begs with ardent eyes
Soon to obtain, and long possess the prize:
The powers gave ear, and granted half his prayer,
The rest, the winds dispersed in empty air.

But now secure the painted vessel glides,
The sun-beams trembling on the floating tides;
While melting music steals upon the sky,
And softened sounds along the waters die;   50
Smooth flow the waves, the zephyrs gently play,
Belinda smiled, and all the world was gay.
All but the sylph – with careful thoughts oppressed,
The impending woe sat heavy on his breast.
He summons straight his denizens of air;
The lucid squadrons round the sails repair:
Soft o'er the shrouds aërial whispers breathe,
That seemed but zephyrs to the train beneath.
Some to the sun their insect-wings unfold,
Waft on the breeze, or sink in clouds of gold;   60

Transparent forms, too fine for mortal sight,
Their fluid bodies half dissolved in light.
Loose to the wind their airy garments flew,
Thin glittering textures of the filmy dew,
Dipped in the richest tincture of the skies,
Where light disports in ever-mingling dyes;
While every beam new transient colours flings,
Colours that change whene'er they wave their wings.
Amid the circle on the gilded mast,
Superior by the head, was Ariel placed;   70
His purple pinions opening to the sun,
He raised his azure wand, and thus begun:
   'Ye sylphs and sylphids, to your chief give ear;
Fays, fairies, genii, elves, and daemons, hear!
Ye know the spheres, and various tasks assigned
By laws eternal to the aërial kind.
Some in the fields of purest ether play,
And bask and whiten in the blaze of day.
Some guide the course of wandering orbs on high,
Or roll the planets through the boundless sky.   80
Some less refined beneath the moon's pale light
Pursue the stars that shoot athwart the night,
Or suck the mists in grosser air below,
Or dip their pinions in the painted bow,
Or brew fierce tempests on the wintry main,
Or o'er the glebe distil the kindly rain.
Others on earth o'er human race preside,
Watch all their ways, and all their actions guide:
Of these the chief the care of nations own,
And guard with arms divine the British throne.   90
   'Our humbler province is to tend the fair,
Not a less pleasing, though less glorious care;
To save the powder from too rude a gale,
Nor let the imprisoned essences exhale;
To draw fresh colours from the vernal flowers;
To steal from rainbows, ere they drop in showers,
A brighter wash; to curl their waving hairs,
Assist their blushes and inspire their airs;
Nay, oft, in dreams, invention we bestow,

To change a flounce, or add a furbelow. 100
'This day, black omens threat the brightest fair
That e'er deserved a watchful spirit's care;
Some dire disaster, or by force, or slight;
But what, or where, the Fates have wrapped in night.
Whether the nymph shall break Diana's law,
Or some frail china jar receive a flaw;
Or stain her honour, or her new brocade;
Forget her prayers, or miss a masquerade;
Or lose her heart, or necklace, at a ball;
Or whether Heaven has doomed that Shock must fall. 110
Haste, then, ye spirits! to your charge repair:
The fluttering fan be Zephyretta's care;
The drops to thee, Brillante, we consign;
And, Momentilla, let the watch be thine;
Do thou, Crispissa, tend her favourite lock;
Ariel himself shall be the guard of Shock.
'To fifty chosen sylphs, of special note,
We trust the important charge, the petticoat:
Oft have we known that seven-fold fence to fail,
Though stiff with hoops, and armed with ribs of whale; 120
Form a strong line about the silver bound,
And guard the wide circumference around.
'Whatever spirit, careless of his charge,
His post neglects, or leaves the fair at large,
Shall feel sharp vengeance soon o'ertake his sins,
Be stopped in vials, or transfixed with pins;
Or plunged in lakes of bitter washes lie,
Or wedged whole ages in a bodkin's eye:
Gums and pomatums shall his flight restrain,
While clogged he beats his silken wings in vain: 130
Or alum styptics with contracting power
Shrink his thin essence like a rivelled flower:
Or, as Ixion fixed, the wretch shall feel
The giddy motion of the whirling mill,
In fumes of burning chocolate shall glow,
And tremble at the sea that froths below!'
He spoke; the spirits from the sails descend;
Some, orb in orb, around the nymph extend;

71

Some thrid the mazy ringlets of her hair;
Some hang upon the pendants of her ear: 140
With beating hearts the dire event they wait,
Anxious, and trembling for the birth of Fate.

Canto III

Close by those meads, for ever crowned with flowers,
Where Thames with pride surveys his rising towers,
There stands a structure of majestic frame,
Which from the neighbouring Hampton takes its name.
Here Britain's statesmen oft the fall foredoom
Of foreign tyrants, and of nymphs at home;
Here thou, great Anna! whom three realms obey,
Dost sometimes counsel take – and sometimes tea.
    Hither the heroes and the nymphs resort,
To taste a while the pleasures of a court; 10
In various talk the instructive hours they passed,
Who gave the ball, or paid the visit last;
One speaks the glory of the British Queen,
And one describes a charming Indian screen;
A third interprets motions, looks, and eyes;
At every word a reputation dies.
Snuff, or the fan, supply each pause of chat,
With singing, laughing, ogling, and all that.
    Meanwhile, declining from the noon of day,
The sun obliquely shoots his burning ray; 20
The hungry judges soon the sentence sign,
And wretches hang that jurymen may dine;
The merchant from the exchange returns in peace,
And the long labours of the toilet cease.
Belinda now, whom thirst of fame invites,
Burns to encounter two adventurous knights,
At ombre singly to decide their doom;
And swells her breast with conquests yet to come.
Straight the three bands prepare in arms to join,
Each band the number of the sacred nine. 30
Soon as she spreads her hand, the aërial guard
Descend, and sit on each important card:

First Ariel perched upon a Matador,
Then each according to the rank they bore;
For sylphs, yet mindful of their ancient race,
Are, as when women, wondrous fond of place. ouch !
  Behold, four Kings in majesty revered,
With hoary whiskers and a forky beard;
And four fair Queens, whose hands sustain a flower,
The expressive emblem of their softer power;   40
Four Knaves in garbs succinct, a trusty band;
Caps on their heads, and halberts in their hand;
And parti-coloured troops, a shining train,
Draw forth to combat on the velvet plain.
  The skilful nymph reviews her force with care:
'Let Spades be trumps!' she said, and trumps they were.
  Now move to war her sable Matadors,
In show like leaders of the swarthy Moors.
Spadillio first, unconquerable lord!
Led off two captive trumps, and swept the board.   50
As many more Manillio forced to yield,
And marched a victor from the verdant field.
Him Basto followed; but his fate more hard
Gained but one trump, and one plebeian card.
With his broad sabre next, a chief in years,
The hoary Majesty of Spades appears,
Puts forth one manly leg, to sight revealed,
The rest, his many-coloured robe concealed.
The rebel Knave, who dares his prince engage,
Proves the just victim of his royal rage.   60
Even mighty Pam, that kings and queens o'erthrew,
And mowed down armies in the fights of Lu,
Sad chance of war! now destitute of aid,
Falls undistinguished by the victor Spade!
  Thus far both armies to Belinda yield;
Now to the baron fate inclines the field.
His warlike Amazon her host invades,
The imperial consort of the crown of Spades.
The Club's black tyrant first her victim died,
Spite of his haughty mien, and barbarous pride: 70
What boots the regal circle on his head,

73

His giant limbs, in state unwieldy spread;
That long behind he trails his pompous robe,
And, of all monarchs, only grasps the globe?
  The baron now his Diamonds pours apace;
The embroidered King who shows but half his face,
And his refulgent Queen, with powers combined
Of broken troops an easy conquest find.
Clubs, Diamonds, Hearts, in wild disorder seen,
With throngs promiscuous strow the level green.   80
Thus when dispersed a routed army runs,
Of Asia's troops, and Afric's sable sons,
With like confusion different nations fly,
Of various habit, and of various dye,
The pierced battalions disunited fall,
In heaps on heaps; one fate o'erwhelms them all.
  The Knave of Diamonds tries his wily arts,
And wins (oh shameful chance!) the Queen of Hearts.
At this, the blood the virgin's cheek forsook,
A livid paleness spreads o'er all her look;   90
She sees, and trembles at the approaching ill,
Just in the jaws of ruin, and Codille.
And now (as oft in some distempered state)
On one nice trick depends the general fate,
An Ace of Hearts steps forth: the King unseen
Lurked in her hand, and mourned his captive Queen:
He springs to vengeance with an eager pace,
And falls like thunder on the prostrate Ace.
The nymph exulting fills with shouts the sky;
The walls, the woods, and long canals reply.   100
  O thoughtless mortals! ever blind to fate,
Too soon dejected, and too soon elate.
Sudden, these honours shall be snatched away,
And cursed for ever this victorious day.
  For lo! the board with cups and spoons is crowned,
The berries crackle, and the mill turns round:
On shining altars of Japan they raise
The silver lamp; the fiery spirits blaze:
From silver spouts the grateful liquors glide,
While China's earth receives the smoking tide: 110

74

At once they gratify their scent and taste,
And frequent cups prolong the rich repast.
Straight hover round the fair her airy band;
Some, as she sipped, the fuming liquor fanned,
Some o'er her lap their careful plumes displayed,
Trembling, and conscious of the rich brocade.
Coffee (which makes the politician wise,
And see through all things with his half-shut eyes)
Sent up in vapours to the baron's brain
New stratagems, the radiant lock to gain.   120
Ah cease, rash youth! desist ere 'tis too late,
Fear the just gods, and think of Scylla's fate!
Changed to a bird, and sent to flit in air,
She dearly pays for Nisus' injured hair!
    But when to mischief mortals bend their will,
How soon they find fit instruments of ill!
Just then, Clarissa drew with tempting grace
A two-edged weapon from her shining case:
So ladies, in romance, assist their knight,
Present the spear, and arm him for the fight.   130
He takes the gift with reverence and extends
The little engine on his fingers' ends;
This just behind Belinda's neck he spread,
As o'er the fragrant steams she bends her head.
Swift to the lock a thousand sprites repair,
A thousand wings, by turns, blow back the hair;
And thrice they twitched the diamond in her ear;
Thrice she looked back, and thrice the foe drew near.
Just in that instant, anxious Ariel sought
The close recesses of the virgin's thought: 140
As on the nosegay in her breast reclined,
He watched the ideas rising in her mind,
Sudden he viewed, in spite of all her art,
An earthly lover lurking at her heart.
Amazed, confused, he found his power expired,
Resigned to fate, and with a sigh retired.
    The peer now spreads the glittering forfex wide,
To enclose the lock; now joins it, to divide.
Even then, before the fatal engine closed,

A wretched sylph too fondly interposed;   150
Fate urged the shears, and cut the sylph in twain,
(But airy substance soon unites again)
The meeting points the sacred hair dissever
From the fair head, for ever, and for ever!
    Then flashed the living lightning from her eyes,
And screams of horror rend the affrighted skies.
Not louder shrieks to pitying Heaven are cast,
When husbands or when lap-dogs breathe their last;
Or when rich China vessels, fallen from high,
In glittering dust and painted fragments lie!   160
    'Let wreaths of triumph now my temples twine,'
(The victor cried) 'the glorious prize is mine!
While fish in streams, or birds delight in air,
Or in a coach and six the British fair,
As long as *Atalantis* shall be read,
Or the small pillow grace a lady's bed,
While visits shall be paid on solemn days,
When numerous wax-lights in bright order blaze,
While nymphs take treats, or assignations give,
So long my honour, name, and praise shall live!'   170
    What Time would spare, from steel receives its date,
And monuments, like men, submit to fate!
Steel could the labour of the gods destroy,
And strike to dust the imperial towers of Troy;
Steel could the works of mortal pride confound,
And hew triumphal arches to the ground.
What wonder then, fair nymph! thy hairs should feel
The conquering force of unresisted steel?

Canto IV

But anxious cares the pensive nymph oppressed,
And secret passions laboured in her breast.
Not youthful kings in battle seized alive,
Not scornful virgins who their charms survive,
Not ardent lovers robbed of all their bliss,
Not ancient ladies when refused a kiss,
Not tyrants fierce that unrepenting die,

76

Not Cynthia when her manteau's pinned awry,
E'er felt such rage, resentment, and despair,
As thou, sad virgin! for thy ravished hair.   10
  For, that sad moment, when the sylphs withdrew,
And Ariel weeping from Belinda flew,
Umbriel, a dusky, melancholy sprite,
As ever sullied the fair face of light,
Down to the central earth, his proper scene,   *the seat of bad temper*
Repaired to search the gloomy Cave of Spleen.
  Swift on his sooty pinions flits the gnome,
And in a vapour reached the dismal dome.
No cheerful breeze this sullen region knows,
The dreaded east is all the wind that blows.   20
Here, in a grotto, sheltered close from air,
And screened in shades from day's detested glare,
She sighs for ever on her pensive bed,
Pain at her side, and Megrim at her head.
  Two handmaids wait the throne: alike in place,
But differing far in figure and in face.
Here stood Ill-nature like an ancient maid,
Her wrinkled form in black and white arrayed;
With store of prayers, for mornings, nights, and noons,
Her hand is filled; her bosom with lampoons.   30
  There Affectation, with a sickly mien,
Shows in her cheek the roses of eighteen,
Practised to lisp, and hang the head aside,
Faints into airs, and languishes with pride,
On the rich quilt sinks with becoming woe,
Wrapped in a gown, for sickness, and for show.
The fair ones feel such maladies as these,
When each new night-dress gives a new disease.
  A constant vapour o'er the palace flies;
Strange phantoms rising as the mists arise;   40
Dreadful, as hermits' dreams in haunted shades,
Or bright, as visions of expiring maids.
Now glaring fiends, and snakes on rolling spires,
Pale spectres, gaping tombs, and purple fires:
Now lakes of liquid gold, Elysian scenes,
And crystal domes, and angels in machines.

77

Unnumbered throngs on every side are seen
Of bodies changed to various forms by Spleen.
Here living tea-pots stand, one arm held out,
One bent; the handle this, and that the spout: 50
A pipkin there, like Homer's tripod walks;
Here sighs a jar, and there a goose-pie talks:
Men prove with child, as powerful fancy works,
And maids turned bottles call aloud for corks.
  Safe passed the gnome through this fantastic band,
A branch of healing spleenwort in his hand.
Then thus addressed the power: 'Hail, wayward Queen!
Who rule the sex to fifty from fifteen;
Parent of vapours, and of female wit,
Who give the hysteric or poetic fit;   60
On various tempers act by various ways,
Make some take physic, others scribble plays;
Who cause the proud their visits to delay,
And send the godly in a pet to pray;
A nymph there is, that all thy power disdains,
And thousands more in equal mirth maintains.
But oh! if e'er thy gnome could spoil a grace,
Or raise a pimple on a beauteous face,
Like citron waters matrons' cheeks inflame,
Or change complexions at a losing game;   70
If e'er with airy horns I planted heads,
Or rumpled petticoats, or tumbled beds,
Or caused suspicion when no soul was rude,
Or discomposed the head-dress of a prude,
Or e'er to costive lap-dog gave disease,
Which not the tears of brightest eyes could ease;
Hear me, and touch Belinda with chagrin,
That single act gives half the world the spleen.'
  The Goddess with a discontented air
Seems to reject him, though she grants his prayer.   80
A wondrous bag with both her hands she binds,
Like that where once Ulysses held the winds;
There she collects the force of female lungs,
Sighs, sobs, and passions, and the war of tongues.
A vial next she fills with fainting fears,

78

Soft sorrows, melting griefs, and flowing tears.
The gnome rejoicing bears her gifts away,
Spreads his black wings, and slowly mounts to day.
    Sunk in Thalestris' arms the nymph he found,
Her eyes dejected, and her hair unbound.   90
Full o'er their heads the swelling bag he rent,
And all the furies issued at the vent.
Belinda burns with more than mortal ire,
And fierce Thalestris fans the rising fire;
'O wretched maid!' she spread her hands, and cried,
(While Hampton's echoes, 'Wretched maid!' replied)
'Was it for this you took such constant care
The bodkin, comb, and essence to prepare?
For this your locks in paper durance bound?
For this with torturing irons wreathed around?   100
For this with fillets strained your tender head,
And bravely bore the double loads of lead?
Gods! shall the ravisher display your hair,
While the fops envy and the ladies stare?
Honour forbid! at whose unrivalled shrine
Ease, pleasure, virtue, all our sex resign.
Methinks already I your tears survey,
Already hear the horrid things they say,
Already see you a degraded toast,
And all your honour in a whisper lost!   110
How shall I then your helpless fame defend?
'Twill then be infamy to seem your friend!
And shall this prize, the inestimable prize,
Exposed through crystal to the gazing eyes,
And heightened by the diamond's circling rays,
On that rapacious hand for ever blaze?
Sooner shall grass in Hyde Park Circus grow,
And wits take lodgings in the sound of Bow;
Sooner let earth, air, sea, to Chaos fall,
Men, monkeys, lap-dogs, parrots, perish all!'   120
    She said; then raging to Sir Plume repairs,
And bids her beau demand the precious hairs:
(Sir Plume of amber snuff-box justly vain,
And the nice conduct of a clouded cane)

With earnest eyes, and round, unthinking face,
He first the snuff-box opened, then the case,
And then broke out – 'My Lord, why, what the devil!
Zounds! damn the lock! 'fore Gad, you must be civil!
Plague on't! 'tis past a jest – nay prithee, pox!
Give her the hair' – he spoke, and rapped his box.   130
'It grieves me much' (replied the peer again)
'Who speaks so well should ever speak in vain,
But by this lock, this sacred lock, I swear,
(Which never more shall join its parted hair;
Which never more its honours shall renew,
Clipped from the lovely head where late it grew)
That while my nostrils draw the vital air,
This hand, which won it, shall for ever wear.'
He spoke, and speaking, in proud triumph spread
The long-contended honours of her head.   140

  But Umbriel, hateful gnome! forbears not so;
He breaks the vial whence the sorrows flow.
Then see! the nymph in beauteous grief appears,
Her eyes half-languishing, half-drowned in tears;
On her heaved bosom hung her drooping head,
Which, with a sigh, she raised; and thus she said:

  'For ever cursed be this detested day,
Which snatched my best, my fav'rite curl away!
Happy! ah ten times happy had I been,
If Hampton Court these eyes had never seen!   150
Yet am I not the first mistaken maid,
By love of courts to numerous ills betrayed,
Oh had I rather unadmired remained
In some lone isle, or distant northern land;
Where the gilt chariot never marks the way,
Where none learn ombre, none e'er taste bohea!
There kept my charms concealed from mortal eye,
Like roses that in deserts bloom and die.
What moved my mind with youthful lords to roam?
Oh had I stayed, and said my prayers at home!   160
'Twas this the morning omens seemed to tell:
Thrice from my trembling hand the patch-box fell;
The tottering china shook without a wind;

Nay, Poll sat mute, and Shock was most unkind!
A sylph too warned me of the threats of Fate,
In mystic visions, now believed too late!
See the poor remnants of these slighted hairs!
My hands shall rend what even thy rapine spares:
These in two sable ringlets taught to break,
Once gave new beauties to the snowy neck;   170
The sister-lock now sits uncouth, alone,
And in its fellow's fate foresees its own;
Uncurled it hangs, the fatal shears demands,
And tempts, once more, thy sacrilegious hands.
Oh hadst thou, cruel! been content to seize
Hairs less in sight, or any hairs but these!'

Canto V

She said: the pitying audience melt in tears;
But Fate and Jove had stopped the baron's ears.
In vain Thalestris with reproach assails,
For who can move when fair Belinda fails?
Not half so fixed the Trojan could remain,
While Anna begged and Dido raged in vain.
Then grave Clarissa graceful waved her fan;
Silence ensued, and thus the nymph began:
'Say, why are beauties praised and honoured most,
The wise man's passion, and the vain man's toast?   10
Why decked with all that land and sea afford?
Why angels called, and angel-like adored?
Why round our coaches crowd the white-gloved beaux?
Why bows the side-box from its inmost rows?
How vain are all these glories, all our pains,
Unless good sense preserve what beauty gains;
That men may say, when we the front-box grace,
"Behold the first in virtue as in face!"
Oh! if to dance all night, and dress all day,
Charmed the small-pox, or chased old age away;   20
Who would not scorn what housewife's cares produce,
Or who would learn one earthly thing of use?
To patch, nay, ogle, might become a saint,

Nor could it sure be such a sin to paint.
But since, alas! frail beauty must decay,
Curled or uncurled, since locks will turn to grey;
Since painted, or not painted, all shall fade,
And she who scorns a man must die a maid;
What then remains, but well our power to use,
And keep good humour still, whate'er we lose?   30
And trust me, dear, good humour can prevail,
When airs, and flights, and screams, and scolding fail.
Beauties in vain their pretty eyes may roll;
Charms strike the sight, but merit wins the soul.'
    So spoke the dame, but no applause ensued;
Belinda frowned, Thalestris called her prude.
'To arms, to arms!' the fierce virago cries,
And swift as lightning to the combat flies.
All side in parties, and begin the attack:
Fans clap, silks rustle, and tough whalebones crack;   40
Heroes' and heroines' shouts confusedly rise,
And bass and treble voices strike the skies.
No common weapons in their hands are found,
Like gods they fight, nor dread a mortal wound.
    So when bold Homer makes the gods engage,
And heavenly breasts with human passions rage;
'Gainst Pallas, Mars; Latona, Hermes arms;
And all Olympus rings with loud alarms;
Jove's thunder roars, Heaven trembles all around,
Blue Neptune storms, the bellowing deeps resound: 50
Earth shakes her nodding towers, the ground gives way,
And the pale ghosts start at the flash of day!
    Triumphant Umbriel on a sconce's height
Clapped his glad wings, and sat to view the fight:
Propped on their bodkin spears, the sprites survey
The growing combat, or assist the fray.
    While through the press enraged Thalestris flies,
And scatters death around from both her eyes,
A beau and witling perished in the throng,
One died in metaphor, and one in song.   60
'O cruel nymph! a living death I bear,'
Cried Dapperwit, and sunk beside his chair.

A mournful glance Sir Fopling upwards cast,
'Those eyes are made so killing,' – was his last.
Thus on Maeander's flowery margin lies
The expiring swan, and as he sings he dies.

    When bold Sir Plume had drawn Clarissa down,
Chloe stepped in, and killed him with a frown;
She smiled to see the doughty hero slain,
But, at her smile, the beau revived again.   70

    Now Jove suspends his golden scales in air,
Weighs the men's wits against the lady's hair:
The doubtful beam long nods from side to side;
At length the wits mount up, the hairs subside.

    See fierce Belinda on the baron flies,
With more than usual lightning in her eyes:
Nor feared the chief the unequal fight to try,
Who sought no more than on his foe to die.
But this bold lord with manly strength endued,
She with one finger and a thumb subdued: 80
Just where the breath of life his nostrils drew,
A charge of snuff the wily virgin threw;
The gnomes direct, to every atom just,
The pungent grains of titillating dust.
Sudden, with starting tears each eye o'erflows,
And the high dome re-echoes to his nose.

    'Now meet thy fate,' incensed Belinda cried,
And drew a deadly bodkin from her side.
(The same, his ancient personage to deck,
Her great-great-grandsire wore about his neck,   90
In three seal rings; which after, melted down,
Formed a vast buckle for his widow's gown:
Her infant grandame's whistle next it grew,
The bells she jingled, and the whistle blew;
Then in a bodkin graced her mother's hairs,
Which long she wore, and now Belinda wears.)

    'Boast not my fall,' (he cried) 'insulting foe!
Thou by some other shalt be laid as low.
Nor think, to die dejects my lofty mind:
All that I dread, is leaving you behind!   100
Rather than so, ah let me still survive,

And burn in Cupid's flames – but burn alive.'
  'Restore the lock!' she cries; and all around
'Restore the lock!' the vaulted roofs rebound.
Not fierce Othello in so loud a strain
Roared for the handkerchief that caused his pain.
But see how oft ambitious aims are crossed,
And chiefs contend till all the prize is lost!
The lock, obtained with guilt, and kept with pain,
In every place is sought, but sought in vain: 110
With such a prize no mortal must be blest,
So Heaven decrees! with Heaven who can contest?
  Some thought it mounted to the lunar sphere,
Since all things lost on earth are treasured there.
There heroes' wits are kept in ponderous vases,
And beaux' in snuff-boxes and tweezer-cases.
There broken vows, and death-bed alms are found,
And lovers' hearts with ends of riband bound,
The courtier's promises, and sick man's prayers,
The smiles of harlots, and the tears of heirs,   120
Cages for gnats, and chains to yoke a flea,
Dried butterflies, and tomes of casuistry.
  But trust the Muse – she saw it upward rise,
Though marked by none but quick, poetic eyes:
(So Rome's great founder to the heavens withdrew,
To Proculus alone confessed in view)
A sudden star it shot through liquid air,
And drew behind a radiant trail of hair.
Not Berenice's locks first rose so bright,
The heavens bespangling with dishevelled light.   130
The sylphs behold it kindling as it flies,
And pleased pursue its progress through the skies.
  This the beau-monde shall from the Mall survey,
And hail with music its propitious ray.
This the blest lover shall for Venus take,
And send up vows from Rosamonda's lake.
This Partridge soon shall view in cloudless skies,
When next he looks through Galileo's eyes;
And hence the egregious wizard shall foredoom
The fate of Louis, and the fall of Rome.   140

Then cease, bright nymph! to mourn thy ravished hair,
Which adds new glory to the shining sphere!
Not all the tresses that fair head can boast
Shall draw such envy as the lock you lost.
For, after all the murders of your eye,
When, after millions slain, yourself shall die;
When those fair suns shall set, as set they must,
And all those tresses shall be laid in dust;
This lock, the Muse shall consecrate to fame,
And 'midst the stars inscribe Belinda's name.   150

Composed 1712-14   First published in five cantos 1714

EPISTLE TO MISS BLOUNT,
ON HER LEAVING THE TOWN,
AFTER THE CORONATION

As some fond virgin, whom her mother's care
Drags from the town to wholesome country air,
Just when she learns to roll a melting eye,
And hear a spark, yet think no danger nigh;
From the dear man unwilling she must sever,
Yet takes one kiss before she parts for ever:
Thus from the world fair Zephalinda flew,
Saw others happy, and with sighs withdrew;
Not that their pleasures caused her discontent,
She sighed not that they stayed, but that she went.   10
   She went to plain-work, and to purling brooks,
Old-fashioned halls, dull aunts, and croaking rooks:
She want from opera, park, assembly, play,
To morning walks, and prayers three hours a-day;
To pass her time 'twixt reading and bohea,
To muse, and spill her solitary tea,
Or o'er cold coffee trifle with the spoon,
Count the slow clock, and dine exact at noon;
Divert her eyes with pictures in the fire,
Hum half a tune, tell stories to the squire;   20
Up to her godly garret after seven,
There starve and pray, for that's the way to Heaven.

Some squire, perhaps, you take delight to rack;
Whose game is whisk, whose treat a toast in sack;
Who visits with a gun, presents you birds,
Then gives a smacking buss and cries – No words!
Or with his hound comes hallooing from the stable,
Makes love with nods, and knees beneath a table;
Whose laughs are hearty, though his jests are coarse,
And loves you best of all things – but his horse.   30

In some fair evening, on your elbow laid,
You dream of triumphs in the rural shade;
In pensive thought recall the fancied scene,
See coronations rise on every green;
Before you pass the imaginary sights
Of lords, and earls, and dukes, and gartered knights,
While the spread fan o'ershades your closing eyes;
Then give one flirt, and all the vision flies.
Thus vanish sceptres, coronets, and balls,
And leave you in lone woods, or empty walls!   40

So when your slave, at some dear idle time,
(Not plagued with head-aches, or the want of rhyme)
Stands in the streets, abstracted from the crew,
And while he seems to study, thinks of you;
Just when his fancy points your sprightly eyes,
Or sees the blush of soft Parthenia rise,
Gay pats my shoulder, and you vanish quite,
Streets, chairs, and coxcombs rush upon my sight;
Vexed to be still in town, I knit my brow,
Look sour, and hum a tune as you may now.   50

Composed 1714   First published 1717

ELOISA TO ABELARD

The Argument

Abelard and Eloisa flourished in the twelfth century; they
were two of the most distinguished persons of their age in
learning and beauty, but for nothing more famous than
for their unfortunate passion. After a long course of

calamities, they retired each to a several convent and
consecrated the remainder of their days to religion. It was
many years after this separation that a letter of Abelard's
to a friend, which contained the history of his misfortune,
fell into the hands of Eloisa. This awakening all her
tenderness, occasioned those celebrated letters (out of   10
which the following is partly extracted) which give so
lively a picture of the struggle of grace and nature, virtue
and passion.

In these deep solitudes and awful cells,
Where heavenly-pensive Contemplation dwells,
And ever-musing Melancholy reigns,
What means this tumult in a Vestal's veins?
Why rove my thought beyond this last retreat?
Why feels my heart its long-forgotten heat?
Yet, yet I love! From Abelard it came,
And Eloisa yet must kiss the name.
 Dear fatal name! rest ever unrevealed,
Nor pass these lips in holy silence sealed: 10
Hide it, my heart, within that close disguise,
Where, mixed with God's, his loved idea lies:
Oh, write it not, my hand – the name appears
Already written – wash it out, my tears!
In vain lost Eloisa weeps and prays,
Her heart still dictates, and her hand obeys.
 Relentless walls! whose darksome round contains
Repentant sighs, and voluntary pains:
Ye rugged rocks! which holy knees have worn;
Ye grots and caverns shagged with horrid thorn!   20
Shrines! where their vigils pale-eyed virgins keep,
And pitying saints, whose statues learn to weep!
Though cold like you, unmoved and silent grown,
I have not yet forgot myself to stone.
All is not Heaven's while Abelard has part,
Still rebel nature holds out half my heart;
Nor prayers nor fasts its stubborn pulse restrain,
Nor tears for ages taught to flow in vain.
 Soon as thy letters trembling I unclose,
That well-known name awakens all my woes.   30

Oh name for ever sad! for ever dear!
Still breathed in sighs, still ushered with a tear.
I tremble too, where'er my own I find,
Some dire misfortune follows close behind.
Line after line my gushing eyes o'erflow,
Led through a sad variety of woe;
Now warm in love, now withering in thy bloom,
Lost in a convent's solitary gloom!
There stern religion quenched the unwilling flame,
There died the best of passions, Love and Fame.   40

 Yet write, oh write me all, that I may join
Griefs to thy grief, and echo sighs to thine.
Nor foes nor fortune take this power away;
And is my Abelard less kind than they?
Tears still are mine, and those I need not spare,
Love but demands what else were shed in prayer;
No happier task these faded eyes pursue;
To read and weep is all they now can do.

 Then share thy pain, allow that sad relief;
Ah, more than share it, give me all thy grief.   50
Heaven first taught letters for some wretch's aid,
Some banished lover, or some captive maid:
They live, they speak, they breathe what love inspires,
Warm from the soul, and faithful to its fires;
The virgin's wish without her fears impart,
Excuse the blush, and pour out all the heart;
Speed the soft intercourse from soul to soul,
And waft a sigh from Indus to the pole.

 Thou knowest how guiltless first I met thy flame,
When love approached me under friendship's name;   60
My fancy formed thee of angelic kind,
Some emanation of the all-beauteous Mind.
Those smiling eyes, attempering every ray,
Shone sweetly lambent with celestial day.
Guiltless I gazed; Heaven listened while you sung;
And truths divine came mended from that tongue.
From lips like those what precepts failed to move?
Too soon they taught me 'twas no sin to love:
Back through the paths of pleasing sense I ran,

Nor wished an angel whom I loved a man.   70
Dim and remote the joys of saints I see;
Nor envy them that Heaven I lose for thee.
  How oft, when pressed to marriage, have I said,
Curse on all laws but those which love has made!
Love, free as air, at sight of human ties,
Spreads his light wings, and in a moment flies.
Let wealth, let honour, wait the wedded dame,
August her deed, and sacred be her fame;
Before true passion all those views remove;
Fame, wealth, and honour! what are you to love?   80
The jealous god, when we profane his fires,
Those restless passions in revenge inspires,
And bids them make mistaken mortals groan,
Who seek in love for aught but love alone.
Should at my feet the world's great master fall,
Himself, his throne, his world, I'd scorn them all:
Not Caesar's empress would I deign to prove;
No, make me mistress to the man I love;
If there be yet another name more free,
More fond than mistress, make me that to thee!   90
Oh, happy state! when souls each other draw,
When love is liberty, and nature law:
All then is full, possessing, and possessed,
No craving void left aching in the breast:
Even thought meets thought ere from the lips it part,
And each warm wish springs mutual from the heart.
This sure is bliss, if bliss on earth there be,
And once the lot of Abelard and me.
  Alas, how changed! what sudden horrors rise!
A naked lover bound and bleeding lies!   100
Where, where was Eloïse? her voice, her hand,
Her poniard had opposed the dire command.
Barbarian, stay! that bloody stroke restrain;
The crime was common, common be the pain.
I can no more, by shame, by rage suppressed,
Let tears, and burning blushes speak the rest.
  Canst thou forget that sad, that solemn day,
When victims at yon altar's foot we lay?

89

Canst thou forget what tears that moment fell,
When, warm in youth, I bade the world farewell? 110
As with cold lips I kissed the sacred veil,
The shrines all trembled, and the lamps grew pale:
Heaven scarce believed the conquest it surveyed,
And saints with wonder heard the vows I made.
Yet then, to those dread altars as I drew,
Not on the cross my eyes were fixed, but you:
Not grace, or zeal, love only was my call;
And if I lose thy love, I lose my all.
Come! with thy looks, thy words, relieve my woe;
Those still at least are left thee to bestow. 120
Still on that breast enamoured let me lie,
Still drink delicious poison from thy eye,
Pant on thy lip, and to thy heart be pressed;
Give all thou canst – and let me dream the rest.
Ah no! instruct me other joys to prize,
With other beauties charm my partial eyes;
Full in my view set all the bright abode,
And make my soul quit Abelard for God.
    Ah, think at least thy flock deserves thy care,
Plants of thy hand, and children of thy prayer. 130
From the false world in early youth they fled,
By thee to mountains, wilds, and deserts led.
You raised these hallowed walls; the desert smiled,
And Paradise was opened in the wild.
No weeping orphan saw his father's stores
Our shrines irradiate, or emblaze the floors;
No silver saints by dying misers given,
Here bribed the rage of ill-requited Heaven:
But such plain roofs as piety could raise,
And only vocal with Maker's praise. 140
In these lone walls, (their day's eternal bound)
These moss-grown domes with spiry turrets crowned,
Where awful arches make a noon-day night,
And the dim windows shed a solemn light;
Thy eyes diffused a reconciling ray,
And gleams of glory brightened all the day.
But now no face divine contentment wears,

'Tis all blank sadness, or continual tears.
See how the force of others' prayers I try,
(O pious fraud of amorous charity!)   150
But why should I on others' prayers depend?
Come thou, my father, brother, husband, friend!
Ah, let thy handmaid, sister, daughter move,
And all those tender names in one, thy love!
The darksome pines that o'er yon rocks reclined
Wave high, and murmur to the hollow wind,
The wandering streams that shine between the hills,
The grots that echo to the tinkling rills,
The dying gales that pant upon the trees,
The lakes that quiver to the curling breeze;   160
No more these scenes my meditation aid,
Or lull to rest the visionary maid.
But o'er the twilight groves and dusky caves,
Long-sounding aisles, and intermingled graves,
Black Melancholy sits, and round her throws
A death-like silence, and a dread repose:
Her gloomy presence saddens all the scene,
Shades every flower, and darkens every green,
Deepens the murmur of the falling floods,
And breathes a browner horror on the woods.   170
  Yet here for ever, ever must I stay;
Sad proof how well a lover can obey!
Death, only death, can break the lasting chain;
And here, even then, shall my cold dust remain,
Here all its frailties, all its flames resign,
And wait till 'tis no sin to mix with thine.
  Ah, wretch! believed the spouse of God in vain,
Confessed within the slave of love and man.
Assist me, Heaven! but whence arose that prayer?
Sprung it from piety, or from despair?   180
Even here, where frozen chastity retires,
Love finds an altar for forbidden fires.
I ought to grieve, but cannot what I ought;
I mourn the lover, not lament the fault;
I view my crime, but kindle at the view,
Repent old pleasures, and solicit new:

Now turned to Heaven, I weep my past offence,
Now think of thee, and curse my innocence.
Of all affliction taught a lover yet,
'Tis sure the hardest science to forget!   190
How shall I lose the sin, yet keep the sense,
And love the offender, yet detest the offence?
How the dear object from the crime remove,
Or how distinguish penitence from love?
Unequal task! a passion to resign,
For hearts so touched, so pierced, so lost as mine.
Ere such a soul regains its peaceful state,
How often must it love, how often hate!
How often hope, despair, resent, regret,
Conceal, disdain, – do all things but forget!   200
But let Heaven seize it, all at once 'tis fired;
Not touched, but rapt; not wakened, but inspired!
Oh come! oh teach me nature to subdue,
Renounce my love, my life, myself – and you.
Fill my fond heart with God alone, for He
Alone can rival, can succeed to thee.

　　How happy is the blameless Vestal's lot!
The world forgetting, by the world forgot:
Eternal sunshine of the spotless mind!
Each prayer accepted, and each wish resigned;   210
Labour and rest that equal periods keep;
'Obedient slumbers that can wake and weep';
Desires composed, affections ever even;
Tears that delight, and sighs that waft to Heaven.
Grace shines around her with serenest beams,
And whispering angels prompt her golden dreams.
For her the unfading rose of Eden blooms,
And wings of seraphs shed divine perfumes;
For her the Spouse prepares the bridal ring,
For her white virgins hymeneals sing;   220
To sounds of heavenly harps she dies away,
And melts in visions of eternal day.

　　Far other dreams my erring soul employ,
Far other raptures, of unholy joy:
When at the close of each sad, sorrowing day,

Fancy restores what vengeance snatched away,
Then conscience sleeps, and leaving nature free,
All my loose soul unbounded springs to thee.
O cursed, dear horrors of all-conscious night!
How glowing guilt exalts the keen delight!   230
Provoking demons all restraint remove,
And stir within me every source of love.
I hear thee, view thee, gaze o'er all thy charms,
And round thy phantom glue my clasping arms.
I wake: – no more I hear, no more I view,
The phantom flies me, as unkind as you.
I call aloud; it hears not what I say:
I stretch my empty arms; it glides away.
To dream once more I close my willing eyes;
Ye soft illusions, dear deceits, arise!   240
Alas, no more! methinks we wandering go
Through dreary wastes, and weep each other's woe,
Where round some mouldering tower pale ivy creeps,
And low-browed rocks hang nodding o'er the deeps.
Sudden you mount, you beckon from the skies;
Clouds interpose, waves roar, and winds arise.
I shriek, start up, the same sad prospect find,
And wake to all the griefs I left behind.
    For thee the Fates, severely kind, ordain
A cool suspense from pleasure and from pain;   250
Thy life a long dead calm of fixed repose;
No pulse that riots, and no blood that glows.
Still as the sea, ere winds were taught to blow,
Or moving spirit bade the waters flow;
Soft as the slumbers of a saint forgiven,
And mild as opening gleams of promised Heaven.
    Come, Abelard! for what hast thou to dread?
The torch of Venus burns not for the dead.
Nature stands checked; religion disapproves:
Even thou art cold – yet Eloisa loves.   260
Ah hopeless, lasting flames! like those that burn
To light the dead, and warm the unfruitful urn.
    What scenes appear where'er I turn my view?
The dear ideas, where I fly, pursue,

Rise in the grove, before the altar rise,
Stain all my soul, and wanton in my eyes.
I waste the matin lamp in sighs for thee,
Thy image steals between my God and me,
Thy voice I seem in every hymn to hear,
With every bead I drop too soft a tear.   270
When from the censer clouds of fragrance roll,
And swelling organs lift the rising soul,
One thought of thee puts all the pomp to flight,
Priests, tapers, temples, swim before my sight:
In seas of flame my plunging soul is drowned,
While altars blaze, and angels tremble round.

    While prostrate here in humble grief I lie,
Kind, virtuous drops just gathering in my eye,
While praying, trembling, in the dust I roll,
And dawning grace is opening on my soul: 280
Come, if thou darest, all charming as thou art!
Oppose thyself to Heaven; dispute my heart;
Come, with one glance of those deluding eyes
Blot out each bright idea of the skies;
Take back that grace, those sorrows, and those tears;
Take back my fruitless penitence and prayers;
Snatch me, just mounting, from the blest abode;
Assist the fiends and tear me from my God!

    No, fly me, fly me, far as pole from pole;
Rise Alps between us! and whole oceans roll!   290
Ah, come not, write not, think not once of me,
Nor share one pang of all I felt for thee,
Thy oaths I quit, thy memory resign;
Forget, renounce me, hate whate'er was mine.
Fair eyes, and tempting looks, (which yet I view!)
Long loved, adored ideas, all adieu!
O grace serene! O virtue heavenly fair!
Divine oblivion of low-thoughted care!
Fresh blooming hope, gay daughter of the sky!
And faith, our early immortality!   300
Enter, each mild, each amicable guest:
Receive, and wrap me in eternal rest!

    See in her cell sad Eloisa spread,

Propped on some tomb, a neighbour of the dead.
In each low wind methinks a spirit calls,
And more than echoes talk along the walls.
Here, as I watched the dying lamps around,
From yonder shrine I heard a hollow sound.
'Come, sister, come!' (it said, or seemed to say)
'Thy place is here, sad sister, come away!   310
Once, like thyself, I trembled, wept, and prayed,
Love's victim then, though now a sainted maid:
But all is calm in this eternal sleep;
Here grief forgets to groan, and love to weep,
Even superstition loses every fear:
For God, not man, absolves our frailties here.'
   I come, I come! prepare your roseate bowers,
Celestial palms, and ever-blooming flowers.
Thither, where sinners may have rest, I go,
Where flames refined in breasts seraphic glow: 320
Thou, Abelard! the last sad office pay,
And smooth my passage to the realms of day;
See my lips tremble, and my eye-balls roll,
Suck my last breath, and catch my flying soul!
Ah no – in sacred vestments may'st thou stand,
The hallowed taper trembling in thy hand,
Present the cross before my lifted eye,
Teach me at once, and learn of me to die.
Ah then, thy once-loved Eloïsa see!
It will be then no crime to gaze on me.   330
See from my cheek the transient roses fly!
See the last sparkle languish in my eye!
Till every motion, pulse, and breath be o'er,
And even my Abelard be loved no more.
O death all-eloquent! you only prove
What dust we dote on, when 'tis man we love.
   Then too, when fate shall thy fair frame destroy,
(That cause of all my guilt, and all my joy,)
In trance ecstatic may thy pangs be drowned,
Bright clouds descend, and angels watch thee round;   340
From opening skies may streaming glories shine,
And saints embrace thee with a love like mine.

95

May one kind grave unite each hapless name,
And graft my love immortal on thy fame!
Then, ages hence, when all my woes are o'er,
When this rebellious heart shall beat no more;
If ever chance two wandering lovers brings
To Paraclete's white walls and silver springs,
O'er the pale marble shall they join their heads,
And drink the falling tears each other sheds; 350
Then sadly say, with mutual pity moved,
'Oh may we never love as these have loved!'
From the full choir when loud Hosannas rise,
And swell the pomp of dreadful sacrifice,
Amid that scene, if some relenting eye
Glance on the stone where our cold relics lie,
Devotion's self shall steal a thought from Heaven,
One human tear shall drop, and be forgiven.
And sure, if fate some future bard shall join,
In sad similitude of griefs to mine, 360
Condemned whole years in absence to deplore,
And image charms he must behold no more;
Such if there be, who loves so long, so well,
Let him our sad, our tender story tell;
The well-sung woes will soothe my pensive ghost;
He best can paint them who shall feel them most.

Composed c. 1716   First published 1717

ELEGY TO THE MEMORY
OF AN UNFORTUNATE LADY

What beckoning ghost along the moonlight shade
Invites my steps, and points to yonder glade?
'Tis she! – but why that bleeding bosom gored,
Why dimly gleams the visionary sword?
Oh, ever beauteous, ever friendly! tell,
Is it, in heaven, a crime to love too well?
To bear too tender or too firm a heart,
To act a lover's or a Roman's part?
Is there no bright reversion in the sky

For those who greatly think, or bravely die?   10
   Why bade ye else, ye powers! her soul aspire
Above the vulgar flight of low desire?
Ambition first sprung from your blest abodes,
The glorious fault of angels and of gods:
Thence to their images on earth it flows,
And in the breasts of kings and heroes glows.
Most souls, 'tis true, but peep out once an age,
Dull, sullen prisoners in the body's cage:
Dim lights of life, that burn a length of years,
Useless, unseen, as lamps in sepulchres;   20
Like Eastern kings a lazy state they keep,
And, close confined to their own palace, sleep.
   From these perhaps (ere nature bade her die)
Fate snatched her early to the pitying sky.
As into air the purer spirits flow,
And separate from their kindred dregs below;
So flew the soul to its congenial place,
Nor left one virtue to redeem her race,
   But thou, false guardian of a charge too good,
Thou, mean deserter of thy brother's blood!   30
See on these ruby lips the trembling breath,
These cheeks now fading at the blast of death;
Cold is that breast which warmed the world before,
And those love-darting eyes must roll no more.
Thus, if eternal justice rules the ball,
Thus shall your wives, and thus your children fall:
On all the line a sudden vengeance waits,
And frequent hearses shall besiege your gates;
There passengers shall stand, and pointing say,
(While the long funerals blacken all the way,)   40
'Lo! these were they, whose souls the Furies steeled,
And cursed with hearts unknowing how to yield.'
Thus unlamented pass the proud away,
The gaze of fools, and pageant of a day!
So perish all, whose breast ne'er learned to glow
For others' good, or melt at others' woe.
   What can atone (oh ever-injured shade!)
Thy fate unpitied, and thy rites unpaid?

97

No friend's complaint, no kind domestic tear
Pleased thy pale ghost, or graced thy mournful bier. 50
By foreign hands thy dying eyes were closed,
By foreign hands thy decent limbs composed,
By foreign hands thy humble grave adorned,
By strangers honoured, and by strangers mourned!
What, though no friends in sable weeds appear,
Grieve for an hour, perhaps, then mourn a year,
And bear about the mockery of woe
To midnight dances, and the public show?
What, though no weeping Loves thy ashes grace,
Nor polished marble emulate thy face? 60
What, though no sacred earth allow thee room,
Nor hallowed dirge be muttered o'er they tomb?
Yet shall thy grave with rising flowers be dressed
And the green turf lie lightly on thy breast:
There shall the morn her earliest tears bestow,
There the first roses of the year shall blow;
While angels with their silver wings o'ershade
The ground, now sacred by thy relics made.

So peaceful rests, without a stone, a name,
What once had beauty, titles, wealth, and fame. 70
How loved, how honoured once, avails thee not,
To whom related, or by whom begot;
A heap of dust alone remains of thee;
'Tis all thou art, and all the proud shall be!

Poets themselves must fall, like those they sung,
Deaf the praised ear, and mute the tuneful tongue.
Even he, whose soul now melts in mournful lays,
Shall shortly want the generous tear he pays;
Then from his closing eyes thy form shall part,
And the last pang shall tear thee from his heart, 80
Life's idle business at one gasp be o'er,
The Muse forgot, and thou beloved no more!

Composed c. 1717   First published 1717

98

from *the preface*

Homer is universally allowed to have had the greatest invention of any writer whatever. The praise of judgement Virgil has justly contested with him, and others may have their pretensions as to particular excellencies; but his invention remains yet unrivalled. Nor is it a wonder if he has ever been acknowledged the greatest of poets, who most excelled in that which is the very foundation of poetry. It is the invention that in different degrees distinguishes all great geniuses; the utmost stretch of human study, learning, and industry, which master 10
everything besides, can never attain to this. It furnishes Art with all her materials, and without it judgement itself can at best but *steal wisely*. For Art is only like a prudent steward that lives on managing the riches of Nature. Whatever praises may be given to works of judgement, there is not even a single beauty in them to which the invention must not contribute. As in the most regular gardens, Art can only reduce the beauties of Nature to more regularity, and such a figure, which the common eye may better take in and is therefore more entertained with. 20
And perhaps the reason why common critics are inclined to prefer a judicious and methodical genius to a great and fruitful one is because they find it easier for themselves to pursue their observations through an uniform and bounded walk of Art than to comprehend the vast and various extent of Nature.

Our author's work is a wild paradise, where, if we cannot see all the beauties so distinctly as in an ordered garden, it is only because the number of them is infinitely greater. 'Tis like a copious nursery which contains the 30
seeds and first productions of every kind, out of which those who followed him have but selected some particular plants, each according to his fancy, to cultivate and beautify. If some things are too luxuriant, it is owing to the richness of the soil; and if others are not arrived to per-

fection or maturity, it is only because they are overrun and oppressed by those of a stronger nature.

It is to the strength of this amazing invention we are to attribute that unequalled fire and rapture which is so forcible in Homer that no man of a true poetical spirit is master of himself while he reads him. What he writes is of the most animated nature imaginable; everything moves, everything lives and is put in action. If a council be called or a battle fought, you are not coldly informed of what was said or done as from a third person; the reader is hurried out of himself by the force of the poet's imagination and turns in one place to a hearer, in another to a spectator. The course of his verses resembles that of the army he describes,

Οἱ δ' ἄρ' ἴσαν ὡς εἴ τε πυρὶ χθὼν πᾶσα νέμοιτο.   50

'They pour along like a fire that sweeps the whole earth before it.' 'Tis however remarkable that his fancy, which is everywhere vigorous, is not discovered immediately at the beginning of his poem in its fullest splendour; it grows in the progress both upon himself and others, and becomes on fire like a chariot-wheel, by its own rapidity. Exact disposition, just thought, correct elocution, polished numbers may have been found in a thousand; but this poetical *fire*, this *vivida vis animi*, in a very few. Even in works where all those are imperfect or neglected, this can overpower criticism and make us admire even while we disapprove. Nay, where this appears, though attended with absurdities, it brightens all the rubbish about it, till we see nothing but its own splendour. This *fire* is discerned in Virgil, but discerned as through a glass, reflected from Homer, and more shining than fierce, but everywhere equal and constant. In Lucan and Statius it bursts out in sudden, short, and interrupted flashes; in Milton it glows like a furnace kept up to an uncommon ardour by the force of art; in Shakespeare it strikes before we are aware, like an accidental fire from Heaven; but in Homer, and in him only, it burns everywhere clearly and everywhere irresistibly.

100

I shall here endeavour to show how this vast invention exerts itself in a manner superior to that of any poet, through all the main consituent parts of his work, as it is the great and peculiar characteristic which distinguishes him from all other authors.

This strong and ruling faculty was like a powerful star, which in the violence of its course drew all things within its vortex. It seemed not enough to have taken in the whole circle of arts and the whole compass of Nature to supply his maxims and reflections; all the inward passions and affections of mankind to furnish his characters and all the outward forms and images of things for his descriptions; but wanting yet an ampler sphere to expatiate in, he opened a new and boundless walk for his imagination and created a world for himself in the invention of *fable*. That which Aristotle calls the 'soul of poetry' was first breathed into it by Homer.

We come now to the characters of his persons, and here we shall find no author has ever drawn so many with so visible and surprising a variety or given us such lively and affecting impressions of them. Every one has something so singularly his own that no painter could have distinguished them more by their features than the poet has by their manners. Nothing can be more exact than the distinctions he has observed in the different degrees of virtues and vices. The single quality of courage is wonderfully diversified in the several characters of the *Iliad*.

The *speeches* are to be considered as they flow from the characters, being perfect or defective as they agree or disagree with the manners of those who utter them. As there is more variety of characters in the *Iliad*, so there is of speeches, than in any other poem. 'Everything in it has manners' (as Aristotle expresses it); that is, everything is acted or spoken. It is hardly credible in a work of such length how small a number of lines are employed in narration. In Virgil the dramatic part is less in proportion to the narrative; and the speeches often consist of general

101

reflections or thoughts which might be equally just in any person's mouth upon the same occasion. As many of his persons have no apparent characters, so many of his speeches escape being applied and judged by the rule of propriety. We oftener think of the author himself when we read Virgil than when we are engaged in Homer. All which are the effects of a colder invention that interests us less in the action described: Homer makes us hearers, and Virgil leaves us readers.

If in the next place we take a view of the *sentiments*, the same presiding faculty is eminent in the sublimity and spirit of his thoughts. Longinus has given his opinion that it was in this part Homer principally excelled.

If we observe his *descriptions*, images, and similes, we shall find the invention still predominant. To what else can we ascribe that vast comprehension of images of every sort, where we see each circumstance of art and individual of Nature summoned together by the extent and fecundity of his imagination, to which all things, in their various views, presented themselves in an instant and had their impressions taken off to perfection at a heat? Nay, he not only gives us the full prospects of things but several unexpected peculiarities and side-views, unobserved by any painter but Homer. Nothing is so surprising as the descriptions of his battles, which take up no less than half the *Iliad* and are supplied with so vast a variety of incidents that no one bears a likeness to another, such different kinds of deaths that no two heroes are wounded in the same manner, and such a profusion of noble ideas that every battle rises above the last in greatness, horror, and confusion. It is certain there is not near that number of images and descriptions in any epic poet, though everyone has assisted himself with a great quantity out of him; and it is evident of Virgil, especially, that he has scarce any comparisons which are not drawn from his master.

If we descend from hence to the *expression*, we see the bright imagination of Homer shining out in the most

102

enlivened forms of it. We acknowledge him the father of poetical diction, the first who taught that language of the 150 gods to men. His expression is like the colouring of some great masters, which discovers itself to be laid on boldly and executed with rapidity. It is indeed the strongest and most glowing imaginable, and touched with the greatest spirit. Aristotle had reason to say he was the only poet who had found out 'living words'; there are in him more daring figures and metaphors than in any good author whatever. An arrow is 'impatient' to be on the wing, a weapon 'thirsts' to drink the blood of an enemy, and the like. Yet his expression is never too big for the sense, but 160 justly great in proportion to it; 'tis the sentiment that swells and fills out the diction, which rises with it and forms itself about it. And in the same degree that a thought is warmer, an expression will be brighter; and as that is more strong, this will become more perspicuous, like glass in the furnace, which grows to a greater magnitude and refines to a greater clearness only as the breath within is more powerful and the heat more intense.

Lastly, if we consider his *versification*, we shall be sen- 170 sible what a share of praise is due to his invention in that also .... It suffices at present to observe of his numbers that they flow with so much ease as to make one imagine Homer had no other care than to transcribe as fast as the Muses dictated, and at the same time with so much force and inspiriting vigour that they awaken and raise us like the sound of a trumpet. They roll along as a plentiful river, always in motion and always full, while we are borne away by a tide of verse the most rapid and yet the most smooth imaginable. 180

Thus, on whatever side we contemplate Homer, what principally strikes us is his *invention*. It is that which forms the character of each part of his work; and accordingly we find it to have made his fable more extensive and copious than any other, his manners more lively and strongly marked, his speeches more affecting and transported, his sentiments more warm and sublime, his images and descriptions more full and animated, his expression more raised and daring, and his numbers more rapid and various. I hope in what has been said of Virgil with regard to any of these heads, I have no way derogated from his character. Nothing is more absurd or endless than the common method of comparing eminent writers by an opposition of particular passages in them and forming a judgement from thence of their merit upon the whole. We ought to have a certain knowledge of the principal character and distinguishing excellence of each; it is in *that* we are to consider him, and in proportion to his degree in *that* we are to admire him. No author or man ever excelled all the world in more than one faculty, and as Homer has done this in invention, Virgil has in judgement. Not that we are to think Homer wanted judgement because Virgil had it in a more eminent degree, or that Virgil wanted invention because Homer possessed a larger share of it: each of these great authors had more of both than perhaps any man besides, and are only said to have less in comparison with one another. Homer was the greater genius, Virgil the better artist. In one we most admire the man, in the other the work. Homer hurries and transports us with a commanding impetuosity, Virgil leads us with an attractive majesty. Homer scatters with a generous profusion, Virgil bestows with a careful magnificence. Homer, like the Nile, pours out his riches with a boundless overflow; Virgil, like a river in its banks, with a gentle and constant stream. When we behold their battles, methinks the two poets resemble the heroes they celebrate: Homer, boundless and irresistible as Achilles, bears all before him, and shines more and more as the tumult increases; Virgil, calmly daring like Aeneas, appears undisturbed in the midst of the action, disposes all about him, and conquers with tranquillity. And when we look upon their machines, Homer seems like his own Jupiter in his terrors, shaking Olympus, scattering the lightnings, and firing the Heavens; Virgil, like the same power in his benevolence,

104

counselling with the gods, laying plans for empires, and regularly ordering his whole creation.

Nothing that belongs to Homer seems to have been more commonly mistaken than the just pitch of his style, some of his translators having swelled into fustian in a proud confidence of the sublime, others sunk into flatness in a cold and timorous notion of simplicity. Methinks I see these different followers of Homer, some sweating and straining after him by violent leaps and bounds (the certain signs of false mettle), others slowly and servilely creeping in his train, while the poet himself is all the time proceeding with an unaffected and equal majesty before them. However, of the two extremes one could sooner pardon frenzy than frigidity; no author is to be envied for such commendations as he may gain by that character of style which his friends must agree together to call simplicity and the rest of the world will call dullness. There is a graceful and dignified simplicity, as well as a bald and sordid one, which differ as much from each other as the air of a plain man from that of a sloven. 'Tis one thing to be tricked up, and another not to be dressed at all. Simplicity is the mean between ostentation and rusticity.

This pure and noble simplicity is nowhere in such perfection as in the Scripture and our author. One may affirm with all respect to the inspired writings that the Divine Spirit made use of no other words but what were intelligible and common to men at that time and in that part of the world; and as Homer is the author nearest to those, his style must of course bear a greater resemblance to the Sacred Books than that of any other writer. This consideration (together with what has been observed of the parity of some of his thoughts) may, methinks, induce a translator, on the one hand, to give in to several of those general phrases and manners of expression which have attained a veneration even in our language from being used in the Old Testament, as, on the other, to avoid those which have been appropriated to the divinity and in a manner consigned to mystery and religion.

For a farther preservation of this air of simplicity, a particular care should be taken to express with all plainness those moral sentences and proverbial speeches which are so numerous in this poet. They have something venerable and, as I may say, oracular in that unadorned gravity and shortness with which they are delivered, a grace which would be utterly lost by endeavouring to   270
give them what we call a more ingenious (that is, a more modern) turn in the paraphrase.

Perhaps the mixture of some Graecisms and old words after the manner of Milton, if done without too much affectation, might not have an ill effect in a version of this particular work, which most of any other seems to require a venerable antique cast. But certainly the use of modern terms of war and government, such as 'platoon', 'campaign', 'junto', or the like, (into which some of his translators have fallen) cannot be allowable, those only   280
excepted without which it is impossible to treat the subjects in any living language.

First published 1715

from *the second book of the Iliad*

The trial of the army
and catalogue of forces

'But now, ye warriors, take a short repast;
And, well refreshed, to bloody conflict haste.
His sharpened spear let every Grecian wield,
And every Grecian fix his brazen shield;
Let all excite the fiery steeds of war,
And all for combat fit the .attling car.
This day, this dreadful day, let each contend;
No rest, no respite, till the shades descend;
Till darkness, or till death, shall cover all:
Let the war bleed, and let the mighty fall;   10
Till bathed in sweat be every manly breast,
With the huge shield each brawny arm depressed,

106

Each aching nerve refuse the lance to throw,
And each spent courser at the chariot blow.
Who dares, inglorious, in his ships to stay,
Who dares to tremble on this signal day;
That wretch, too mean to fall by martial power,
The birds shall mangle, and the dogs devour.'

He said; the monarch issued his commands;
Straight the loud heralds call the gathering bands;   20
The chiefs enclose their king; the hosts divide,
In tribes and nations ranked on either side.
High in the midst the blue-eyed virgin flies;
From rank to rank she darts her ardent eyes;
The dreadful aegis, Jove's immortal shield,
Blazed on her arm, and lightened all the field:
Round the vast orb a hundred serpents rolled,
Formed the bright fringe, and seemed to burn in gold;
With this each Grecian's manly breast she warms,
Swells their bold hearts, and strings their nervous arms,   30
No more they sigh, inglorious, to return,
But breathe revenge, and for the combat burn.
As on some mountain, through the lofty grove,
The crackling flames ascend, and blaze above;
The fires expanding, as the winds arise,
Shoot their long beams, and kindle half the skies:
So from the polished arms, and brazen shields,
A gleamy splendour flashed along the fields.
Not less their number than the embodied cranes,
Or milk-white swans in Asius' watery plains,   40
That, o'er the windings of Caÿster's springs,
Stretch their long necks, and clap their rustling wings,
Now tower aloft, and course in airy rounds,
Now light with noise; with noise the field resounds.
Thus numerous and confused, extending wide,
The legions crowd Scamander's flowery side;
With rushing troops the plains are covered o'er,
And thundering footsteps shake the sounding shore.
Along the river's level meads they stand,
Thick as in spring the flowers adorn the land,   50

107

Or leaves the trees; or thick as insects play,
The wandering nation of a summer's day:
That, drawn by milky steams, at evening hours,
In gathered swarms surround the rural bowers;
From pail to pail with busy murmur run
The gilded legions, glittering in the sun.
So thronged, so close, the Grecian squadrons stood
In radiant arms, and thirst for Trojan blood.
Each leader now his scattered force conjoins
In close array, and forms the deepening lines.   60
Not with more ease the skilful shepherd swain
Collects his flocks from thousands on the plain.
The king of kings, majestically tall,
Towers o'er his armies, and outshines them all;
Like some proud bull, that round the pastures leads
His subject herds, the monarch of the meads,
Great as the gods, the exalted chief was seen,
His strength like Neptune, and like Mars his mien;
Jove o'er his eyes celestial glories spread,
And dawning conquest played around his head.   70

from *the eighth book of the Iliad*

A nightpiece

The troops exulting sat in order round,
And beaming fires illumined all the ground.
As when the moon, refulgent lamp of night,
O'er heaven's clear azure spreads her sacred light,
When not a breath disturbs the deep serene,
And not a cloud o'ercasts the solemn scene,
Around her throne the vivid planets roll,
And stars unnumbered gild the glowing pole,
O'er the dark trees a yellower verdure shed,
And tip with silver every mountain's head: 10
Then shine the vales, the rocks in prospect rise,
A flood of glory bursts from all the skies:
The conscious swains, rejoicing in the sight,
Eye the blue vault, and bless the useful light.

So many flames before proud Ilion blaze,
And lighten glimmering Xanthus with their rays.
The long reflections of the distant fires
Gleam on the walls, and tremble on the spires.
A thousand piles the dusky horrors gild,
And shoot a shady lustre o'er the field.   20
Full fifty guards each flaming pile attend,
Whose umbered arms, by fits, thick flashes send,
Loud neigh the coursers o'er their heaps of corn,
And ardent warriors wait the rising morn.

from *the twelfth and sixteenth books of the Iliad*

The episode of Sarpedon

from *The Argument*

Sarpedon, the son of Jupiter, commanded the Lycians who
came to the aid of Troy. In the first battle when Diomedes had
put the Trojans to flight, he encouraged Hector to rally and
signalized himself by the death of Tlepolemus. Afterwards
when the Greeks had raised a fortification to cover their fleet,
which the Trojans endeavoured to overthrow, this prince was
the occasion of effecting it. He incites Glaucus to second him in
this action by an admirable speech.

Thus godlike Hector and his troops contend
To force the ramparts, and the gates to rend:
Nor Troy could conquer, nor the Greeks would yield,
Till great Sarpedon towered amid the field:
For mighty Jove inspired with martial flame
His matchless son, and urged him on to fame.
In arms he shines, conspicuous from afar,
And bears aloft his ample shield in air;
Within whose orb the thick bull-hides were rolled,
Ponderous with brass, and bound with ductile gold: 10
And while two pointed javelins arm his hands,
Majestic moves along, and leads his Lycian bands.
  So pressed with hunger, from the mountain's brow

109

Descends a lion on the flocks below;
So stalks the lordly savage o'er the plain,
In sullen majesty, and stern disdain:
In vain loud mastiffs bay him from afar,
And shepherds gall him with an iron war;
Regardless, furious, he pursues his way;
He foams, he roars, he rends the panting prey.   20

    Resolved alike, divine Sarpedon glows
With generous rage that drives him on the foes.
He views the towers, and meditates their fall,
To sure destruction dooms the aspiring wall;
Then casting on his friend an ardent look,
Fired with the thirst of glory, thus he spoke:
    'Why boast we, Glaucus! our extended reign,
Where Xanthus' streams enrich the Lycian plain,
Our numerous herds that range the fruitful field,
And hills where vines their purple harvest yield,   30
Our foaming bowls with purer nectar crowned,
Our feasts enhanced with music's sprightly sound?
Why on those shores are we with joy surveyed,
Admired as heroes, and as gods obeyed,
Unless great acts superior merit prove,
And vindicate the bounteous powers above?
'Tis ours, the dignity they give to grace;
The first in valour, as the first in place;
That when with wondering eyes our martial bands
Behold our deeds transcending our commands,   40
Such, they may cry, deserve the sovereign state,
Whom those that envy dare not imitate!
Could all our care elude the gloomy grave,
Which claims no less the fearful than the brave,
For lust of fame I should not vainly dare
In fighting fields, nor urge thy soul to war.
But since, alas! ignoble age must come,
Disease, and death's inexorable doom;
The life, which others pay, let us bestow,
And give to fame what we to nature owe;   50
Brave though we fall, and honoured if we live,
Or let us glory gain, or glory give!'

He said; his words the listening chief inspire
With equal warmth, and rouse the warrior's fire;
The troops pursue their leaders with delight,
Rush to the foe, and claim the promised fight.
Menestheus from on high the storm beheld
Threatening the fort, and blackening in the field:
Around the walls he gazed, to view from far
What aid appeared to avert the approaching war,　　60
And saw where Teucer with the Ajaces stood,
Of fight insatiate, prodigal of blood.
In vain he calls; the din of helms and shields
Rings to the skies, and echoes through the fields,
The brazen hinges fly, the walls resound,
Heaven trembles, roar the mountains, thunders all the ground.

Nor could the Greeks repel the Lycian powers,
Nor the bold Lycians force the Grecian towers.
As on the confines of adjoining grounds,
Two stubborn swains with blows dispute their bounds;　　70
They tug, they sweat; but neither gain, nor yield,
One foot, one inch, of the contended field;
Thus obstinate to death, they fight, they fall;
Nor these can keep, nor those can win the wall.
Their manly breasts are pierced with many a wound,
Loud strokes are heard, and rattling arms resound;
The copious slaughter covers all the shore,
And the high ramparts drop with human gore.
　　As when two scales are charged with doubtful loads,
From side to side the trembling balance nods,　　80
(While some laborious matron, just and poor,
With nice exactness weighs her woolly store,)
Till poised aloft, the resting beam suspends
Each equal weight; nor this, nor that, descends:
So stood the war, till Hector's matchless might,
With fates prevailing, turned the scale of fight.
Fierce as a whirlwind up the walls he flies.
And fires his host with loud repeated cries.
'Advance, ye Trojans! lend your valiant hands,
Haste to the fleet, and toss the blazing brands!'　　90

111

They hear, they run; and, gathering at his call,
Raise scaling engines, and ascend the wall:
Around the works a wood of glittering spears
Shoots up, and all the rising host appears.
A ponderous stone bold Hector heaved to throw,
Pointed above, and rough and gross below:
Not two strong men the enormous weight could raise,
Such men as live in these degenerate days:
Yet this, as easy as a swain could bear
The snowy fleece, he tossed, and shook in air;   100
For Jove upheld, and lightened of its load
The unwieldy rock, the labour of a god.
Thus armed, before the folded gates he came,
Of massy substance, and stupendous frame;
With iron bars and brazen hinges strong,
On lofty beams of solid timber hung:
Then thundering through the planks with forceful sway,
Drives the sharp rock; the solid beams give way,
The folds are shattered; from the crackling door
Leap the resounding bars, the flying hinges roar.   110
Now rushing in, the furious chief appears,
Gloomy as night! and shakes two shining spears:
A dreadful gleam from his bright armour came,
And from his eye-balls flashed the living flame.
He moves a god, resistless in his course,
And seems a match for more than mortal force.
Then pouring after, through the gaping space,
A tide of Trojans flows, and fills the place;
The Greeks behold, they tremble, and they fly;
The shore is heaped with death, and tumult rends the sky.   120

The wall being forced by Hector, an obstinate battle was
fought before the ships, one of which was set on fire by the
Trojans. Patroclus thereupon obtaining of Achilles to lead out
the Myrmidons to the assistance of the Greeks, made a great
slaughter of the enemy, 'till he was opposed by Sarpedon. The
combat betwixt these two, and the death of the latter, with the
grief of Jupiter for his son, are described in the ensuing
translation from the sixteenth book of the *Iliad*.

112

When now Sarpedon his brave friends beheld
Grovelling in dust, and gasping on the field,
With this reproach his flying host he warms:
'Oh stain to honour! oh disgrace to arms!
Forsake, inglorious, the contended plain;
This hand unaided shall the war sustain:
The task be mine this hero's strength to try,
Who mows whole troops, and makes an army fly.'
    He spake: and, speaking, leaps from off the car:
Patroclus lights, and sternly waits the war.   130
As when two vultures on the mountain's height
Stoop with resounding pinions to the fight;
They cuff, they tear, they raise a screaming cry;
The desert echoes, and the rocks reply:
The warriors thus opposed in arms, engage
With equal clamours, and with equal rage.
    Jove viewed the combat: whose event foreseen,
He thus bespoke his sister and his queen:
'The hour draws on; the destinies ordain,
My godlike son shall press the Phrygian plain: 140
Already on the verge of death he stands,
His life is owed to fierce Patroclus' hands,
What passions in a parent's breast debate!
Say, shall I snatch him from impending fate,
And send him safe to Lycia, distant far
From all the dangers and the toils of war;
Or to his doom my bravest offspring yield,
And fatten, with celestial blood, the field?'
    Then thus the goddess with the radiant eyes:
'What words are these, O sovereign of the skies?   150
Short is the date prescribed to mortal man;
Shall Jove for one extend the narrow span,
Whose bounds were fixed before his race began?
How many sons of gods, foredoomed to death,
Before proud Ilion must resign their breath!
Were thine exempt, debate would rise above,
And murmuring powers condemn their partial Jove.
Give the bold chief a glorious fate in fight;
And when the ascending soul has winged her flight,

Let Sleep and Death convey, by thy command,   160
The breathless body to his native land.
His friends and people, to his future praise,
A marble tomb and pyramid shall raise,
And lasting honours to his ashes give;
His fame ('tis all the dead can have!) shall live.'
    She said: the cloud-compeller, overcome,
Assents to fate, and ratifies the doom.
Then touched with grief, the weeping heavens distilled
A shower of blood o'er all the fatal field:
The god, his eyes averting from the plain,   170
Laments his son, predestined to be slain,
Far from the Lycian shores, his happy native reign.
    Now met in arms, the combatants appear;
Each heaved the shield, and poised the lifted spear;
From strong Patroclus' hand the javelin fled,
And passed the groin of valiant Thrasymed;
The nerves unbraced no more his bulk sustain,
He falls, and falling bites the bloody plain.
Two sounding darts the Lycian leader threw:
The first aloof with erring fury flew,   180
The next transpierced Achilles' mortal steed,
The generous Pedasus of Theban breed:
Fixed in the shoulder's joint, he reeled around,
Rolled in the bloody dust, and pawed the slippery ground.
His sudden fall the entangled harness broke;
Each axle crackled, and the chariot shook:
When bold Automedon, to disengage
The starting coursers, and restrain their rage,
Divides the traces with his sword, and freed
The encumbered chariot from the dying steed: 190
The rest move on, obedient to the rein:
The car rolls slowly o'er the dusty plain.
    The towering chiefs to fiercer fight advance:
And first Sarpedon whirled his weighty lance,
Which o'er the warrior's shoulder took its course,
And spent in empty air its dying force.
Not so Patroclus' never-erring dart;
Aimed at his breast it pierced a mortal part,
Where the strong fibres bind the solid heart.

Then as the mountain oak, or poplar tall,   200
Or pine (fit mast for some great admiral)
Nods to the axe, till with a groaning sound
It sinks, and spreads its honours on the ground,
Thus fell the king; and laid on earth supine,
Before his chariot stretched his form divine:
He grasped the dust distained with streaming gore,
And, pale in death, lay groaning on the shore.
So lies a bull beneath the lion's paws,
While the grim savage grinds with foamy jaws
The trembling limbs, and sucks the smoking blood;   210
Deep groans, and hollow roars, re-bellow through the wood.
   Then to the leader of the Lycian band
The dying chief addressed his last command;
'Glaucus, be bold; thy task be first to dare
The glorious dangers of destructive war,
To lead my troops, to combat at their head,
Incite the living, and supply the dead.
Tell them, I charged them with my latest breath
Not unrevenged to bear Sarpedon's death.
What grief, what shame, must Glaucus undergo,   220
If these spoiled arms adorn a Grecian foe!
Then as a friend, and as a warrior fight;
Defend my body, conquer in my right:
That, taught by great examples, all may try
Like thee to vanquish, or like me to die.'
He ceased; the Fates suppressed his labouring breath,
And his eyes darkened with the shades of death.
The insulting victor with disdain bestrode
The prostrate prince, and on his bosom trod;
Then drew the weapon from this panting heart   230
The reeking fibres clinging to the dart;
From the wide wound gushed out a stream of blood,
And the soul issued in the purple flood.
His flying steeds the Myrmidons detain,
Unguided now, their mighty master slain.

Now great Sarpedon on the sandy shore,
His heavenly form defaced with dust and gore,
And stuck with darts by warring heroes shed,

115

Lies undistinguished from the vulgar dead.
His long-disputed corpse the chiefs enclose,   240
On every side the busy combat grows;
Thick as beneath some shepherd's thatched abode
(The pails high foaming with a milky flood)
The buzzing flies, a persevering train,
Incessant swarm, and chased return again.
   Jove viewed the combat with a stern survey,
And eyes that flashed intolerable day.
Fixed on the field his sight, his breast debates
The vengeance due, and meditates the fates:
Whether to urge their prompt effect, and call   250
The force of Hector to Patroclus' fall,
This instant see his short-lived trophies won,
And stretch him breathless on his slaughtered son;
Or yet, with many a soul's untimely flight,
Augment the fame and horror of the fight.
To crown Achilles' valiant friend with praise
At length he dooms; and, that his last of days
Shall set in glory, bids him drive the foe;
Nor unattended see the shades below.
Then Hector's mind he fills with dire dismay;   260
He mounts his car, and calls his hosts away;
Sunk with Troy's heavy fates, he sees decline
The scales of Jove, and pants with awe divine.
   Then, nor before, the hardy Lycians fled,
And left their monarch with the common dead:
Around, in heaps on heaps, a dreadful wall
Of carnage rises, as the heroes fall.
(So Jove decreed!) At length the Greeks obtain
The prize contested, and despoil the slain.
The radiant arms are by Patroclus borne;   270
Patroclus' ships the glorious spoils adorn.
   Then thus to Phoebus, in the realms above,
Spoke from his throne the cloud-compelling Jove:
'Descend, my Phœbus! on the Phrygian plain,
And from the fight convey Sarpedon slain;
Then bathe his body in the crystal flood,
With dust dishonoured, and deformed with blood;

116

O'er all his limbs ambrosial odours shed,
And with celestial robes adorn the dead.
Those rites discharged, his sacred corpse bequeath   280
To the soft arms of silent Sleep and Death.
They to his friends the mournful charge shall bear;
His friends a tomb and pyramid shall rear:
What honours mortals after death receive,
Those unavailing honours we may give!'
  Apollo bows, and from mount Ida's height,
Swift to the field precipitates his flight;
Thence from the war the breathless hero bore,
Veiled in a cloud, to silver Simois' shore;
There bathed his honourable wounds, and dressed   290
His manly members in the immortal vest;
And with perfumes of sweet ambrosial dews
Restores his freshness, and his form renews.
Then Sleep and Death, two twins of winged race,
Of matchless swiftness, but of silent pace,
Received Sarpedon, at the god's command,
And in a moment reached the Lycian land;
The corpse amidst his weeping friends they laid,
Where endless honours wait the sacred shade.

from *the eighteenth book of the Iliad*

The grief of Achilles,
and new armour made him by Vulcan

  While the long night extends her sable reign,
Around Patroclus mourned the Grecian train.
Stern in superior grief Pelides stood;
Those slaughtering arms, so used to bathe in blood,
Now clasp his clay-cold limbs: then gushing start
The tears, and sighs burst from his swelling heart.
The lion thus, with dreadful anguish stung,
Roars through the desert, and demands his young;
When the grim savage, to his rifled den
Too late returning, snuffs the track of men,   10
And o'er the vales and o'er the forest bounds;

117

His clamorous grief the bellowing wood resounds.
So grieves Achilles; and, impetuous, vents
To all his Myrmidons his loud laments.
  'In what vain promise, gods! did I engage,
When to console Menoetius' feeble age,
I vowed his much-loved offspring to restore,
Charged with rich spoils, to fair Opuntia's shore?
But mighty Jove cuts short, with just disdain,
The long, long views of poor designing man!   20
One fate the warrior and the friend shall strike,
And Troy's black sands must drink our blood alike:
Me too a wretched mother shall deplore,
An aged father never see me more!
Yet, my Patroclus! yet a space I stay,
Then swift pursue thee on the darksome way.
Ere thy dear relics in the grave are laid,
Shall Hector's head be offered to thy shade;
That, with his arms, shall hang before thy shrine;
And twelve, the noblest of the Trojan line,   30
Sacred to vengeance, by this hand expire;
Their lives effused around thy flaming pyre.
Thus let me lie till then! thus, closely pressed,
Bathe thy cold face, and sob upon thy breast!
While Trojan captives here thy mourners stay,
Weep all the night and murmur all the day:
Spoils of my arms, and thine; when, wasting wide,
Our swords kept time, and conquered side by side.'
  He spoke, and bid the sad attendants round
Cleanse the pale corpse, and wash each honoured wound. 40
A massy cauldron of stupendous frame
They brought, and placed it o'er the rising flame:
Then heaped the lighted wood; the flame divides
Beneath the vase, and climbs around the sides:
In its wide womb they pour the rushing stream;
The boiling water bubbles to the brim.
The body then they bathe with pious toil,
Embalm the wounds, anoint the limbs with oil,
High on a bed of state extended laid,
And decent covered with a linen shade;   50

118

Last o'er the dead the milk-white veil they threw;
That done, their sorrows and their sighs renew.

   Thus having said, the father of the fires
To the black labours of his forge retires.
Soon as he bade them blow, the bellows turned
Their iron mouths; and where the furnace burned,
Resounding breathed: at once the blast expires,
And twenty forges catch at once the fires;
Just as the god directs, now loud, now low,
They raise a tempest, or they gently blow;   60
In hissing flames huge silver bars are rolled,
And stubborn brass, and tin, and solid gold;
Before, deep fixed, the eternal anvils stand;
The ponderous hammer loads his better hand,
His left with tongs turns the vexed metal round,
And thick, strong strokes, the doubling vaults rebound.
   Then first he formed the immense and solid shield;
Rich various artifice emblazed the field;
Its utmost verge a threefold circle bound;
A silver chain suspends the massy round;   70
Five ample plates the broad expanse compose,
And godlike labours on the surface rose.
There shone the image of the master-mind:
There earth, there heaven, there ocean he designed;
The unwearied sun, the moon completely round;
The starry lights that heaven's high convex crowned;
The Pleiads, Hyads, with the northern team;
And great Orion's more refulgent beam;
To which, around the axle of the sky,
The Bear, revolving, points his golden eye,   80
Still shines exalted on the ethereal plain,
Nor bathes his blazing forehead in the main.
   Two cities radiant on the shield appear,
The image one of peace, and one of war,
Here sacred pomp and genial feast delight,
And solemn dance, and hymeneal rite;
Along the street the new-made brides are led,
With torches flaming to the nuptial bed:

The youthful dancers in a circle bound
To the soft flute, and cithern's silver sound: 90
Through the fair streets the matrons in a row
Stand in their porches, and enjoy the show.
   There in the forum swarm a numerous train;
The subject of debate, a townsman slain:
One pleads the fine discharged, which one denied,
And bade the public and the laws decide:
The witness is produced on either hand:
For this, or that, the partial people stand:
The appointed heralds still the noisy bands,
And form a ring, with sceptres in their hands: 100
On seats of stone, within the sacred place,
The reverend elders nodded o'er the case;
Alternate, each the attesting sceptre took,
And rising solemn, each his sentence spoke.
Two golden talents lay amidst, in sight,
The prize of him who best adjudged the right.
   Another part (a prospect differing far)
Glowed with refulgent arms, and horrid war.
Two mighty hosts a leaguered town embrace,
And one would pillage, one would burn the place.   110
Meantime the townsmen, armed with silent care,
A secret ambush on the foe prepare:
Their wives, their children, and the watchful band
Of trembling parents, on the turrets stand.
They march; by Pallas and by Mars made bold:
Gold were the gods, their radiant garments gold,
And gold their armour: these the squadron led,
August, divine, superior by the head!
A place for ambush fit they found, and stood,
Covered with shields, beside a silver flood.   120
Two spies at distance lurk, and watchful seem
If sheep or oxen seek the winding stream.
Soon the white flocks proceeded o'er the plains,
And steers slow-moving, and two shepherd swains;
Behind them piping on their reeds they go,
Nor fear an ambush, nor suspect a foe.
In arms the glittering squadron rising round

Rush sudden; hills of slaughter heap the ground;
Whole flocks and herds lie bleeding on the plains,
And, all amidst them, dead, the shepherd swains!   130
The bellowing oxen the besiegers hear;
They rise, take horse, approach, and meet the war:
They fight, they fall, beside the silver flood;
The waving silver seemed to blush with blood.
There Tumult, there Contention stood confessed;
One reared a dagger at a captive's breast;
One held a living foe, that freshly bled
With new-made wounds; another dragged a dead;
Now here, now there, the carcases they tore:
Fate stalked amidst them, grim with human gore.   140
And the whole war came out, and met the eye;
And each bold figure seemed to live or die.

A field deep furrowed next the god designed,
The third time laboured by the sweating hind;
The shining shares full many ploughmen guide,
And turn their crooked yokes on every side.
Still as at either end they wheel around,
The master meets them with his goblet crowned;
The hearty draught rewards, renews their toil,
Then back the turning ploughshares cleave the soil: 150
Behind, the rising earth in ridges rolled;
And sable looked, though formed of molten gold.

Another field rose high with waving grain;
With bended sickles stand the reaper train:
Here stretched in ranks the levelled swarths are found,
Sheaves heaped on sheaves here thicken up the ground.
With sweeping stroke the mowers strow the lands;
The gatherers follow, and collect in bands;
And last the children, in whose arms are borne
(Too short to gripe them) the brown sheaves of corn.   160
The rustic monarch of the field descries,
With silent glee, the heaps around him rise.
A ready banquet on the turf is laid,
Beneath an ample oak's expanded shade.
The victim ox the sturdy youth prepare;
The reaper's due repast, the woman's care.

Next, ripe in yellow gold, a vineyard shines,
Bent with the ponderous harvest of its vines;
A deeper dye the dangling clusters show,
And curled on silver props, in order glow: 170
A darker metal mixed entrenched the place;
And pales of glittering tin the enclosure grace.
To this, one pathway gently winding leads,
Where march a train with baskets on their heads.
(Fair maids and blooming youths) that smiling bear
The purple product of the autumnal year.
To these a youth awakes the warbling strings,
Whose tender lay the fate of Linus sings;
In measured dance behind him move the train,
Tune soft the voice, and answer to the strain.   180

Here herds of oxen march, erect and bold,
Rear high their horns, and seem to low in gold,
And speed to meadows on whose sounding shores
A rapid torrent through the rushes roars:
Four golden herdsmen as their guardians stand,
And nine sour dogs complete the rustic band.
Two lions rushing from the wood appeared;
And seized a bull, the master of the herd:
He roared: in vain the dogs, the men withstood;
They tore his flesh, and drank his sable blood.   190
The dogs (oft cheered in vain) desert the prey,
Dread the grim terrors, and at distance bay.

Next this, the eye the art of Vulcan leads
Deep through fair forests, and a length of meads,
And stalls, and folds, and scattered cots between;
And fleecy flocks, that whiten all the scene.

A figured dance succeeds; such once was seen
In lofty Gnossus for the Cretan queen,
Formed by Daedalean art; a comely band
Of youths and maidens, bounding hand in hand.   200
The maids in soft simars of linen dressed;
The youths all graceful in the glossy vest:
Of those the locks with flowery wreath inrolled;
Of these the sides adorned with swords of gold,
That glittering gay, from silver belts depend.
Now all at once they rise, at once descend,

With well-taught feet: now shape in oblique ways,
Confusedly regular, the moving maze:
Now forth at once, too swift for sight, they spring,
And undistinguished blend the flying ring: 210
So whirls a wheel, in giddy circle tossed,
And, rapid as it runs, the single spokes are lost.
The gazing multitudes admire around:
Two active tumblers in the centre bound:
Now high, now low, their pliant limbs they bend:
And general songs the sprightly revel end.

    Thus the broad shield complete the artist crowned
With his last hand, and poured the ocean round:
In living silver seemed the waves to roll,
And beat the buckler's verge, and bound the whole.   220

    This done, whate'er a warrior's use requires
He forged; the cuirass that outshone the fires,
The greaves of ductile tin, the helm impressed
With various sculpture, and the golden crest.
At Thetis' feet the finished labour lay:
She, as a falcon cuts the aërial way,
Swift from Olympus' snowy summit flies,
And bears the blazing present through the skies.

from *the nineteenth book of the Iliad*

*Thetis brings to her son
the armour made by Vulcan....
He arms for the fight*

Soon as Aurora heaved her orient head
Above the waves, that blushed with early red,
(With new-born day to gladden mortal sight,
And gild the courts of heaven with sacred light,)
The immortal arms the goddess-mother bears
Swift to her son: her son she finds in tears
Stretched o'er Patroclus' corpse; while all the rest
Their sovereign's sorrows in their own expressed.
A ray divine her heavenly presence shed,
And thus, his hand soft touching, Thetis said: 10

'Suppress, my son, this rage of grief, and know
It was not man, but heaven, that gave the blow;
Behold what arms by Vulcan are bestowed,
Arms worthy thee, or fit to grace a god.'
Then drops the radiant burden on the ground;
Clang the strong arms, and ring the shores around;
Back shrink the Myrmidons with dread surprise,
And from the broad effulgence turn their eyes.
Unmoved the hero kindles at the show,
And feels with rage divine his bosom glow;   20
From his fierce eyeballs living flames expire,
And flash incessant like a stream of fire:
He turns the radiant gift: and feeds his mind
On all the immortal artist had designed.

Now issued from the ships the warrior-train,
And like a deluge poured upon the plain.
As when the piercing blasts of Boreas blow,
And scatter o'er the fields the driving snow;
From dusky clouds the fleecy winter flies,
Whose dazzling lustre whitens all the skies: 30
So helms succeeding helms, so shields from shields,
Catch the quick beams, and brighten all the fields;
Broad glittering breastplates, spears with pointed rays,
Mix in one stream, reflecting blaze on blaze;
Thick beats the centre as the coursers bound;
With splendour flame the skies, and laugh the fields around.
Full in the midst, high-towering o'er the rest,
His limbs in arms divine Achilles dressed;
Arms which the father of the fire bestowed,
Forged on the eternal anvils of the god.   40
Grief and revenge his furious heart inspire,
His glowing eyeballs roll with living fire;
He grinds his teeth, and furious with delay
O'erlooks the embattled host, and hopes the bloody day.
The silver cuishes first his thighs infold;
Then o'er his breast was braced the hollow gold;
The brazen sword a various baldric tied,
That, starred with gems, hung glittering at his side;

124

And, like the moon, the broad refulgent shield
Blazed with long rays, and gleamed athwart the field.   50
  So to night-wandering sailors, pale with fears,
Wide o'er the watery waste, a light appears,
Which on the far-seen mountain blazing high,
Streams from some lonely watch-tower to the sky:
With mournful eyes they gaze, and gaze again;
Loud howls the storm, and drives them o'er the main.
  Next, his high head the helmet graced; behind
The sweepy crest hung floating in the wind:
Like the red star, that from his flaming hair
Shakes down diseases, pestilence, and war;   60
So streamed the golden honours from his head,
Trembled the sparkling plumes, and the loose glories shed.
The chief beholds himself with wondering eyes;
His arms he poises, and his motions tries;
Buoyed by some inward force, he seems to swim,
And feels a pinion lifting every limb.
  And now he shakes his great paternal spear,
Ponderous and huge, which not a Greek could rear,
From Pelion's cloudy top an ash entire
Old Chiron felled, and shaped it for his sire;   70
A spear which stern Achilles only wields,
The death of heroes, and the dread of fields.
  Automedon and Alcimus prepare
The immortal coursers, and the radiant car;
(The silver traces sweeping at their side;)
Their fiery mouths resplendent bridles tied;
The ivory-studded reins, returned behind,
Waved o'er their backs, and to the chariot joined.
The charioteer then whirled the lash around,
And swift ascended at one active bound.   80
All bright in heavenly arms, above his squire
Achilles mounts, and sets the field on fire;
Not brighter Phoebus in the ethereal way
Flames from his chariot, and restores the day.
High o'er the host, all terrible he stands,
And thunders to his steeds these dread commands:
  'Xanthus and Balius! of Podarges' strain,

(Unless ye boast that heavenly race in vain,)
Be swift, be mindful of the load ye bear,
And learn to make your master more your care: 90
Through falling squadrons bear my slaughtering sword,
Nor, as ye left Patroclus, leave your lord.'

  The generous Xanthus, as the words he said,
Seemed sensible of woe, and drooped his head:
Trembling he stood before the golden wain,
And bowed to dust the honours of his mane.
When, strange to tell! (so Juno willed) he broke
Eternal silence, and portentous spoke.
'Achilles! yes! this day at least we bear
Thy rage in safety through the files of war: 100
But come it will, the fatal time must come,
Not ours the fault, but God decrees thy doom.
Not through our crime, or slowness in the course,
Fell thy Patroclus, but by heavenly force;
The bright far-shooting god who gilds the day
(Confessed we saw him) tore his arms away.
No – could our swiftness o'er the winds prevail,
Or beat the pinions of the western gale,
All were in vain – the Fates thy death demand,
Due to a mortal and immortal hand.'   110

  Then ceased for ever, by the Furies tied,
His fateful voice. The intrepid chief replied
With unabated rage – 'So let it be!
Portents and prodigies are lost on me.
I know my Fates: to die, to see no more
My much-loved parents, and my native shore –
Enough – when heaven ordains, I sink in night:
Now perish Troy!' He said, and rushed to fight.

from *the twenty-first book of the Iliad*

The battle in the River Scamander

And now to Xanthus' gliding stream they drove,
Xanthus, immortal progeny of Jove.
The river here divides the flying train,

Part to the town fly diverse o'er the plain,
Where late their troops triumphant bore the fight,
Now chased, and trembling in ignoble flight:
(These with a gathered mist Saturnia shrouds,
And rolls behind the rout a heap of clouds:)
Part plunge into the stream: old Xanthus roars,
The flashing billows beat the whitened shores: 10
With cries promiscuous all the banks resound,
And here, and there, in eddies whirling round,
The flouncing steeds and shrieking warriors drowned.
As the scorched locusts from their fields retire,
While fast behind them runs the blaze of fire;
Driven from the land before the smoky cloud,
The clustering legions rush into the flood:
So, plunged in Xanthus by Achilles' force,
Roars the resounding surge with men and horse.
His bloody lance the hero casts aside,   20
(Which spreading tamarisks on the margin hide,)
Then, like a god, the rapid billows braves,
Armed with his sword, high brandished o'er the waves:
Now down he plunges, now he whirls it round,
Deep groaned the waters with the dying sound;
Repeated wounds the reddening river dyed,
And the warm purple circled on the tide.
Swift through the foamy flood the Trojans fly,
And close in rocks or winding caverns lie:
So the huge dolphin tempesting the main,   30
In shoals before him fly the scaly train,
Confusedly heaped they seek their inmost caves,
Or pant and heave beneath the floating waves.
Now, tired with slaughter, from the Trojan band
Twelve chosen youths he drags alive to land;
With their rich belts their captive arms constrains
(Late their proud ornaments, but now their chains).
These his attendants to the ships conveyed,
Sad victims destined to Patroclus' shade.
  Then, as once more he plunged amid the flood,   40
The young Lycaon in his passage stood;
The son of Priam; whom the hero's hand

But late made captive in his father's land....
Ten days were past, since in his father's reign
He felt the sweets of liberty again;
The next, that god whom men in vain withstand
Gives the same youth to the same conquering hand;
Now never to return! and doomed to go
A sadder journey to the shades below.
His well-known face when great Achilles eyed,   50
(The helm and visor he had cast aside
With wild affright, and dropped upon the field
His useless lance and unavailing shield,)
As trembling, panting, from the stream he fled,
And knocked his faltering knees, the hero said:
   'Ye mighty gods! what wonders strike my view!
Is it in vain our conquering arms subdue?
Sure I shall see yon heaps of Trojans killed
Rise from the shades, and brave me on the field:
As now the captive, whom so late I bound   60
And sold to Lemnos, stalks on Trojan ground!
Not him the sea's unmeasured deeps detain,
That bar such numbers from their native plain:
Lo! he returns. Try, then, my flying spear!
Try, if the grave can hold the wanderer;
If earth at length this active prince can seize,
Earth, whose strong grasp has held down Hercules.'
   Thus while he spoke, the Trojan pale with fears
Approached, and sought his knees with suppliant tears.
Loth as he was to yield his youthful breath,   70
And his soul shivering at the approach of death.
Achilles raised the spear, prepared to wound;
He kissed his feet, extended on the ground:
And while, above, the spear suspended stood,
Longing to dip its thirsty point in blood,
On hand embraced them close, one stopped the dart,
While thus these melting words attempt his heart:
   'Thy well-known captive, great Achilles! see,
Once more Lycaon trembles at thy knee.
Some pity to a suppliant's name afford,   80
Who shared the gifts of Ceres at thy board;

128

Whom late thy conquering arm to Lemnos bore,
Far from his father, friends, and native shore;
A hundred oxen were his price that day,
Now sums immense thy mercy shall repay.
Scarce respited from woes I yet appear,
And scarce twelve morning suns have seen me here;
Lo! Jove again submits me to thy hands,
Again, her victim cruel Fate demands!....
How from that arm of terror shall I fly?   90
Some demon urges! 'tis my doom to die!
If ever yet soft pity touched thy mind,
Ah! think not me too much of Hector's kind!
Not the same mother gave thy suppliant breath,
With his, who wrought thy loved Patroclus' death.'
   These words, attended with a shower of tears,
The youth addressed to unrelenting ears:
'Talk not of life, or ransom' (he replies):
'Patroclus dead, whoever meets me, dies:
In vain a single Trojan sues for grace;   100
But least, the sons of Priam's hateful race.
Die then, my friend! what boots it to deplore?
The great, the good Patroclus is no more!
He, far thy better, was foredoomed to die,
'And thou, dost thou bewail mortality?'
Seest thou not me, whom nature's gifts adorn,
Sprung from a hero, from a goddess born?
The day shall come (which nothing can avert)
When by the spear, the arrow, or the dart,
By night, or day, by force, or by design,   110
Impending death and certain fate are mine!
Die then,' – He said; and as the word he spoke,
The fainting stripling sunk, before the stroke:
His hand forgot its grasp, and left the spear,
While all his trembling frame confessed his fear:
Sudden, Achilles his broad sword displayed,
And buried in his neck the reeking blade.
Prone fell the youth; and panting on the land,
The gushing purple dyed the thirsty sand.
The victor to the stream the carcase gave,   120

And thus insults him, floating on the wave:
  'Lie there, Lycaon! let the fish surround
Thy bloated corpse, and suck thy gory wound:
There no sad mother shall thy funerals weep,
But swift Scamander roll thee to the deep,
Whose every wave, some watery monster brings,
To feast unpunished on the fat of kings.
So perish Troy, and all the Trojan line!
Such ruin theirs, and such compassion mine.
What boots ye now Scamander's worshipped stream,   130
His earthly honours, and immortal name?
In vain your immolated bulls are slain,
Your living coursers glut his gulfs in vain!
Thus he rewards you, with this bitter fate;
Thus, till the Grecian vengeance is complete:
Thus is atoned Patroclus' honoured shade,
And the short absence of Achilles paid.'
  These boastful words provoked the raging god;
With fury swells the violated flood.

  'O first of mortals! (for the gods are thine)   140
In valour matchless, and in force divine!
If Jove have given thee every Trojan head,
'Tis not on me thy rage should heap the dead.
See! my choked streams no more their course can keep,
Nor roll their wonted tribute to the deep.
Turn then, impetuous! from our injured flood;
Content, thy slaughters could amaze a god.'
  In human form, confessed before his eyes,
The river thus; and thus the chief replies:
'O sacred stream! thy word we shall obey;   150
But not till Troy the destined vengeance pay,
Not till within her towers the perjured train
Shall pant, and tremble at our arms again;
Not till proud Hector, guardian of her wall,
Or stain this lance, or see Achilles fall.'
  He said; and drove with fury on the foe.
Then to the godhead of the silver bow
The yellow flood began: 'O son of Jove!

Was not the mandate of the sire above
Full and express, that Phoebus should employ   160
His sacred arrows in defence of Troy,
And make her conquer, till Hyperion's fall
In awful darkness hid the face of all?'
    He spoke in vain – the chief without dismay
Ploughs through the boiling surge his desperate way.
Then rising in his rage above the shores,
From all his deep the bellowing river roars,
Huge heaps of slain disgorges on the coast,
And round the banks the ghastly dead are tossed.
While all before, the billows ranged on high,   170
(A watery bulwark,) screen the bands who fly.
Now bursting on his head with thundering sound,
The falling deluge whelms the hero round:
His loaded shield bends to the rushing tide;
His feet, upborne, scarce the strong flood divide,
Sliddering, and staggering. On the border stood
A spreading elm, that overhung the flood;
He seized a bending bough, his steps to stay;
The plant uprooted to his weight gave way.
Heaving the bank, and undermining all;   180
Loud flash the waters to the rushing fall
Of the thick foliage. The large trunk displayed
Bridged the rough flood across: the hero stayed
On this his weight, and raised upon his hand,
Leaped from the channel, and regained the land.
Then blackened the wild waves: the murmur rose;
The god pursues, a huger billow throws,
And bursts the bank, ambitious to destroy
The man whose fury is the fate of Troy.
He like the warlike eagle speeds his pace   190
(Swiftest and strongest of the aërial race);
Far as a spear can fly, Achilles springs;
At every bound his clanging armour rings:
Now here, now there, he turns on every side,
And winds his course before the following tide;
The waves flow after, wheresoe'er he wheels,
And gather fast, and murmur at his heels.

131

So when a peasant to his garden brings
Soft rills of water from the bubbling springs,
And calls the floods from high, to bless his bowers,   200
And feed with pregnant streams the plants and flowers:
Soon as he clears whate'er their passage stayed,
And marks the future current with his spade,
Swift o'er the rolling pebbles, down the hills,
Louder and louder purl the falling rills;
Before him scattering, they prevent his pains,
And shine in mazy wanderings o'er the plains.
  Still flies Achilles, but before his eyes
Still swift Scamander rolls where'er he flies:
Not all his speed escapes the rapid floods;   210
The first of men, but not a match for gods.
Oft as he turned the torrent to oppose,
And bravely try if all the powers were foes;
So oft the surge, in watery mountains spread,
Beats on his back, or bursts upon his head.
Yet dauntless still the adverse flood he braves,
And still indignant bounds above the waves.
Tired by the tides, his knees relax with toil;
Washed from beneath him slides the slimy soil;
When thus (his eyes on heaven's expansion thrown)   220
Forth bursts the hero with an angry groan:
  'Is there no god Achilles to befriend,
No power to avert his miserable end?
Prevent, O Jove! this ignominious date,
And make my future life the sport of fate.
Of all heaven's oracles believed in vain,
But most of Thetis must her son complain;
By Phoebus' darts she prophesied my fall,
In glorious arms before the Trojan wall.
Oh! had I died in fields of battle warm,   230
Stretched like a hero, by a hero's arm!
Might Hector's spear this dauntless bosom rend,
And my swift soul o'ertake my slaughtered friend.
Ah no! Achilles meets a shameful fate,
Oh how unworthy of the brave and great!
Like some vile swain, whom on a rainy day,

132

Crossing a ford, the torrent sweeps away,
An unregarded carcase to the sea.'
    Neptune and Pallas haste to his relief,
And thus in human form address the chief: 240
The power of ocean first: 'Forbear thy fear,
O son of Peleus! Lo, thy gods appear!
Behold! from Jove descending to thy aid,
Propitious Neptune, and the blue-eyed maid.
Stay, and the furious flood shall cease to rave,
'Tis not thy fate to glut his angry wave.
But thou, the counsel heaven suggests, attend!
Nor breathe from combat, nor thy sword suspend,
Till Troy receive her flying sons, till all
Her routed squadrons pant behind their wall: 250
Hector alone shall stand his fatal chance,
And Hector's blood shall smoke upon thy lance.
Thine is the glory doomed.' Thus spake the gods:
Then swift ascended to the bright abodes.
    Stung with new ardour, thus by heaven impelled,
He springs impetuous, and invades the field:
O'er all the expanded plain the waters spread;
Heaved on the bounding billows danced the dead,
Floating 'midst scattered arms; while casques of gold
And turned-up bucklers glittered as they rolled.   260
High o'er the surging tide, by leaps and bounds,
He wades, and mounts; the parted wave resounds.
Not a whole river stops the hero's course,
While Pallas fills him with immortal force.
With equal rage, indignant Xanthus roars,
And lifts his billows, and o'erwhelms his shores.
    Then thus to Simoïs: 'Haste, my brother flood;
And check this mortal that controls a god;
Our bravest heroes else shall quit the fight,
And Ilion tumble from her towery height.   270
Call then thy subject streams, and bid them roar,
From all thy fountains swell thy watery store,
With broken rocks, and with a load of dead,
Charge the black surge, and pour it on his head.
Mark how resistless through the floods he goes,

133

And boldly bids the warring gods be foes!
But nor that force, nor form divine to sight,
Shall aught avail him, if our rage unite:
Whelmed under our dark gulfs those arms shall lie,
That blaze so dreadful in each Trojan eye;   280
And deep beneath a sandy mountain hurled,
Immersed remain this terror of the world.
Such ponderous ruin shall confound the place,
No Greek shall e'er his perished relics grace,
No hand his bones shall gather, or inhume;
These his cold rites, and this his watery tomb.'
    He said; and on the chief descends amain,
Increased with gore, and swelling with the slain.
Then, murmuring from his beds, he boils, he raves,
And a foam whitens on the purple waves: 290
At every step, before Achilles stood
The crimson surge, and deluged him with blood.
Fear touched the queen of heaven: she saw dismayed,
She called aloud, and summoned Vulcan's aid.
    'Rise to the war! the insulting flood requires
Thy wasteful arm! assemble all thy fires!
While to their aid, by our command enjoined,
Rush the swift eastern and the western wind:
These from old ocean at my word shall blow,
Pour the red torrent on the watery foe,   300
Corpses and arms to one bright ruin turn,
And hissing rivers to their bottoms burn.
Go, mighty in thy rage! display thy power,
Drink the whole flood, the crackling trees devour.
Scorch all the banks! and (till our voice reclaim)
Exert the unwearied furies of the flame!'
    The power ignipotent her word obeys:
Wide o'er the plain he pours the boundless blaze;
At once consumes the dead, and dries the soil,
And the shrunk waters in their channel boil.   310
As when autumnal Boreas sweeps the sky,
And instant blows the watered gardens dry:
So looked the field, so whitened was the ground,
While Vulcan breathed the fiery blast around.

134

Swift on the sedgy reeds the ruin preys;
Along the margin winds the running blaze:
The trees in flaming rows to ashes turn,
The flowering lotus and the tamarisk burn,
Broad elm, and cypress rising in a spire;
The watery willows hiss before the fire.   320
Now glow the waves, the fishes pant for breath,
The eels lie twisting in the pangs of death:
Now flounce aloft, now dive the scaly fry,
Or, gasping, turn their bellies to the sky.
At length the river reared his languid head,
And thus, short-panting, to the god he said:
   'Oh, Vulcan! oh! what power resists thy might?
I faint, I sink, unequal to the fight——
I yield——Let Ilion fall; if fate decree——
Ah——bend no more thy fiery arms on me!'   330
   He ceased; wide conflagration blazing round;
The bubbling waters yield a hissing sound.
As when the flames beneath a cauldron rise,
To melt the fat of some rich sacrifice,
Amid the fierce embrace of circling fires
The waters foam, the heavy smoke aspires.
So boils the imprisoned flood, forbid to flow,
And choked with vapours feels his bottom glow.
To Juno then, imperial queen of air,
The burning river sends his earnest prayer: 340
   'Ah why, Saturnia; must thy son engage
Me, only me, with all his wasteful rage?
On other gods his dreadful arm employ,
For mightier gods assert the cause of Troy.
Submissive I desist, if thou command;
But ah! withdraw this all-destroying hand.
Hear then my solemn oath, to yield to fate
Unaided Ilion, and her destined state,
Till Greece shall gird her with destructive flame,
And in one ruin sink the Trojan name.'   350
   His warm entreaty touched Saturnia's ear:
She bade the ignipotent his rage forbear,
Recall the flame, nor in a mortal cause

135

Infest a god: the obedient flame withdraws:
Again the branching streams begin to spread.
And soft remurmur in their wonted bed.

THE ODYSSEY OF HOMER

from *the tenth book of the Odyssey*

Adventures with . . . Circe

Now dropped our anchors in the Aeaean bay,
Where Circe dwelt, the daughter of the Day!...
Goddess, and queen, to whom the powers belong
Of dreadful magic and commanding song.
Some god directing to this peaceful bay
Silent we came, and melancholy lay,
Spent and o'erwatched. Two days and nights rolled on,
And now the third succeeding morning shone.
I climbed a cliff, with spear and sword in hand,
Whose ridge o'erlooked a shady length of land;   10
To learn if aught of mortal works appear,
Or cheerful voice of mortal strike the ear?
From the high point I marked, in distant view,
A stream of curling smoke ascending blue,
And spiry tops, the tufted trees above,
Of Circe's palace bosomed in the grove.
  Thither to haste, the region to explore,
Was first my thought: but speeding back to shore
I deemed it best to visit first my crew,
And send our spies the dubious coast to view.   20

In equal parts I straight divide my band,
And name a chief each party to command;
I led the one, and of the other side
Appointed brave Eurylochus the guide.
Then in the brazen helm the lots we throw,
And fortune casts Eurylochus to go;
He marched with twice eleven in his train;
Pensive they march, and pensive we remain.

The palace in a woody vale they found,
High raised of stone; a shaded space around;   30
Where mountain wolves and brindled lions roam,
(By magic tamed,) familiar to the dome.
With gentle blandishment our men they meet,
And wag their tails, and fawning lick their feet.
As from some feast a man returning late,
His faithful dogs all meet him at the gate,
Rejoicing round, some morsel to receive,
(Such as the good man ever used to give,)
Domestic thus the grisly beasts drew near;
They gaze with wonder not unmixed with fear.   40
Now on the threshold of the dome they stood,
And heard a voice resounding through the wood:
Placed at her loom within, the goddess sung;
The vaulted roofs and solid pavement rung.
O'er the fair web the rising figures shine,
Immortal labour! worthy hands divine.
Polites to the rest the question moved
(A gallant leader, and a man I loved):

'What voice celestial, chanting to the loom
(Or nymph, or goddess), echoes from the room?   50
Say, shall we seek access?' With that they call;
And wide unfold the portals of the hall.

The goddess, rising, asks her guests to stay,
Who blindly follow where she leads the way.
Eurylochus alone of all the band,
Suspecting fraud, more prudently remained.
On thrones around with downy coverings graced,
With semblance fair, the unhappy men she placed.
Milk newly pressed, the sacred flour of wheat,
And honey fresh, and Pramnian wines the treat: 60
But venomed was the bread, and mixed the bowl,
With drugs of force to darken all the soul:
Soon in the luscious feast themselves they lost;
And drank oblivion of their native coast.
Instant her circling wand the goddess waves,
To hogs transforms them, and the sty receives.
No more was seen the human form divine;

137

Head, face, and members, bristle into swine:
Still cursed with sense, their mind remains alone,
And their own voice affrights them when they groan.   70
Meanwhile the goddess in disdain bestows
The mast and acorn, brutal food! and strows
The fruits and cornel, as their feast, around;
Now prone and grovelling on unsavoury ground.

  Eurylochus, with pensive steps and slow,
Aghast returns; the messenger of woe,
And bitter fate. To speak he made essay,
In vain essayed, nor would his tongue obey.
His swelling heart denied the words their way.
But speaking tears the want of words supply,   80
And the full soul bursts copious from his eye.
Affrighted, anxious for our fellows' fates,
We press to hear what sadly he relates:

  'We went, Ulysses! (such was thy command)
Through the lone thicket and the desert land.
A palace in a woody vale we found
Brown with dark forests, and with shades around.
A voice celestial echoed from the dome,
Or nymph or goddess, chanting to the loom.
Access we sought, nor was access denied: 90
Radiant she came: the portals opened wide:
The goddess mild invites the guests to stay:
They blindly follow where she leads the way.
I only wait behind of all the train:
I waited long, and eyed the doors in vain:
The rest are vanished, none repassed the gate,
And not a man appears to tell their fate.'

  I heard, and instant o'er my shoulder flung
The belt in which my weighty falchion hung
(A beamy blade): then seized the bended bow,   100
And bade him guide the way, resolved to go.
He, prostrate falling, with both hands embraced
My knees, and weeping thus his suit addressed:

  'O king, beloved of Jove, thy servant spare,
And ah, thyself the rash attempt forbear!
Never, alas! thou never shalt return,

138

Or see the wretched for whose loss we mourn.
With what remains from certain ruin fly,
And save the few not fated yet to die.'
  I answered stern: 'Inglorious then remain,   110
Here feast and loiter, and desert thy train.
Alone, unfriended, will I tempt my way;
The laws of fate compel, and I obey.'
This said, and scornful turning from the shore
My haughty step, I stalked the valley o'er.
Till now approaching nigh the magic bower,
Where dwelt the enchantress skilled in herbs of power,
A form divine forth issued from the wood
(Immortal Hermes with the golden rod)
In human semblance. On his bloomy face   120
Youth smiled celestial, with each opening grace.
He seized my hand, and gracious thus began:
'Ah whither roam'st thou, much-enduring man?
O blind to fate! what led thy steps to rove
The horrid mazes of this magic grove?
Each friend you seek in yon enclosure lies,
All lost their form, and habitants of sties.
Thinkest thou by wit to model their escape?
Sooner shalt thou, a stranger to thy shape,
Fall prone their equal: first thy danger know,   130
Then take the antidote the gods bestow.
The plant I give through all the direful bower
Shall guard thee, and avert the evil hour.
Now hear her wicked arts: Before thy eyes
The bowl shall sparkle, and the banquet rise;
Take this, nor from the faithless feast abstain,
For tempered drugs and poisons shall be vain.
Soon as she strikes her wand, and gives the word,
Draw forth and brandish thy refulgent sword,
And menace death: those menaces shall move   140
Her altered mind to blandishment and love.
Nor shun the blessing proffered to thy arms.
Ascend her bed, and taste celestial charms:
So shall thy tedious toils a respite find,
And thy lost friends return to humankind.

139

But swear her first by those dread oaths that tie
The powers below, the blessed in the sky;
Lest to thee naked secret fraud be meant,
Or magic bind thee cold and impotent.
    Thus while he spoke, the sovereign plant he drew   150
Where on the all-bearing earth unmarked it grew,
And showed its nature and its wondrous power:
Black was the root, but milky white the flower;
Moly the name, to mortals hard to find,
But all is easy to the ethereal kind.
This Hermes gave, then, gliding off the glade,
Shot to Olympus from the woodland shade.
    While full of thought, revolving fates to come,
I speed my passage to the enchanted dome.
Arrived, before the lofty gates I stayed;   160
The lofty gates the goddess wide displayed:
She leads before, and to the feast invites;
I follow sadly to the magic rites.
Radiant with starry studs, a silver seat
Received my limbs: a footstool eased my feet,
She mixed the potion, fraudulent of soul;
The poison mantled in the golden bowl.
I took, and quaffed it, confident in heaven:
Then waved the wand, and then the word was given.
'Hence to thy fellows!' (dreadful she began:)   170
'Go, be a beast!' – I heard, and yet was man.
    Then, sudden whirling like a waving flame,
My beamy falchion, I assault the dame.
Struck with unusual fear, she trembling cries,
She faints, she falls; she lifts her weeping eyes.
    'What art thou? say! from whence, from whom you came?
O more than human! tell thy race, thy name.
Amazing strength, these poisons to sustain!
Not mortal thou, nor mortal is thy brain.
Or art thou he, the man to come (foretold   180
By Hermes, powerful with the wand of gold),
The man from Troy, who wandered ocean round;
The man for wisdom's various arts renowned,
Ulysses? Oh! thy threatening fury cease,

140

Sheathe thy bright sword, and join our hands in peace!
Let mutual joys our mutual trust combine,
And love, and love-born confidence, be thine.'
　'And how, dread Circe!' (furious I rejoin)
'Can love, and love-born confidence, be mine,
Beneath thy charms when my companions groan,　　　190
Transformed to beasts, with accents not their own?
O thou of fraudful heart, shall I be led
To share thy feast-rites, or ascend thy bed;
That, all unarmed, thy vengenance may have vent,
And magic bind me, cold and impotent?
Celestial as thou art, yet stand denied;
Or swear that oath by which the gods are tied,
Swear, in thy soul no latent frauds remain,
Swear by the vow which never can be vain.'
　The goddess swore: then seized my hand, and led　　200
To the sweet transports of the genial bed.
Ministrant to their queen, with busy care
Four faithful handmaids the soft rites prepare;
Nymphs sprung from fountains, or from shady woods,
Or the fair offspring of the sacred floods.
One o'er the couches painted carpets threw,
Whose purple lustre glowed against the view:
White linen lay beneath. Another placed
The silver stands, with golden flaskets graced:
With dulcet beverage this the beaker crowned,　　　210
Fair in the midst, with gilded cups around,
That in the tripod o'er the kindled pile
The water pours; the bubbling waters boil;
An ample vase receives the smoking wave;
And, in the bath prepared, my limbs I lave:
Reviving sweets repair the mind's decay,
And take the painful sense of toil away.
A vest and tunic o'er me next she threw,
Fresh from the bath, and dropping balmy dew;
Then led and placed me on the sovereign seat,　　　220
With carpets spread; a footstool at my feet.
The golden ewer a nymph obsequious brings,
Replenished from the cool translucent springs;

With copious water the bright vase supplies
A silver laver of capacious size.
I washed. The table in fair order spread.
They heap the glittering canisters with bread:
Viands of various kinds allure the taste,
Of choicest sort and savour, rich repast!
Circe in vain invites the feast to share;   230
Absent I ponder, and absorbed in care:
While scenes of woe rose anxious in my breast,
The queen beheld me, and these words addressed:
    'Why sits Ulysses silent and apart,
Some hoard of grief close harboured at his heart?
Untouched before thee stand the cates divine,
And unregarded laughs the rosy wine.
Can yet a doubt or any dread remain,
When sworn that oath which never can be vain?'
    I answered: 'Goddess! human is my breast,   240
By justice swayed, by tender pity pressed:
Ill fits it me, whose friends are sunk to beasts,
To quaff thy bowls, or riot in thy feasts.
Me would'st thou please? for them thy cares employ,
And them to me restore, and me to joy.'
    With that she parted: in her potent hand
She bore the virtue of the magie wand.
Then, hastening to the sties, set wide the door,
Urged forth, and drove the bristly herd before;
Unwieldy, out they rushed with general cry,   250
Enormous beasts, dishonest to the eye.
Now touched by counter-charms they change again,
And stand majestic, and recalled to men.
Those hairs of late that bristled every part,
Fall off, miraculous effect of art!
Till all the form in full proportion rise,
More young, more large, more graceful to my eyes.
They saw, they knew me, and with eager pace
Clung to their master in a long embrace:
Sad, pleasing sight! with tears each eye ran o'er,   260
And sobs of joy re-echoed through the bower;
E'en Circe wept, her adamantine heart

142

Felt pity enter, and sustained her part.
  'Son of Laertes!' (then the queen began)
'Oh much-enduring, much-experienced man!
Haste to thy vessel on the sea-beat shore,
Unload thy treasures, and the galley moor;
Then bring thy friends, secure from future harms,
And in our grottoes stow thy spoils and arms.'
  She said. Obedient to her high command   270
I quit the place, and hasten to the strand;
My sad companions on the beach I found,
Their wistful eyes in floods of sorrow drowned.
As from fresh pastures and the dewy field
(When loaded cribs their evening banquet yield)
The lowing herds return; around them throng
With leaps and bounds their late imprisoned young,
Rush to their mothers with unruly joy,
And echoing hills return the tender cry:
So round me pressed, exulting at my sight,   280
With cries and agonies of wild delight,
The weeping sailors; nor less fierce their joy
Than if returned to Ithaca from Troy.
'Ah master! ever honoured, ever dear!'
(These tender words on every side I hear)
'What other joy can equal thy return?
Not that loved country for whose sight we mourn,
The soil that nursed us, and that gave us breath:
But ah! relate our lost companions' death.'
  I answered cheerful: 'Haste, your galley moor,   290
And bring our treasures and our arms ashore:
Those in yon hollow caverns let us lay,
Then rise, and follow where I lead the way.
Your fellows live; believe your eyes, and come
To taste the joys of Circe's sacred dome.'
  With ready speed the joyful crew obey;
Alone Eurylochus persuades their stay.
'Whither (he cried), ah whither will ye run?
Seek ye to meet those evils ye should shun?
Will you the terrors of the dome explore,   300
In swine to grovel, or in lions roar,

143

Or wolf-like howl away the midnight hour
In dreadful watch around the magic bower?
Remember Cyclops, and his bloody deed;
The leader's rashness made the soldiers bleed.'

    I heard incensed, and first resolved to speed
My flying falchion at the rebel's head.
Dear as he was, by ties of kindred bound,
This hand had stretched him breathless on the ground,
But all at once my interposing train   310
For mercy pleaded, nor could plead in vain.
'Leave here the man who dares his prince desert,
Leave to repentance and his own sad heart,
To guard the ship. Seek we the sacred shades
Of Circe's palace, where Ulysses leads.'

    This with one voice declared, the rising train
Left the black vessel by the murmuring main.
Shame touched Eurylochus his altered breast;
He feared my threats, and followed with the rest.

    Meanwhile the goddess, with indulgent cares   320
And social joys, the late transformed repairs;
The bath, the feast, their fainting soul renews:
Rich in refulgent robes, and dropping balmy dews:
Brightening with joy, their eager eyes behold
Each other's face, and each his story told;
Then gushing tears the narrative confound,
And with their sobs the vaulted roofs resound.
When hushed their passion, thus the goddess cries:
'Ulysses, taught by labours to be wise,
Let this short memory of grief suffice.   330
To me are known the various woes ye bore,
In storms by sea, in perils on the shore;
Forget whatever was in Fortune's power,
And share the pleasures of this genial hour.
Such be your mind as ere ye left your coast,
Or learned to sorrow for a country lost.
Exiles and wanderers now, where'er ye go,
Too faithful memory renews your woe:
The cause removed, habitual griefs remain,
And the soul saddens by the use of pain.'   340

Her kind entreaty moved the general breast;
Tired with long toil, we willing sunk to rest.
We plied the banquet, and the bowl we crowned,
Till the full circle of the year came round.
But when the seasons, following in their train,
Brought back the months, the days, and hours again;
As from a lethargy at once they rise,
And urge their chief with animating cries:
   'Is this, Ulysses, our inglorious lot?
And is the name of Ithaca forgot?   350
Shall never the dear land in prospect rise,
Or the loved palace glitter in our eyes?'
   Melting I heard; yet till the sun's decline
Prolonged the feast, and quaffed the rosy wine:
But when the shades came on at evening hour,
And all lay slumbering in the dusky bower,
I came as suppliant to fair Circe's bed.
The tender moment seized, and thus I said:
'Be mindful, goddess! of thy promise made;
Must sad Ulysses ever be delayed?   360
Around their lord my sad companions mourn,
Each breast beats homeward, anxious to return:
If but a moment parted from thy eyes,
Their tears flow round me, and my heart complies.'
   'Go then' (she cried), 'ah go! yet think, not I,
Not Circe, but the Fates, your wish deny.
Ah, hope not yet to breathe thy native air!
Far other journey first demands thy care;
To tread the uncomfortable paths beneath,
And view the realms of darkness and of death.'   370

from *the postscript*

I cannot dismiss this work without a few observations on
the true character and style of it. Whoever reads the
Odyssey with an eye to the *Iliad*, expecting to find it of the
same character or of the same sort of spirit, will be griev-
ously deceived and err against the first principle of criticism, which is to consider the nature of the piece and the

intent of its author. The *Odyssey* is a moral and political work, instructive to all degrees of men and filled with images, examples, and precepts of civil and domestic life.... The *Odyssey* is the reverse of the *Iliad* in moral,   10 subject, manner, and style, to which it has no sort of relation but as the story happens to follow in order of time and as some of the same persons are actors in it. Yet from this incidental connection many have been misled to regard it as a continuation or second part, and thence to expect a parity of character inconsistent with its nature.

The *Odyssey* is a perpetual source of poetry; the stream is not the less full for being gentle, though it is true (when we speak only with regard to the sublime) that a river foaming and thundering in cataracts from rocks and pre-   20 cipices is what more strikes, amazes, and fills the mind than the same body of water flowing afterwards through peaceful vales and agreeable scenes of pasturage.

The *Odyssey* (as I have before said) ought to be considered according to its own nature and design, not with an eye to the *Iliad*. To censure Homer because it is unlike what it was never meant to resemble is as if a gardener who had purposely cultivated two beautiful trees of contrary natures, as a specimen of his skill in the several kinds, should be blamed for not bringing them into pairs;   30 when in root, stem, leaf, and flower each was so entirely different that one must have been spoiled in the endeavour to match the other.

From the nature of the poem, we shall form an idea of the *style*. The diction is to follow the images and to take its colour from the complexion of the thoughts. Accordingly, the *Odyssey* is not always clothed in the majesty of verse proper to tragedy, but sometimes descends into the plainer narrative, and sometimes even to that familiar dialogue essential to comedy. However, where it cannot   40 support a sublimity, it always preserves a dignity or at least a propriety.

There is a real beauty in an easy, pure, perspicuous

146

description even of a low action. There are numerous instances of this both in Homer and Virgil, and perhaps those natural passages are not the least pleasing of their works. It is often the same in history, where the representations of common or even domestic things in clear, plain, and natural words, are frequently found to make the liveliest impression on the reader.   50

Indeed the true reason that so few poets have imitated Homer in these lower parts has been the extreme difficulty of preserving that mixture of ease and dignity essential to them. For it is as hard for an epic poem to stoop to the narrative with success as for a prince to descend to be familiar without diminution to his greatness.

Homer, in his lowest narrations or speeches, is ever easy, flowing, copious, clear, and harmonious. He shows not less invention in assembling the humbler than the   60 greater thoughts and images; nor less judgement in proportioning the style and the versification to these than to the other. Let it be remembered that the same genius that soared the highest, and from whom the greatest models of the sublime are derived, was also he who stooped the lowest and gave to the simple narrative its utmost perfection. Which of these was the harder task to Homer himself I cannot pretend to determine; but to his translator I can affirm (however unequal all his imitations must be) that of the latter has been much the more difficult.   70

First published 1726

from the PREFACE TO THE WORKS OF SHAKESPEARE

If ever any author deserved the name of an *original*, it was Shakespeare. Homer himself drew not his art so immediately from the fountains of Nature; it proceeded through Egyptian strainers and channels and came to him not without some tincture of the learning or some cast of the models of those before him. The poetry of Shakespeare was inspiration indeed; he is not so much an imitator as an instrument of Nature; and 'tis not so just to say that he speaks from her, as that she speaks through him.

His *characters* are so much Nature herself that 'tis a sort of injury to call them by so distant a name as copies of her. Those of other poets have a constant resemblance, which shows that they received them from one another and were but multipliers of the same image: each picture, like a mock rainbow, is but the reflection of a reflection. But every single character in Shakespeare is as much an individual as those in life itself; it is as impossible to find any two alike; and such as from their relation or affinity in any respect appear most to be twins will upon comparison be found remarkably distinct. To this life and variety of character, we must add the wonderful preservation of it, which is such throughout his plays that, had all the speeches been printed without the very names of the persons, I believe one might have applied them with certainty to every speaker.

The power over our *passions* was never possessed in a more eminent degree or displayed in so different instances. Yet all along, there is seen no labour, no pains to raise them, no preparation to guide our guess to the effect or be perceived to lead toward it. But the heart swells and the tears burst out just at the proper places. We are surprised the moment we weep; and yet upon reflection find the passion so just that we should be surprised if we had not wept, and wept at that very moment.

How astonishing is it again that the passions directly opposite to these, laughter and spleen, are no less at his command! that he is not more a master of the great than of the ridiculous in human nature; of our noblest tendernesses, than of our vainest foibles; of our strongest emotions, than of our idlest sensations!

Nor does he only excel in the passions: in the coolness of reflection and reasoning he is full as admirable. His *sentiments* are not only in general the most pertinent and judicious upon every subject; but by a talent very peculiar, something between penetration and felicity, he hits

148

upon that particular point on which the bent of each
argument turns or the force of each motive depends. This
is perfectly amazing from a man of no education or experience in those great and public scenes of life which are
usually the subject of his thoughts; so that he seems to   50
have known the world by intuition, to have looked
through human nature at one glance, and to be the only
author that gives ground for a very new opinion, that the
philosopher and even the man of the world may be *born*,
as well as the poet.

I will conclude by saying of Shakespeare, that with all
his faults and with all the irregularity of his drama, one
may look upon his works, in comparison of those that are
more finished and regular, as upon an ancient majestic
piece of Gothic architecture, compared with a neat mo-   60
dern building. The latter is more elegant and glaring, but
the former is more strong and more solemn. It must be
allowed that in one of these there are materials enough to
make many of the other. It has much the greater variety
and much the nobler apartments, though we are often
conducted to them by dark, odd, and uncouth passages.
Nor does the whole fail to strike us with greater reverence, though many of the parts are childish, ill-placed,
and unequal to its grandeur.

First published 1725

TO MRS M.B. ON HER BIRTHDAY

Oh be thou blest with all that Heaven can send,
Long health, long youth, long pleasure, and a friend:
Not with those toys the female world admire,
Riches that vex, and vanities that tire.
With added years, if life bring nothing new,
But like a sieve let every blessing through,
Some joy still lost, as each vain year runs o'er,
And all we gain, some sad reflection more;
Is that a birthday? 'tis alas! too clear,

'Tis but the funeral of the former year.   10
    Let joy or ease, let affluence or content,
And the gay conscience of a life well spent,
Calm every thought, inspirit every grace,
Glow in thy heart and smile upon thy face.
Let day improve on day, and year on year,
Without a pain, a trouble, or a fear;
Till death unfelt that tender frame destroy,
In some soft dream, or ecstasy of joy,
Peaceful sleep out the Sabbath of the tomb,
And wake to raptures in a life to come.   20

Composed 1723   First published 1724

EPITAPH. ON MRS CORBETT, WHO DIED OF A CANCER IN HER BREAST

Here rests a woman, good without pretence,
Blessed with plain reason, and with sober sense:
No conquests she, but o'er herself, desired;
Nor arts essayed, but not to be admired.
Passion and pride were to her soul unknown,
Convinced that virtue only is our own.
So unaffected, so composed a mind;
So firm, yet soft; so strong, yet so refined;
Heaven, as its purest gold, by tortures tried!
The saint sustained it, but the woman died.   10

Composed c. 1730   First published 1730

EPITAPH. ON MR ELIJAH FENTON. AT EASTHAMSTEAD IN BERKS, 1730

This modest stone, what few vain marbles can,
May truly say, Here lies an honest man;
A poet blest beyond the poet's fate,
Whom Heaven kept sacred from the proud and great:
Foe to loud praise, and friend to learned ease,
Content with science in the vale of peace,

Calmly he looked on either life, and here
Saw nothing to regret, or there to fear;
From Nature's temperate feast rose satisfied,
Thanked Heaven that he had lived, and that he died.   10

Composed 1730   First published 1730

EPITAPH. ON MR GAY.
IN WESTMINSTER ABBEY, 1732

Of manners gentle, of affections mild;
In wit, a man; simplicity, a child:
With native humour tempering virtuous rage,
Formed to delight at once and lash the age:
Above temptation in a low estate,
And uncorrupted, even among the great:
A safe companion, and an easy friend,
Unblamed through life, lamented in thy end.
These are thy honours! not that here thy bust
Is mixed with heroes, or with kings thy dust;   10
But that the worthy and the good shall say,
Striking their pensive bosoms – Here lies Gay.

Composed 1733   First published 1733

AN ESSAY ON MAN

from *the first epistle*

Of the nature and state of man
with respect to the universe

Awake, my St John! leave all meaner things
To low ambition and the pride of kings.
Let us (since life can little more supply
Than just to look about us, and to die)
Expatiate free o'er all this scene of man;
A mighty maze! but not without a plan:
A wild, where weeds and flowers promiscuous shoot;
Or garden, tempting with forbidden fruit.

151

Together let us beat this ample field,
Try what the open, what the covert yield!   10
The latent tracts, the giddy heights explore
Of all who blindly creep, or sightless soar;
Eye Nature's walks, shoot folly as it flies,
And catch the manners living as they rise:
Laugh where we must, be candid where we can;
But vindicate the ways of God to man.

Heaven from all creatures hides the book of Fate,
All but the page prescribed, their present state:
From brutes what men, from men what spirits know:
Or who could suffer being here below?   20
The lamb thy riot dooms to bleed today,
Had he thy reason, would he skip and play?
Pleased to the last, he crops the flowery food,
And licks the hand just raised to shed his blood.
Oh blindness to the future! kindly given,
That each may fill the circle marked by Heaven:
Who sees with equal eye, as God of all,
A hero perish, or a sparrow fall,
Atoms or systems into ruin hurled,
And now a bubble burst, and now a world.   30

The bliss of man (could pride that blessing find)
Is not to act or think beyond mankind;
No powers of body or of soul to share,
But what his nature and his state can bear.
Why has not man a microscopic eye?
For this plain reason, man is not a fly.
Say what the use, were finer optics given,
To inspect a mite, not comprehend the heaven?
Or touch, if trembling alive all o'er,
To smart and agonize at every pore?   40
Or quick effluvia darting through the brain,
Die of a rose in aromatic pain?
If nature thundered in his opening ears,
And stunned him with the music of the spheres,
How would he wish that Heaven had left him still

The whispering zephyr, and the purling rill?
Who finds not Providence all good and wise,
Alike in what it gives and what denies?

All are but parts of one stupendous whole,
Whose body Nature is, and God the soul;   50
That, changed through all, and yet in all the same;
Great in the earth, as in the ethereal frame;
Warms in the sun, refreshes in the breeze,
Glows in the stars, and blossoms in the trees;
Lives through all life, extends through all extent;
Spreads undivided, operates unspent!
Breathes in our soul, informs our mortal part,
As full, as perfect, in a hair as heart;
As full, as perfect in vile man that mourns,
As the rapt seraph that adores and burns: 60
To him no high, no low, no great, no small;
He fills, he bounds, connects, and equals all.

from *the second epistle*

Of the nature and state of man,
with respect to himself,
as an individual

Know then thyself, presume not God to scan;
The proper study of mankind is man.
Placed on this isthmus of a middle state,
A being darkly wise, and rudely great:
With too much knowledge for the Sceptic side,
With too much weakness for the Stoic's pride,
He hangs between; in doubt to act, or rest;
In doubt to deem himself a god, or beast;
In doubt his mind or body to prefer;
Born but to die, and reasoning but to err;   10
Alike in ignorance, his reason such,
Whether he thinks too little, or too much:
Chaos of thought and passion, all confused;
Still by himself abused or disabused;

Created half to rise, and half to fall;
Great lord of all things, yet a prey to all;
Sole judge of truth, in endless error hurled:
The glory, jest, and riddle òf the world!
   Go, wondrous creature! mount where Science guides,
Go, measure earth, weigh air, and state the tides;   20
Instruct the planets in what orbs to run,
Correct old Time, and regulate the sun;
Go, soar with Plato to the empyreal sphere,
To the first good, first perfect, and first fair;
Or tread the mazy round his followers trod,
And quitting sense call imitating God;
As Eastern priests in giddy circles run,
And turn their heads to imitate the sun.
Go, teach Eternal Wisdom how to rule –
Then drop into thyself, and be a fool!   30
   Superior beings, when of late they saw
A mortal man unfold all Nature's law,
Admired such wisdom in an earthly shape,
And showed a Newton as we show an ape.
   Could he, whose rules the rapid comet bind,
Describe or fix one movement of his mind?
Who saw its fires here rise, and there descend,
Explain his own beginning, or his end?
Alas what wonder! man's superior part
Unchecked may rise, and climb from art to art;   40
But when his own great work is but begun,
What reason weaves, by passion is undone.

Two principles in human nature reign;
Self-love, to urge, and Reason, to restrain;
Nor this a good, nor that a bad we call,
Each works its end, to move or govern all:
And to their proper operation still,
Ascribe all good; to their improper, ill.
   Self-love, the spring of motion, acts the soul;
Reason's comparing balance rules the whole.   50
Man, but for that, no action could attend,
And, but for this, were active to no end:

Fixed like a plant on his peculiar spot,
To draw nutrition, propagate, and rot:
Or, meteor-like, flame lawless through the void,
Destroying others, by himself destroyed.

from *the third epistle*

Of the nature and state of man,
with respect to society

Look round our world; behold the chain of Love
Combining all below and all above.
See plastic Nature working to this end,
The single atoms each to other tend,
Attract, attracted to, the next in place
Formed and impelled its neighbour to embrace.
See Matter next, with various life endued,
Press to one centre still, the general good.
See dying vegetables life sustain,
See life dissolving vegetate again: 10
All forms that perish other forms supply;
(By turns we catch the vital breath, and die)
Like bubbles on the sea of Matter borne,
They rise, they break, and to that sea return.
Nothing is foreign: parts relate to whole;
One all-extending, all-preserving soul
Connects each being, greatest with the least;
Made beast in aid of man, and man of beast;
All served, all serving: nothing stands alone:
The chain holds on, and where it ends, unknown.   20

See him from Nature rising slow to Art!
To copy instinct then was reason's part;
Thus then to man the voice of Nature spake:
'Go, from the creatures thy instructions take:
Learn from the birds what food the thickets yield;
Learn from the beasts the physic of the field;
Thy arts of building from the bee receive;
Learn of the mole to plough, the worm to weave;

155

Learn of the little nautilus to sail,
Spread the thin oar, and catch the driving gale.   30
Here too all forms of social union find,
And hence let reason, late, instruct mankind:
Here subterranean works and cities see;
There towns aerial on the waving tree.
Learn each small people's genius, policies,
The ants' republic, and the realm of bees;
How those in common all their wealth bestow,
And anarchy without confusion know;
And these for ever, though a monarch reign,
Their separate cells and properties maintain.   40
Mark what unvaried laws preserve each state,
Laws wise as Nature, and as fixed as fate.
In vain thy reason finer webs shall draw,
Entangle Justice in her net of law,
And right, too rigid, harden into wrong;
Still for the strong too weak, the weak too strong.
Yet go! and thus o'er all the creatures sway,
Thus let the wiser make the rest obey:
And for those arts mere instinct could afford,
Be crowned as monarchs, or as gods adored.'   50

'Twas then the studious head or generous mind,
Follower of God, or friend of human kind,
Poet or patriot, rose but to restore
The faith and moral Nature gave before;
Relumed her ancient light, not kindled new,
If not God's image, yet his shadow drew;
Taught power's due use to people and to kings,
Taught nor to slack, nor strain its tender strings,
The less, or greater, set so justly true,
That touching one must strike the other too: 60
Till jarring interests of themselves create
The according music of a well-mixed state.
Such is the world's great harmony, that springs
From order, union, full consent of things:
Where small and great, where weak and mighty, made
To serve, not suffer – strengthen, not invade;

More powerful each as needful to the rest,
And, in proportion as it blesses, blest;
Draw to one point, and to one centre bring
Beast, man, or angel, servant, lord, or king.   70

from *the fourth epistle*

Of the nature and state of man,
with respect to happiness

Come, then, my friend! my genius! come along;
Oh master of the poet and the song!
And while the Muse now stoops, or now ascends,
To man's low passions, or their glorious ends,
Teach me, like thee, in various nature wise,
To fall with dignity, with temper rise;
Formed by thy converse happily to steer
From grave to gay, from lively to severe;
Correct, with spirit; eloquent, with ease;
Intent to reason, or polite to please.   10
Oh! while along the stream of time thy name
Expanded flies, and gathers all its fame;
Say, shall my little bark attendant sail,
Pursue the triumph, and partake the gale?
When statesmen, heroes, kings, in dust repose,
Whose sons shall blush their fathers were thy foes,
Shall then this verse to future age pretend
Thou wert my guide, philosopher, and friend?
That, urged by thee, I turned the tuneful art
From sounds to things, from fancy to the heart;   20
For Wit's false mirror held up Nature's light;
Showed erring Pride, – Whatever is, is right!
That reason, passion, answer one great aim;
That true self-love and social are the same;
That virtue only makes our bliss below;
And all our knowledge is, – Ourselves to know.

Composed 1730–2   First published 1733–4

See Crit pages 236 - 239

EPISTLE TO A LADY.
OF THE CHARACTERS OF WOMEN

Personal – like a letter – as indeed

he contradicts himself – gives a list of not too pleasant characters

Nothing so true as what you once let fall:
'Most women have no characters at all.'
Matter too soft a lasting mark to bear,
And best distinguished by black, brown, or fair. *true*

  How many pictures of one nymph we view,
All how unlike each other, all how true!
Arcadia's Countess, here, in ermined pride,
Is there, Pastora by a fountain side.
Here Fannia, leering on her own good man,
And there, a naked Leda with a swan.   10
Let then the fair one beautifully cry
In Magdalen's loose hair and lifted eye,
Or dressed in smiles of sweet Cecilia shine,
With simpering angels, palms, and harps divine;
Whether the charmer sinner it, or saint it,
If folly grow romantic, I must paint it.
  Come, then, the colours and the ground prepare!
Dip in the rainbow, trick her off in air;
Choose a firm cloud before it fall, and in it
Catch, ere she change, the Cynthia of this minute.   20
  Rufa, whose eye quick glancing o'er the park
Attracts each light gay meteor of a spark,
Agrees as ill with Rufa studying Locke, *saying she shouldn't*
As Sappho's diamonds with her dirty smock; *Locke – its too intel[lectual]*
Or Sappho at her toilet's greasy task, *for her.*
With Sappho fragrant at an evening mask:
So morning insects, that in muck begun,
Shine, buzz, and fly-blow in the setting sun.
  How soft is Silia! fearful to offend;
The frail one's advocate, the weak one's friend.   30
To her, Calista proved her conduct nice;
And good Simplicius asks of her advice.
Sudden, she storms! she raves! You tip the wink,
But spare your censure – Silia does not drink.
All eyes may see from what the change arose,
All eyes may see – a pimple on her nose.

implies women change too quickly

158

Papillia, wedded to her doting spark,
Sighs for the shades – 'How charming is a park!'
A park is purchased, but the fair he sees
All bathed in tears – 'Oh odious, odious trees!'

childish tone captured here

  Ladies, like variegated tulips, show,
'Tis to their changes half their charms we owe;
Their happy spots the nice admirer take,
Fine by defect, and delicately weak.
'Twas thus Calypso once each heart alarmed,
Awed without virtue, without beauty charmed;
Her tongue bewitched as oddly as her eyes,
Less wit than mimic, more a wit than wise;
Strange graces still, and stranger flights she had,
Was just not ugly, and was just not mad;
Yet ne'er so sure our passion to create,
As when she touched the brink of all we hate.
  Narcissa's nature, tolerably mild,
To make a wash would hardly stew a child;
Has even been proved to grant a lover's prayer,
And paid a tradesman once, to make him stare;
Gave alms at Easter, in a Christian trim,
And made a widow happy for a whim.
Why then declare good-nature is her scorn,
When 'tis by that alone she can be borne?
Why pique all mortals, yet affect a name?
A fool to pleasure, yet a slave to fame:
Now deep in Taylor and the Book of Martyrs,
Now drinking citron with his Grace and Chartres:
Now conscience chills her, and now passion burns;
And atheism and religion take their turns;
A very heathen in the carnal part,
Yet still a sad, good Christian at her heart.
  See Sin in state, majestically drunk;
Proud as a peeress, prouder as a punk;
Chaste to her husband, frank to all beside,
A teeming mistress, but a barren bride.
What then? let blood and body bear the fault,
Her head's untouched, that noble seat of thought:
Such this day's doctrine – in another fit

40

50

60

70

She sins with poets through pure love of wit.
What has not fired her bosom or her brain?
Cæsar and Tall-boy, Charles and Charlemagne.
As Helluo, late dictator of the feast,
The nose of hautgout and the tip of taste,   80
Critiqued your wine, and analysed your meat,
Yet on plain pudding deigned at home to eat:
So Philomedé, lecturing all mankind
On the soft passion, and the taste refined,
The address, the delicacy – stoops at once,
And makes her hearty meal upon a dunce.
  Flavia's a wit, has too much sense to pray;
To toast our wants and wishes is her way;
Nor asks of God, but of her stars, to give
The mighty blessing, 'While we live, to live.'   90
Then all for death, that opiate of the soul!
Lucretia's dagger, Rosamonda's bowl.
Say, what can cause such impotence of mind?
A spark too fickle, or a spouse too kind.
Wise wretch! with pleasures too refined to please;
With too much spirit to be e'er at ease;
With too much quickness ever to be taught;
With too much thinking to have common thought;
You purchase pain with all that joy can give,
And die of nothing but a rage to live.   100
    Turn then from wits; and look on Simo's mate,
No ass so meek, no ass so obstinate.
Or her that owns her faults, but never mends,
Because she's honest, and the best of friends.
Or her whose life the church and scandal share,
For ever in a passion or a prayer.
Or her who laughs at hell, but (like her grace)
Cries, 'Ah! how charming if there's no such place!'
Or who in sweet vicissitude appears
Of mirth and opium, ratafie and tears,   110
The daily anodyne, and nightly draught,
To kill those foes to fair ones, time and thought.
Woman and fool are two hard things to hit;
For true no-meaning puzzles more than wit.

160

But what are these to great Atossa's mind?
Scarce once herself, by turns all womankind! → never behaves like
            herself but like every
            one else
Who, with herself, or others, from her birth
Finds all her life one warfare upon earth:
Shines in exposing knaves and painting fools,
Yet is whate'er she hates and ridicules.   120
No thought advances, but her eddy brain
Whisks it about, and down it goes again.
Full sixty years the world has been her trade,
The wisest fool much time has ever made.
From loveless youth to unrespected age,
No passion gratified, except her rage,
So much the fury still outran the wit,
The pleasure missed her, and the scandal hit.
Who breaks with her, provokes revenge from hell,
But he's a bolder man who dares be well.   130
Her every turn with violence pursued,
No more a storm her hate than gratitude:
To that each passion turns, or soon or late;
Love, if it makes her yield, must make her hate.
Superiors? death! and equals? what a curse!
But an inferior not dependant? worse!
Offend her, and she knows not to forgive;
Oblige her, and she'll hate you while you live:
But die, and she'll adore you – then the bust
And temple rise – then fall again to dust.   140
Last night, her lord was all that's good and great;
A knave this morning, and his will a cheat.
Strange! by the means defeated of the ends, → warmth of temper
By spirit robbed of power, by warmth of friends,
By wealth of followers! without one distress,
Sick of herself, through very selfishness!
Atossa, cursed with every granted prayer,
Childless with all her children, wants an heir.
To heirs unknown descends the unguarded store,
Or wanders, heaven-directed, to the poor.   150
   Pictures like these, dear Madam, to design,
Asks no firm hand, and no unerring line;
Some wandering touches, some reflected light,

Some flying stroke alone can hit them right:
For how should equal colours do the knack?
Cameleons who can paint in white and black?
  'Yet Chloe sure was formed without a spot.' –
Nature in her then erred not, but forgot.
'With every pleasing, every prudent part,
Say, what can Chloe want?' – She wants a heart.   160
She speaks, behaves, and acts, just as she ought,
But never, never reached one generous thought.
Virtue she finds too painful an endeavour,
Content to dwell in decencies for ever.
So very reasonable, so unmoved,
As never yet to love, or to be loved.
She, while her lover pants her breast,
Can mark the figures on an Indian chest;
And when she sees her friend in deep despair,
Observes how much a chintz exceeds mohair!   170
Forbid it, Heaven, a favour or a debt
She e'er should cancel – but she may forget.
Safe is your secret still in Chloe's ear;
But none of Chloe's shall you ever hear.
Of all her dears she never slandered one,
But cares not if a thousand are undone.
Would Chloe know if you're alive or dead?
She bids her footman put it in her head.
Chloe is prudent – would you too be wise?
Then never break your heart when Chloe dies.   180
  One certain portrait may (I grant) be seen,
Which Heaven has varnished out, and made a queen:
The same for ever! and described by all
With truth and goodness, as with crown and ball.
Poets heap virtues, painters gems, at will,
And show their zeal, and hide their want of skill.
'Tis well – but artists! who can paint or write,
To draw the naked is your true delight.
That robe of quality so struts and swells,
None see what parts of nature it conceals: 190
The exactest traits of body or of mind,
We owe to models of an humble kind.

162

If Queensberry to strip there's no compelling,
'Tis from a handmaid we must take a Helen.
From peer or bishop 'tis no easy thing
To draw the man who loves his God or king:
Alas! I copy (or my draught would fail)
From honest Mahomet, or plain Parson Hale.

    But grant, in public, men sometimes are shown,
A woman's seen in private life alone: 200
Our bolder talents in full light displayed;
Your virtues open fairest in the shade.
Bred to disguise, in public 'tis you hide;
There, none distinguish 'twixt your shame or pride,
Weakness or delicacy; all so nice,
That each may seem a virtue or a vice.

    In men we various ruling passions find;
In women, two almost divide the kind;
Those, only fixed, they first or last obey,
The love of pleasure, and the love of sway.   210

    That, Nature gives; and where the lesson taught
Is but to please, can pleasure seem a fault?
Experience, this; by man's oppression cursed,
They seek the second not to lose the first.

Men, some to business, some to pleasure take;
But every woman is at heart a rake:
Men, some to quiet, some to public strife;
But every lady would be queen for life.

    Yet mark the fate of a whole sex of queens!
Power all their end, but beauty all the means: 220
In youth they conquer with so wild a rage,
As leaves them scarce a subject in their age:
For foreign glory, foreign joy, they roam;
No thought of peace or happiness at home.
But wisdom's triumph is well-timed retreat,
As hard a science to the fair as great!
Beauties, like tyrants, old and friendless grown,
Yet hate repose, and dread to be alone,
Worn out in public, weary every eye,
Nor leave one sigh behind them when they die.   230

    Pleasures the sex, as children birds, pursue,

Still out of reach, yet never out of view;
Sure, if they catch, to spoil the toy at most,
To covet flying, and regret when lost:
At last, to follies youth could scarce defend,
It grows their age's prudence to pretend;
Ashamed to own they gave delight before,
Reduced to feign it, when they give no more:
As hags hold sabbaths, less for joy than spite,
So these their merry, miserable night;   240
Still round and round the ghosts of beauty glide,
And haunt the places where their honour died.
  See how the world its veterans rewards!
A youth of frolics, an old age of cards;
Fair to no purpose, artful to no end,
Young without lovers, old without a friend;
A fop their passion, but their prize a sot,
Alive, ridiculous, and dead, forgot!
  Ah, friend! to dazzle let the vain design;
To raise the thought and touch the heart be thine!   250
That charm shall grow, while what fatigues the Ring,
Flaunts and goes down, an unregarded thing:
So when the sun's broad beam has tired the sight,
All mild ascends the moon's more sober light,
Serene in virgin modesty she shines,
And unobserved the glaring orb declines.
  Oh! blest with temper, whose unclouded ray
Can make tomorrow cheerful as today;
She who can love a sister's charms, or hear
Sighs for a daughter with unwounded ear;   260
She who ne'er answers till a husband cools,
Or, if she rules him, never shows she rules;
Charms by accepting, by submitting sways,
Yet has her humour most when she obeys;
Let fops or fortune fly which way they will,
Disdains all loss of tickets, or codille;
Spleen, vapours, or small-pox, above them all,
And mistress of herself, though China fall.
  And yet, believe me, good as well as ill,
Woman's at best a contradiction still.   270

164

Heaven, when it strives to polish all it can
Its last best work, but forms a softer man;
Picks from each sex, to make the favourite blest,
Your love of pleasure, our desire of rest:
Blends, in exception to all general rules,
Your taste of follies, with our scorn of fools:
Reserve with frankness, art with truth allied,
Courage with softness, modesty with pride;
Fixed principles, with fancy ever new;
Shakes all together, and produces – you!   280
　Be this a woman's fame; with this unblest,
Toasts live a scorn, and queens may die a jest.
This Phoebus promised (I forget the year)
When those blue eyes first opened on the sphere;
Ascendant Phoebus watched that hour with care,
Averted half your parents' simple prayer;
And gave you beauty, but denied the pelf → *riches*
That buys your sex a tyrant o'er itself.
The generous god, who wit and gold refines,
And ripens spirits as he ripens mines,   290
Kept dross for duchesses, the world shall know it,
To you gave sense, good humour, and a poet.

Composed 1732–4   First published 1735

EPISTLE TO BURLINGTON

Argument: of the use of riches

The vanity of expense in people of wealth and quality.
The abuse of the word taste, ver. 13. That the first principle and foundation in this, as in everything else, is good
sense, ver. 39. The chief proof of it is to follow Nature,
even in works of mere luxury and elegance. Instanced in
architecture and gardening, where all must be adapted to
the genius and use of the place, and the beauties not
forced into it, but resulting from it, ver. 47. How men
are disappointed in their most expensive undertakings for
want of this true foundation, without which nothing can   10

please long, if at all; and the best examples and rules will be but perverted into something burdensome or ridiculous, ver. 65, etc., to 98. A description of the false taste of magnificence; the first grand error of which is to imagine that greatness consists in the size and dimension, instead of the proportion and harmony of the whole, ver. 99; and the second, either in joining together parts incoherent, or too minutely resembling, or in the repetition of the same too frequently, ver. 105, etc. A word or two of false taste in books, in music, in painting, even in preaching and prayer, and lastly in entertainments, ver. 133, etc. Yet Providence is justified in giving wealth to be squandered in this manner, since it is dispersed to the poor and laborious part of mankind, ver. 169 (recurring to what is laid down in the *Essay on Man*, Epistle II., and in the epistle preceding, ver. 159, etc.). What are the proper objects of magnificence, and a proper field for the expense of great men, ver. 177, etc.; and finally, the great and public works which become a prince, ver. 191 to the end.

'Tis strange, the miser should his cares employ
To gain those riches he can ne'er enjoy:
Is it less strange, the prodigal should waste
His wealth to purchase what he ne'er can taste?
Not for himself he sees, or hears, or eats;
Artists must choose his pictures, music, meats:
He buys for Topham drawings and designs,
For Pembroke statues, dirty gods, and coins;
Rare monkish manuscripts for Hearne alone,
And books for Mead, and butterflies for Sloane.
Think we all these are for himself? no more
Than his fine wife, alas! or finer whore.
   For what has Virro painted, built, and planted?
Only to show how many tastes he wanted.
What brought Sir Visto's ill-got wealth to waste?
Some demon whispered, 'Visto! have a taste.'
Heaven visits with a taste the wealthy fool,
And needs no rod but Ripley with a rule.
See! sportive fate, to punish awkward pride,

Bids Bubo build, and sends him such a guide: 20
A standing sermon, at each year's expense,
That never coxcomb reached magnificence!

    You show us Rome was glorious, not profuse,
And pompous buildings once were things of use.
Yet shall (my lord) your just, your noble rules
Fill half the land with imitating fools;
Who random drawings from your sheets shall take,
And of one beauty many blunders make;
Load some vain church with old theatric state,
Turn arcs of triumph to a garden-gate;   30
Reverse your ornaments, and hang them all
On some patched dog-hole eked with ends of wall;
Then clap four slices of pilaster on 't,
That, laced with bits of rustic, makes a front;
Or call the winds through long arcades to roar,
Proud to catch cold at a Venetian door;
Conscious they act a true Palladian part,
And, if they starve, they starve by rules of art.
    Oft have you hinted to your brother peer
A certain truth, which many buy too dear: 40
Something there is more needful than expense,
And something previous even to taste – 'tis sense:
Good sense, which only is the gift of Heaven,
And, though no science, fairly worth the seven:
A light, which in yourself you must perceive;
Jones and Le Nôtre have it not to give.
    To build, to plant, whatever you intend,
To rear the column, or the arch to bend,
To swell the terrace, or to sink the grot,
In all, let Nature never be forgot,   50
But treat the goddess like a modest fair,
Nor over-dress, nor leave her wholly bare;
Let not each beauty everywhere be spied,
Where half the skill is decently to hide.
He gains all points, who pleasingly confounds,
Surprises, varies, and conceals the bounds.
    Consult the genius of the place in all:
That tells the waters or to rise or fall;

Or helps the ambitious hill the heavens to scale,
Or scoops in circling theatres the vale;   60
Calls in the country, catches opening glades,
Joins willing woods, and varies shades from shades;
Now breaks, or now directs, the intending lines;
Paints, as you plant, and, as you work, designs.

   Still follow sense, of every art the soul,
Parts answering parts shall slide into a whole,
Spontaneous beauties all around advance,
Start even from difficulty, strike from chance;
Nature shall join you; Time shall make it grow
A work to wonder at – perhaps a Stowe.   70

   Without it, proud Versailles! thy glory falls;
And Nero's terraces desert their walls:
The vast parterres a thousand hands shall make,
Lo! Cobham comes, and floats them with a lake:
Or cut wide views through mountains to the plain,
You'll wish your hill or sheltered seat again.
Even in an ornament its place remark,
Nor in an hermitage set Dr Clarke.

   Behold Villario's ten years' toil complete;
His quincunx darkens, his espaliers meet;   80
The wood supports the plain, the parts unite,
And strength of shade contends with strength of light;
A waving glow his bloomy beds display,
Blushing in bright diversities of day,
With silver-quivering rills meandered o'er –
Enjoy them, you! Villario can no more:
Tired of the scene parterres and fountains yield,
He finds at last he better likes a field.

   Through his young woods how pleased Sabinus strayed,
Or sate delighted in the thickening shade,   90
With annual joy the reddening shoots to greet,
Or see the stretching branches long to meet!
His son's fine taste an opener vista loves,
Foe to the Dryads of his father's groves;
One boundless green, or flourished carpet views,
With all the mournful family of yews:
The thriving plants, ignoble broomsticks made,

168

Now sweep those alleys they were born to shade.
  At Timon's villa let us pass a day,
Where all cry out, 'What sums are thrown away!'   100
So proud, so grand: of that stupendous air,
Soft and agreeable come never there.
Greatness, with Timon, dwells in such a draught
As brings all Brobdignag before your thought.
To compass this, his building is a town,
His pond an ocean, his parterre a down:
Who but must laugh, the master when he sees,
A puny insect, shivering at a breeze!
Lo, what huge heaps of littleness around!
The whole, a laboured quarry above ground,   110
Two cupids squirt before: a lake behind
Improves the keenness of the northern wind.
His gardens next your admiration call,
On every side you look, behold the wall!
No pleasing intricacies intervene,
No artful wildness to perplex the scene:
Grove nods at grove, each alley has a brother,
And half the platform just reflects the other.
The suffering eye inverted Nature sees,
Trees cut to statues, statues thick as trees;   120
With here a fountain, never to be played;
And there a summer-house, that knows no shade:
Here Amphitrite sails through myrtle bowers;
There gladiators fight, or die, in flowers;
Unwatered see the drooping sea-horse mourn,
And swallows roost in Nilus' dusty urn.
  My Lord advances with majestic mien,
Smit with the mighty pleasure to be seen:
But soft – by regular approach – not yet –
First through the length of yon hot terrace sweat;   130
And when up ten steep slopes you've dragged your thighs,
Just at his study-door he'll bless your eyes.
  His study! with what authors is it stored?
In books, not authors, curious is my Lord;
To all their dated backs he turns you round;
These Aldus printed, those Du Sueil has bound.

Lo, some are vellum, and the rest as good
For all his Lordship knows, but they are wood.
For Locke or Milton 'tis in vain to look,
These shelves admit not any modern book.   140
    And now the chapel's silver bell you hear,
That summons you to all the pride of prayer:
Light quirks of music, broken and uneven,
Make the soul dance upon a jig to Heaven.
On painted ceilings you devoutly stare,
Where sprawl the saints of Verrio or Laguerre,
Or gilded clouds in fair expansion lie,
And bring all Paradise before your eye.
To rest, the cushion and soft dean invite,
Who never mentions Hell to ears polite.   150
    But hark! the chiming clocks to dinner call;
A hundred footsteps scrape the marble hall:
The rich buffet well-coloured serpents grace,
And gaping Tritons spew to wash your face.
Is this a dinner? this a genial room?
No, 'tis a temple, and a hecatomb.
A solemn sacrifice, performed in state,
You drink by measure, and to minutes eat.
So quick retires each flying course, you'd swear
Sancho's dread doctor and his wand were there.   160
Between each act the trembling salvers ring,
From soup to sweet-wine, and God bless the king.
In plenty starving, tantalized in state,
And complaisantly helped to all I hate,
Treated, caressed, and tired, I take my leave,
Sick of his civil pride from morn to eve;
I curse such lavish cost, and little skill,
And swear no day was ever passed so ill.
    Yet hence the poor are clothed, the hungry fed;
Health to himself, and to his infants bread,   170
The labourer bears: what his hard heart denies,
His charitable vanity supplies.
    Another age shall see the golden ear
Imbrown the slope, and nod on the parterre,
Deep harvests bury all his pride has planned,
And laughing Ceres reassume the land.

170

Who then shall grace, or who improve the soil? –
Who plants like Bathurst, or who builds like Boyle.
'Tis use alone that sanctifies expense,
And splendour borrows all her rays from sense.   180
    His father's acres who enjoys in peace,
Or makes his neighbours glad, if he increase:
Whose cheerful tenants bless their yearly toil,
Yet to their lord owe more than to the soil;
Whose ample lawns are not ashamed to feed
The milky heifer and deserving steed;
Whose rising forests, not for pride or show,
But future buildings, future navies grow:
Let his plantations stretch from down to down,
First shade a country, and then raise a town.   190
    You too proceed! make falling arts your care,
Erect new wonders, and the old repair;
Jones and Palladio to themselves restore,
And be whate'er Vitruvius was before:
'Till kings call forth the ideas of your mind,
Proud to accomplish what such hands designed,
Bid harbours open, public ways extend,
Bid temples, worthier of the god, ascend;
Bid the broad arch the dangerous flood contain,
The mole projected break the roaring main;   200
Back to his bounds their subject sea command,
And roll obedient rivers through the land;
These honours Peace to happy Britain brings,
These are imperial works, and worthy kings.

Composed 1730–1   First published 1731

TO DR ARBUTHNOT, 26 JULY 1734 [ON HIS SATIRE]

I thank you for your letter, which has all those genuine
marks of a good mind by which I have ever distinguished
yours, and for which I have so long loved you. Our
friendship has been constant; because it was grounded on
good principles, and therefore not only uninterrupted by
any distrust, but by any vanity, much less any interest.

What you recommend to me with the solemnity of a last request shall have its due weight with me. That disdain and indignation against vice is (I thank God) the only disdain and indignation I have. It is sincere, and it will be a lasting one. But sure it is as impossible to have a just abhorrence of vice without hating the vicious as to bear a true love for virtue without loving the good. To reform and not to chastise I am afraid is impossible, and that the best precepts, as well as the best laws, would prove of small use if there were no examples to enforce them. To attack vices in the abstract, without touching persons, may be safe fighting indeed, but it is fighting with shadows. General propositions are obscure, misty, and uncertain, compared with plain, full, and home examples. Precepts only apply to our reason, which in most men is but weak; examples are pictures, and strike the senses, nay raise the passions, and call in those (the strongest and most general of all motives) to the aid of reformation. Every vicious man makes the case his own; and that is the only way by which such men can be affected, much less deterred. So that to chastise is to reform. The only sign by which I found my writings ever did any good, or had any weight, has been that they raised the anger of bad men. And my greatest comfort and encouragement to proceed has been to see that those who have no shame and no fear of anything else have appeared touched by my satires.

As to your kind concern for my safety, I can guess what occasions it at this time. Some characters I have drawn are such that, if there be any who deserve them, 'tis evidently a service to mankind to point those men out, yet such as, if all the world gave them, none I think will own they take to themselves. But if they should, those of whom all the world think in such a manner must be men I cannot fear. Such in particular as have the meanness to do mischiefs in the dark have seldom the courage to justify them in the face of day; the talents that make a cheat or a whisperer are not the same that qualify a man for an insulter; and, as to private villainy, it is not so safe to join in an assassination as in a libel. I will consult my safety so far as I think becomes a prudent man, but not so far as to omit anything which I think becomes an honest one. As to personal attacks beyond the law, every man is liable to them; as for danger within the 50 law, I am not guilty enough to fear any. For the good opinion of all the world, I know it is not to be had; for that of worthy men, I hope I shall not forfeit it; for that of the great, or those in power, I may wish I had it, but if through misrepresentations (too common about persons in that station) I have it not, I shall be sorry, but not miserable in the want of it.

It is certain much freer satirists than I have enjoyed the encouragement and protection of the princes under whom they lived. Augustus and Maecenas made Horace their 60 companion, though he had been in arms on the side of Brutus; and allow me to remark it was out of the suffering party, too, that they favoured and distinguished Virgil. You will not suspect me of comparing myself with Virgil and Horace, nor even with another court favourite, Boileau. I have always been too modest to imagine my panegyrics were incense worthy of a court; and that, I hope, will be thought the true reason why I have never offered any. I would only have observed that it was under the greatest princes and best ministers that moral satirists 70 were most encouraged, and that then poets exercised the same jurisdiction over the follies as historians did over the vices of men. It may also be worth considering whether Augustus himself makes the greater figure in the writings of the former or of the latter; and whether Nero and Domitian do not appear as ridiculous for their false taste and affectation in Persius and Juvenal as odious for their bad government in Tacitus and Suetonius. In the first of these reigns it was that Horace was protected and caressed, and in the latter that Lucan was put to death and 80 Juvenal banished.

I would not have said so much, but to show you my whole heart on this subject; and to convince you, I am deliberately bent to perform that request which you make

173

your last to me, and to perform it with temper, justice and resolution. As your approbation, (being the testimony of a sound head and an honest heart) does greatly confirm me herein, I wish you may live to see the effect it may hereafter have upon me, in something more deserving of that approbation. But if it be the will of God (which I 90 know will also be yours) that we must separate, I hope it will be better for you than it can be for me. You are fitter to live, or to die, than any man I know. Adieu, my dear friend! and may God preserve your life easy, or make your death happy.

AN EPISTLE TO DR ARBUTHNOT

Advertisement

This paper is a sort of bill of complaint, begun many years since, and drawn up by snatches, as the several occasions offered. I had no thoughts of publishing it, till it pleased some persons of rank and fortune (the authors of *Verses to the Imitator of Horace*, and of an *Epistle to a Doctor of Divinity from a Nobleman at Hampton Court*) to attack, in a very extraordinary manner, not only my writings (of which, being public, the public judge), but my person, morals, and family, whereof, to those who know me not, a truer information may be requisite. Be- 10 ing divided between the necessity to say something of myself and my own laziness to undertake so awkward a task, I thought it the shortest way to put the last hand to this Epistle. If it have anything pleasing, it will be that by which I am most desirous to please, the truth and the sentiment; and if anything offensive, it will be only to those I am least sorry to offend, the vicious or the un-generous.

Many will know their own pictures in it, there being not a circumstance but what is true; but I have for the 20 most part spared their names, and they may escape being laughed at if they please.

I would have some of them know it was owing to the request of the learned and candid friend to whom it is

174

inscribed that I make not as free use of theirs as they have
done of mine. However, I shall have this advantage and
honour on my side, that whereas, by their proceeding,
any abuse may be directed at any man, no injury can
possibly be done by mine, since a nameless character can
never be found out but by its truth and likeness.   30

Shut, shut the door, good John! fatigued, I said;
Tie up the knocker, say I'm sick, I'm dead.
The dog-star rages! nay 'tis past a doubt,
All Bedlam, or Parnassus, is let out:
Fire in each eye, and papers in each hand,
They rave, recite, and madden round the land.
    What walls can guard me, or what shades can hide?
They pierce my thickets, through my grot they glide,
By land, by water, they renew the charge,
They stop the chariot, and they board the barge.   10
No place is sacred, not the church is free,
Even Sunday shines no Sabbath-day to me:
Then from the Mint walks forth the man of rhyme,
Happy! to catch me, just at dinner-time.
    Is there a parson, much bemused in beer,
A maudlin poetess, a rhyming peer,
A clerk, foredoomed his father's soul to cross,
Who pens a stanza, when he should engross?
Is there, who, locked from ink and paper, scrawls
With desperate charcoal round his darkened walls?   20
All fly to Twit'nam, and in humble strain
Apply to me, to keep them mad or vain.
Arthur, whose giddy son neglects the laws,
Imputes to me and my damned works the cause:
Poor Cornus sees his frantic wife elope,
And curses wit, and poetry, and Pope.
    Friend to my life! (which did not you prolong,
The world had wanted many an idle song)
What drop or nostrum can this plague remove?
Or which must end me, a fool's wrath or love?   30
A dire dilemma! either way I'm sped,
If foes, they write, if friends, they read me dead.

175

Seized and tied down to judge, how wretched I!
Who can't be silent, and who will not lie:
To laugh, were want of goodness and of grace,
And to be grave, exceeds all power of face.
I sit with sad civility, I read
With honest anguish, and an aching head;
And drop at last, but in unwilling ears,
This saving counsel, – 'Keep your piece nine years.'   40
    'Nine years!' cries he, who, high in Drury Lane,
Lulled by soft zephyrs through the broken pane,
Rhymes ere he wakes, and prints before Term ends,
Obliged by hunger, and request of friends:
'The piece, you think, is incorrect? why take it,
I'm all submission; what you'd have it, make it.'
    Three things another's modest wishes bound,
My friendship, and a prologue, and ten pound.
    Pitholeon sends to me: 'You know his grace,
I want a patron; ask him for a place.'   50
Pitholeon libelled me – 'But here's a letter
Informs you, Sir, 'twas when he knew no better.
Dare you refuse him? Curll invites to dine,
He'll write a journal, or he'll turn divine.'
    Bless me! a packet. ''Tis a stranger sues,
A virgin tragedy, an orphan Muse.'
If I dislike it, 'Furies, death and rage!'
If I approve, 'Commend it to the stage.'
There (thank my stars) my whole commission ends,
The players and I are, luckily, no friends;   60
Fired that the house reject him, ''Sdeath! I'll print it,
And shame the fools – your interest, Sir, with Lintot.'
Lintot, dull rogue! will think your price too much:
'Not, Sir, if you revise it, and retouch.'
All my demurs but double his attacks:
And last he whispers, 'Do; and we go snacks.'
Glad of a quarrel, straight I clap the door:
Sir, let me see your works and you no more.
    'Tis sung, when Midas' ears began to spring
(Midas, a sacred person and a king),   70
His very minister who spied them first

176

(Some say his queen) was forced to speak or burst:
And is not mine, my friend, a sorer case,
When every coxcomb perks them in my face?
'Good friend, forbear! you deal in dangerous things,
I'd never name queens, ministers, or kings:
Keep close to ears, and those let asses prick,
'Tis nothing' – Nothing? if they bite and kick?
Out with it, *Dunciad*! let the secret pass,
That secret to each fool, that he's an ass: 80
The truth once told (and wherefore should we lie?)
The Queen of Midas slept, and so may I.
    You think this cruel? Take it for a rule,
No creature smarts so little as a fool.
Let peals of laughter, Codrus! round thee break,
Thou unconcerned canst hear the mighty crack:
Pit, box, and gallery in convulsions hurled,
Thou standest unshook amidst a bursting world.
Who shames a scribbler? break one cobweb through,
He spins the slight, self-pleasing thread anew: 90
Destroy his fib or sophistry, in vain,
The creature's at his dirty work again,
Throned in the centre of his thin designs,
Proud of a vast extent of flimsy lines!
Whom have I hurt? has poet yet, or peer,
Lost the arched eyebrow, or Parnassian sneer?
And has not Colley still his lord, and whore?
His butchers Henley, his freemasons Moore?
Does not one table Bavius still admit?
Still to one bishop Philips seem a wit?   100
Still Sappho—'Hold! for God's sake – you'll offend:
No names – be calm – learn prudence of a friend.
I too could write, and I am twice as tall;
But foes like these'—One flatterer's worse than all.
Of all mad creatures, if the learned are right,
It is the slaver kills, and not the bite.
A fool quite angry is quite innocent:
Alas! 'tis ten times worse when they repent.
    One dedicates in high heroic prose,
And ridicules beyond a hundred foes: 110

177

One from all Grub Street will my fame defend,
And, more abusive, calls himself my friend.
This prints my Letters, that expects a bribe,
And others roar aloud, 'Subscribe, subscribe!'
    There are, who to my person pay their court:
I cough like Horace, and, though lean, am short.
Ammon's great son one shoulder had too high –
Such Ovid's nose, – and, 'Sir! you have an eye.'
Go on, obliging creatures, make me see
All that disgraced my betters met in me.   120
Say, for my comfort, languishing in bed,
'Just so immortal Maro held his head';
And, when I die, be sure you let me know
Great Homer died three thousand years ago.
    Why did I write? what sin to me unknown
Dipped me in ink, my parents', or my own?
As yet a child, nor yet a fool to fame,
I lisped in numbers, for the numbers came.
I left no calling for this idle trade,
No duty broke, no father disobeyed: 130
The Muse but served to ease some friend, not wife,
To help me through this long disease, my life;
To second, Arbuthnot! thy art and care,
And teach the being you preserved to bear.
    But why then publish? Granville the polite,
And knowing Walsh, would tell me I could write;
Well-natured Garth inflamed with early praise,
And Congreve loved, and Swift endured my lays;
The courtly Talbot, Somers, Sheffield read,
Even mitred Rochester would nod the head,   140
And St John's self (great Dryden's friends before)
With open arms received one poet more.
Happy my studies, when by these approved!
Happier their author, when by these beloved!
From these the world will judge of men and books,
Not from the Burnets, Oldmixons, and Cookes.
    Soft were my numbers; who could take offence
While pure description held the place of sense?
Like gentle Fanny's was my flowery theme,

A painted mistress, or a purling stream. 150
Yet then did Gildon draw his venal quill;
I wished the man a dinner, and sat still.
Yet then did Dennis rave in furious fret;
I never answered – I was not in debt.
If want provoked, or madness made them print,
I waged no war with Bedlam or the Mint.
    Did some more sober critic come abroad?
If wrong, I smiled; if right, I kissed the rod.
Pains, reading, study, are their just pretence,
And all they want is spirit, taste, and sense. 160
Commas and points they set exactly right,
And 'twere a sin to rob them of their mite;
Yet ne'er one sprig of laurel graced these ribalds,
From slashing Bentley down to piddling Tibbalds:
Each wight, who reads not, and but scans and spells,
Each word-catcher, that lives on syllables,
Even such small critics, some regard may claim,
Preserved in Milton's or in Shakespeare's name.
Pretty! in amber to observe the forms
Of hairs, or straws, or dirt, or grubs, or worms! 170
The things, we know, are neither rich nor rare,
But wonder how the devil they got there?
    Were others angry? I excused them too;
Well might they rage, I gave them but their due.
A man's true merit 'tis not hard to find;
But each man's secret standard in his mind,
That casting-weight pride adds to emptiness,
This, who can gratify, for who can guess?
The bard whom pilfered Pastorals renown,
Who turns a Persian tale for half-a-crown, 180
Just writes to make his barrenness appear,
And strains from hard-bound brains, eight lines a-year;
He, who still wanting, though he lives on theft,
Steals much, spends little, yet has nothing left:
And he, who now to sense, now nonsense leaning,
Means not, but blunders round about a meaning:
And he, whose fustian's so sublimely bad,
It is not poetry, but prose run mad:

179

All these, my modest satire bade translate,
And owned that nine such poets made a Tate.   190
How did they fume, and stamp, and roar, and chafe!
And swear, not Addison himself was safe.

Peace to all such! but were there one whose fires
True genius kindles, and fair fame inspires;
Blest with each talent, and each art to please,
And born to write, converse, and live with ease;
Should such a man, too fond to rule alone,
Bear, like the Turk, no brother near the throne,
View him with scornful, yet with jealous eyes,
And hate for arts that caused himself to rise;   200
Damn with faint praise, assent with civil leer,
And, without sneering, teach the rest to sneer;
Willing to wound, and yet afraid to strike,
Just hint a fault, and hesitate dislike;
Alike reserved to blame, or to commend,
A timorous foe, and a suspicious friend;
Dreading even fools, by flatterers besieged,
And so obliging, that he ne'er obliged;
Like Cato, give his little senate laws,
And sit attentive to his own applause;   210
While wits and Templars every sentence raise,
And wonder with a foolish face of praise –
Who but must laugh, if such a man there be?
Who would not weep, if Atticus were he?

What though my name stood rubric on the walls,
Or plastered posts, with claps, in capitals?
Or smoking forth, a hundred hawkers load,
On wings of winds came flying all abroad?
I sought no homage from the race that write;
I kept, like Asian monarchs, from their sight: 220
Poems I heeded (now be-rhymed so long)
No more than thou, great George! a birthday song.
I ne'er with wits or witlings passed my days,
To spread about the itch of verse and praise;
Nor like a puppy, daggled through the town,
To fetch and carry, sing-song up and down;
Nor at rehearsals sweat, and mouthed, and cried,

With handkerchief and orange at my side;
But sick of fops, and poetry, and prate,
To Bufo left the whole Castalian state.   230
    Proud as Apollo on his forked hill,
Sat full-blown Bufo, puffed by every quill;
Fed with soft dedication all day long,
Horace and he went hand in hand in song.
His library (where busts of poets dead
And a true Pindar stood without a head)
Received of wits an undistinguished race,
Who first his judgement asked, and then a place:
Much they extolled his pictures, much his seat,
And flattered every day, and some days eat: 240
Till grown more frugal in his riper days,
He paid some bards with port, and some with praise,
To some a dry rehearsal was assigned,
And others (harder still) he paid in kind.
Dryden alone (what wonder?) came not nigh,
Dryden alone escaped this judging eye:
But still the great have kindness in reserve,
He helped to bury whom he helped to starve.
    May some choice patron bless each grey goose quill!
May every Bavius have his Bufo still!   250
So when a statesman wants a day's defence,
Or envy holds a whole week's war with sense,
Or simple pride for flattery makes demands,
May dunce by dunce be whistled off my hands!
Blest be the great! for those they take away,
And those they left me – for they left me Gay;
Left me to see neglected genius bloom,
Neglected die! and tell it on his tomb:
Of all thy blameless life the sole return
My verse, and Queensberry weeping o'er thy urn!   260
Oh let me live my own, and die so too!
('To live and die is all I have to do':)
Maintain a poet's dignity and ease,
And see what friends, and read what books I please:
Above a patron, though I condescend
Sometimes to call a minister my friend.

181

I was not born for courts or great affairs:
I pay my debts, believe, and say my prayers;
Can sleep without a poem in my head,
Nor know if Dennis be alive or dead.   270

  Why am I asked what next shall see the light?
Heavens! was I born for nothing but to write?
Has life no joys for me? or (to be grave)
Have I no friend to serve, no soul to save?
'I found him close with Swift' – 'Indeed? no doubt'
(Cries prating Balbus) 'something will come out.'
'Tis all in vain, deny it as I will:
'No, such a genius never can lie still';
And then for mine obligingly mistakes
The first lampoon Sir Will or Bubo makes.   280
Poor guiltless I! and can I choose but smile,
When every coxcomb knows me by my style?

  Cursed be the verse, how well soe'er it flow,
That tends to make one worthy man my foe,
Give virtue scandal, innocence a fear,
Or from the soft-eyed virgin steal a tear!
But he who hurts a harmless neighbour's peace,
Insults fallen worth, or beauty in distress,
Who loves a lie, lame slander helps about,
Who writes a libel, or who copies out;   290
That fop, whose pride affects a patron's name,
Yet absent, wounds an author's honest fame;
Who can your merit selfishly approve,
And show the sense of it without the love;
Who has the vanity to call you friend,
Yet wants the honour, injured, to defend;
Who tells whate'er you think, whate'er you say,
And if he lie not, must at least betray;
Who to the dean and silver bell can swear,
And sees at Cannons what was never there;   300
Who reads, but with a lust to misapply,
Makes satire a lampoon, and fiction lie;
A lash like mine no honest man shall dread,
But all such babbling blockheads in his stead.

  Let Sporus tremble – 'What? that thing of silk,

Sporus, that mere white curd of ass's milk?
Satire or sense, alas! can Sporus feel,
Who breaks a butterfly upon a wheel?'
Yet let me flap this bug with gilded wings,
This painted child of dirt, that stinks and stings;   310
Whose buzz the witty and the fair annoys,
Yet wit ne'er tastes, and beauty ne'er enjoys:
So well-bred spaniels civilly delight
In mumbling of the game they dare not bite.
Eternal smiles his emptiness betray,
As shallow streams run dimpling all the way.
Whether in florid impotence he speaks,
And, as the prompter breathes, the puppet squeaks;
Or at the ear of Eve, familiar toad!
Half froth, half venom, spits himself abroad,   320
In puns, or politics, or tales, or lies,
Or spite, or smut, or rhymes, or blasphemies.
His wit all see-saw, between that and this,
Now high, now low, now master up, now miss,
And he himself one vile antithesis.
Amphibious thing! that acting either part,
The trifling head, or the corrupted heart;
Fop at the toilet, flatterer at the board,
Now trips a lady, and now struts a lord.
Eve's tempter thus the Rabbins have expressed,   330
A cherub's face, a reptile all the rest.
Beauty that shocks you, parts that none will trust,
Wit that can creep, and pride that licks the dust.

   Not fortune's worshipper, nor fashion's fool,
Not lucre's madman, nor ambition's tool,
Not proud, nor servile; be one poet's praise,
That, if he pleased, he pleased by manly ways:
That flattery, even to kings, he held a shame,
And thought a lie in verse or prose the same;
That not in fancy's maze he wandered long,   340
But stooped to truth, and moralized his song:
That not for fame, but virtue's better end,
He stood the furious foe, the timid friend,
The damning critic, half-approving wit,

The coxcomb hit, or fearing to be hit;
Laughed at the loss of friends he never had,
The dull, the proud, the wicked, and the mad;
The distant threats of vengeance on his head,
The blow unfelt, the tear he never shed;
The tale revived, the lie so oft o'erthrown,　　　　　350
The imputed trash, and dullness not his own;
The morals blackened when the writings 'scape,
The libelled person, and the pictured shape;
Abuse, on all he loved, or loved him, spread,
A friend in exile, or a father dead;
The whisper, that to greatness still too near,
Perhaps yet vibrates on his sovereign's ear –
Welcome for thee, fair Virtue! all the past:
For thee, fair Virtue! welcome even the last!
　'But why insult the poor, affront the great?'　　　360
A knave's a knave, to me, in every state;
Alike my scorn, if he succeed or fail,
Sporus at court, or Japhet in a jail,
A hireling scribbler, or a hireling peer,
Knight of the post corrupt, or of the shire;
If on a pillory, or near a throne,
He gain his prince's ear, or lose his own.
　Yet soft by nature, more a dupe than wit,
Sappho can tell you how this man was bit:
This dreaded satirist Dennis will confess　　　　　370
Foe to his pride, but friend to his distress:
So humble, he has knocked at Tibbald's door,
Has drunk with Cibber, nay has rhymed for Moore.
Full ten years slandered, did he once reply?
Three thousand suns went down on Welsted's lie;
To please a mistress, one aspersed his life;
He lashed him not, but let her be his wife:
Let Budgell charge low Grub Street on his quill,
And write whate'er he pleased, except his will;
Let the two Curlls of town and court abuse　　　　380
His father, mother, body, soul, and Muse.
Yet why? that father held it for a rule,
It was a sin to call our neighbour fool:

184

That harmless mother thought no wife a whore:
Hear this, and spare his family, James Moore!
Unspotted names, and memorable long!
If there be force in virtue, or in song.
  Of gentle blood (part shed in honour's cause,
While yet in Britain honour had applause)
Each parent sprung – 'What fortune, pray?' – Their own,   390
And better got, than Bestia's from the throne.
Born to no pride, inheriting no strife,
Nor marrying discord in a noble wife,
Stranger to civil and religious rage,
The good man walked innoxious through his age.
No courts he saw, no suits would ever try,
Nor dared an oath, nor hazarded a lie.
Unlearned, he knew no schoolman's subtle art,
No language, but the language of the heart.
By nature honest, by experience wise,   400
Healthy by temperance, and by exercise,
His life, though long, to sickness passed unknown,
His death was instant, and without a groan.
O grant me thus to live, and thus to die!
Who sprung from kings shall know less joy than I.
  O friend! may each domestic bliss be thine!
Be no unpleasing melancholy mine:
Me, let the tender office long engage,
To rock the cradle of reposing age,
With lenient arts extend a mother's breath,   410
Make languor smile, and smooth the bed of death.
Explore the thought, explain the asking eye,
And keep awhile one parent from the sky!
On cares like these if length of days attend,
May Heaven, to bless those days, preserve my friend,
Preserve him social, cheerful, and serene,
And just as rich as when he served a queen.
Whether that blessing be denied or given,
Thus far was right, the rest belongs to Heaven.

Composed 1731–4   First published 1735

THE FIRST SATIRE OF THE SECOND BOOK
OF HORACE IMITATED

To Mr Fortescue

P. There are (I scarce can think it, but am told)
There are, to whom my satire seems too bold:
Scarce to wise Peter complaisant enough,
And something said of Chartres much too rough.
The lines are weak, another's pleased to say,
Lord Fanny spins a thousand such a day.
Timorous by nature, of the rich in awe,
I come to Counsel learned in the law:
You'll give me, like a friend both sage and free,
Advice; and (as you use) without a fee.   10
    F. I'd write no more.
                  P. Not write? but then I think,
And, for my soul, I cannot sleep a wink:
I nod in company, I wake at night,
Fools rush into my head, and so I write.
    F. You could not do a worse thing for your life.
Why, if the nights seem tedious – take a wife;
Or rather truly, if your point be rest,
Lettuce and cowslip wine; *Probatum est.*
But talk with Celsus, Celsus will advise
Hartshorn, or something that shall close your eyes.   20
Or, if you needs must write, write Caesar's praise,
You'll gain at least a knighthood or the bays.
    P. What! like Sir Richard, rumbling, rough, and fierce,
With *arms* and *George* and *Brunswick* crowd the verse?
Rend with tremendous sound your ears asunder,
With gun, drum, trumpet, blunderbuss, and thunder?
Or, nobly wild, with Budgell's fire and force,
Paint angels trembling round his falling horse?
    F. Then all your Muse's softer art display,
Let Carolina smooth the tuneful lay,   30
Lull with Amelia's liquid name the Nine,
And sweetly flow through all the Royal line.
    P. Alas! few verses touch their nicer ear;

They scarce can bear their Laureate twice a year;
And justly Caesar scorns the poet's lays, –
It is to history he trusts for praise.
    F. Better be Cibber, I'll maintain it still,
Than ridicule all taste, blaspheme quadrille,
Abuse the City's best good men in metre,
And laugh at peers that put their trust in Peter.   40
Even those you touch not, hate you.
                            P. What should ail them?
    F. A hundred smart in Timon and in Balaam:
The fewer still you name, you wound the more;
Bond is but one, but Harpax is a score.
    P. Each mortal has his pleasure: none deny
Scarsdale his bottle, Darty his ham-pie;
Ridotta sips and dances, till she see
The doubling lustres dance as fast as she;
F— loves the senate, Hockley-hole his brother,
Like, in all else, as one egg to another.   50
I love to pour out all myself, as plain
As downright Shippen, or as old Montaigne:
In them, as certain to be loved as seen,
The soul stood forth, nor kept a thought within;
In my what spots (for spots I have) appear,
Will prove at least the medium must be clear.
In this impartial glass, my Muse intends
Fair to expose myself, my foes, my friends;
Publish the present age; but, where my text
Is vice too high, reserve it for the next: 60
My foes shall wish my life a longer date,
And every friend the less lament my fate.
    My head and heart thus flowing through my quill,
Verse-man or prose-man, term me which you will,
Papist or Protestant, or both between,
Like good Erasmus, in an honest mean,
In moderation placing all my glory,
While Tories call me Whig, and Whigs a Tory.
    Satire's my weapon, but I'm too discreet
To run a-muck, and tilt at all I meet;   70
I only wear it in a land of hectors,

Thieves, supercargoes, sharpers, and directors.
Save but our army! and let Jove incrust
Swords, pikes, and guns, with everlasting rust!
Peace is my dear delight – not Fleury's more:
But touch me, and no minister so sore.
Whoe'er offends, at some unlucky time
Slides into verse, and hitches in a rhyme,
Sacred to ridicule his whole life long,
And the sad burden of some merry song.   80

   Slander or poison dread from Delia's rage,
Hard words or hanging, if your judge be Page.
From furious Sappho scarce a milder fate,
Poxed by her love, or libelled by her hate.
Its proper power to hurt each creature feels;
Bulls aim their horns, and asses lift their heels;
'Tis a bear's talent not to kick, but hug;
And no man wonders he's not stung by Pug:
So drink with Walters, or with Chartres eat,
They'll never poison you, they'll only cheat.   90

   Then, learnèd sir! (to cut the matter short)
Whate'er my fate, or well or ill at Court;
Whether old age, with faint but cheerful ray,
Attends to gild the evening of my day,
Or death's black wing already be displayed,
To wrap me in the universal shade;
Whether the darkened room to muse invite,
Or whitened wall provoke the skewer to write:
In durance, exile, Bedlam, or the Mint,
Like Lee or Budgell, I will rhyme and print.   100

   F. Alas, young man! your days can ne'er be long,
In flower of age you perish for a song!
Plums and directors, Shylock and his wife,
Will club their testers, now, to take your life!
   P. What! armed for virtue, when I point the pen,
Brand the bold front of shameless guilty men;
Dash the proud gamester in his gilded car;
Bare the mean heart that lurks beneath a star;
Can there be wanting, to defend her cause,
Lights of the Church, or guardians of the laws?   110

188

Could pensioned Boileau lash, in honest strain,
Flatterers and bigots even in Louis' reign?
Could Laureate Dryden pimp and frair engage,
Yet neither Charles nor James be in a rage?
And I not strip the gilding off a knave,
Unplaced, unpensioned, no man's heir, or slave?
I will, or perish in the generous cause.
Hear this and tremble! you, who 'scape the laws:
Yes, while I live, no rich or noble knave
Shall walk the world, in credit, to his grave.   120
To VIRTUE ONLY, and HER FRIENDS, A FRIEND:
The world beside may murmur, or commend.
Know, all the distant din that world can keep,
Rolls o'er my grotto, and but soothes my sleep.
There, my retreat the best companions grace,
Chiefs out of war, and statesmen out of place.
There St John mingles with my friendly bowl
The feast of reason and the flow of soul:
And he, whose lightning pierced the Iberian lines,
Now forms my quincunx, and now ranks my vines,   130
Or tames the genius of the stubborn plain,
Almost as quickly as he conquered Spain.
    Envy must own, I live among the great,
No pimp of pleasure, and no spy of state,
With eyes that pry not, tongue that ne'er repeats,
Fond to spread friendships, but to cover heats;
To help who want, to forward who excel; –
This, all who know me, know; who love me, tell:
And who unknown defame me, let them be
Scribblers or peers, alike are mob to me.   140
This is my plea, on this I rest my cause –
What saith my counsel, learned in the laws?
    F. Your plea is good; but still I say, beware!
Laws are explained by men – so have a care.
It stands on record, that in Richard's times
A man was hanged for very honest rhymes;
Consult the statute, *quart.* I think it is,
Edwardi Sext. or *prim. et quint. Eliz.*
See Libels, Satires – here you have it – read.

189

P. Libels and Satires! lawless things indeed!   150
But grave epistles, bringing vice to light,
Such as a king might read, a bishop write;
Such as Sir Robert would approve –
                              F. Indeed?
The case is altered – you may then proceed;
In such a cause the plaintiff will be hissed,
My lords the judges laugh, and you're dismissed.

Composed 1733   First published 1733

THE FIRST EPISTLE OF THE FIRST BOOK
OF HORACE IMITATED

To L. Bolingbroke

St John, whose love indulged my labours past,
Matures my present, and shall bound my last!
Why will you break the Sabbath of my days?
Now sick alike of envy and of praise.
Public too long, ah, let me hide my age!
See modest Cibber now has left the stage:
Our generals now, retired to their estates,
Hang their old trophies o'er the garden gates;
In life's cool evening satiate of applause,
Nor fond of bleeding, even in Brunswick's cause.   10
    A voice there is, that whispers in my ear
('Tis Reason's voice, which sometimes one can hear),
'Friend Pope! be prudent, let your Muse take breath,
And never gallop Pegasus to death;
Lest stiff, and stately, void of fire or force,
You limp, like Blackmore on a Lord Mayor's horse.'
    Farewell, then, verse, and love, and every toy,
The rhymes and rattles of the man or boy;
What right, what true, what fit we justly call,
Let this be all my care, for this is all: 20
To lay this harvest up, and hoard with haste,
What every day will want, and most, the last.
    But ask not, to what doctors I apply?

190

Sworn to no master, of no sect am I:
As drives the storm, at any door I knock:
And house with Montaigne now, or now with Locke;
Sometimes a patriot, active in debate,
Mix with the world, and battle for the state,
Free as young Lyttelton, her cause pursue,
Still true to virtue, and as warm as true;   30
Sometimes with Aristippus, or St Paul,
Indulge my candour, and grow all to all;
Back to my native moderation slide,
And win my way by yielding to the tide.
  Long, as to him who works for debt, the day,
Long as the night to her whose love's away,
Long as the year's dull circle seems to run,
When the brisk minor pants for twenty-one;
So slow the unprofitable moments roll,
That lock up all the functions of my soul;   40
That keep me from myself; and still delay
Life's instant business to a future day:
That task, which as we follow or despise,
The eldest is a fool, the youngest wise:
Which done, the poorest can no wants endure;
And which, not done, the richest must be poor.
  Late as it is, I put myself to school,
And feel some comfort not to be a fool.
Weak though I am of limb, and short of sight,
Far from a lynx, and not a giant quite;   50
I'll do what Mead and Cheselden advise,
To keep these limbs, and to preserve these eyes.
Not to go back, is somewhat to advance,
And men must walk at least before they dance.
  Say, does thy blood rebel, thy bosom move
With wretched avarice, or as wretched love?
Know, there are words, and spells, which can control
Between the fits this fever of the soul:
Know, there are rhymes, which, fresh and fresh applied,
Will cure the arrant'st puppy of his pride.   60
Be furious, envious, slothful, mad or drunk,
Slave to a wife, or vassal to a punk,

191

A Switz, a High-Dutch, or a Low-Dutch bear;
All that we ask is but a patient ear.
    'Tis the first virtue, vices to abhor:
And the first wisdom, to be fool no more.
But to the world no bugbear is so great,
As want of figure, and a small estate.
To either India see the merchant fly,
Scared at the spectre of pale poverty!   70
See him, with pains of body, pangs of soul,
Burn through the tropic, freeze beneath the pole!
Wilt thou do nothing for a nobler end,
Nothing, to make philosophy thy friend?
To stop thy foolish views, thy long desires,
And ease thy heart of all that it admires?
Here wisdom calls: 'Seek virtue first, be bold!
As gold to silver, virtue is to gold.'
There, London's voice: 'Get money, money still!
And then let virtue follow, if she will.'   80
This, this the saving doctrine, preached to all,
From low St James's up to high St Paul!
From him whose quills stand quivered at his ear,
To him who notches sticks at Westminster.
    Barnard in spirit, sense, and truth abounds;
'Pray, then, what wants he?' Fourscore thousand pounds;
A pension, or such harness for a slave
As Bug now has, and Dorimant would have.
Barnard, thou art a *cit*, with all thy worth;
But Bug and D—l, their *honours*, and so forth.   90
    Yet every child another song will sing,
'Virtue, brave boys! 'tis virtue makes a king.'
True, conscious honour is to feel no sin,
He's armed without that's innocent within;
Be this thy screen, and this thy wall of brass;
Compared to this a minister's an ass.
    And say, to which shall our applause belong,
This new Court-jargon, or the good old song?
The modern language of corrupted peers,
Or what was spoke at Cressy and Poitiers?   100
    Who counsels best? who whispers, 'Be but great,

192

With praise or infamy leave that to fate;
Get place and wealth – if possible with grace;
If not, by any means get wealth and place.'
For what? to have a box where eunuchs sing,
And foremost in the circle eye a king.
Or he, who bids thee face with steady view
Proud fortune, and look shallow greatness through:
And, while he bids thee, sets the example too?
If such a doctrine, in St James's air,   110
Should chance to make the well-dressed rabble stare;
If honest S—z take scandal at a spark,
That less admires the palace than the park:
Faith, I shall give the answer Reynard gave:
'I cannot like, dread sir, your royal cave:
Because I see, by all the tracks about,
Full many a beast goes in, but none comes out.'
Adieu to virtue, if you're once a slave:
Send her to Court, you send her to her grave.
   Well, if a king's a lion, at the least   120
The people are a many-headed beast:
Can they direct what measures to pursue,
Who know themselves so little what to do?
Alike in nothing but one lust of gold,
Just half the land would buy, and half be sold:
Their country's wealth our mightier misers drain,
Or cross, to plunder provinces, the main;
The rest, some farm the poor-box, some the pews;
Some keep assemblies, and would keep the stews;
Some with fat bucks on childless dotards fawn;   130
Some win rich widows by their chine and brawn;
While with the silent growth of ten per cent,
In dirt and darkness, hundreds stink content.
   Of all these ways, if each pursues his own,
Satire, be kind, and let the wretch alone:
But show me one who has it in his power
To act consistent with himself an hour.
Sir Job sailed forth, the evening bright and still,
'No place on earth' (he cried) 'like Greenwich hill!'
Up starts a palace, lo, the obedient base   140

Slopes at its foot, the woods its sides embrace,
The silver Thames reflects its marble face.
Now let some whimsy, or that devil within
Which guides all those who know not what they mean,
But give the knight (or give his lady) spleen;
'Away, away! take all your scaffolds down,
For snug's the word: My dear! we'll live in town.'
    At amorous Flavio is the stocking thrown?
That very night he longs to lie alone.
The fool whose wife elopes some thrice a quarter,   150
For matrimonial solace dies a martyr.
Did ever Proteus, Merlin, any witch,
Transform themselves so strangely as the rich?
'Well, but the poor' – the poor have the same itch;
They change their weekly barber, weekly news,
Prefer a new japanner to their shoes.
Discharge their garrets, move their beds, and run
(They know not whither) in a chaise and one;
They hire their sculler, and, when once aboard,
Grow sick, and damn the climate – like a lord.   160
    You laugh, half beau, half sloven if I stand,
My wig all powder, and all snuff my band;
You laugh, if coat and breeches strangely vary,
White gloves, and linen worthy Lady Mary!
But, when no prelate's lawn with hair-shirt lined
Is half so incoherent as my mind;
When (each opinion with the next at strife,
One ebb and flow of follies all my life)
I plant, root up; I build, and then confound;
Turn round to square, and square again to round;   170
You never change one muscle of your face,
You think this madness but a common case,
Nor once to Chancery, nor to Hale apply,
Yet hang your lip, to see a seam awry!
Careless how ill I with myself agree,
Kind to my dress, my figure, not to me.
Is this my guide, philosopher, and friend?
This he who loves me, and who ought to mend;
Who ought to make me (what he can, or none),
That man divine whom wisdom calls her own;   180

194

Great without title, without fortune blessed;
Rich, even when plundered, honoured while oppressed;
Loved without youth, and followed without power;
At home, though exiled – free, though in the Tower;
In short, that reasoning, high, immortal thing,
Just less than Jove, and much above a king,
Nay, half in Heaven – except (what's mighty odd)
A fit of vapours clouds this demi-god.

Composed c. 1737   First published 1738

THE FIRST ODE
OF THE FOURTH BOOK OF HORACE

To Venus

Again? new tumults in my breast?
Ah spare me, Venus! let me, let me rest!
  I am not now, alas! the man
As in the gentle reign of my Queen Anne.
  Ah, sound no more thy soft alarms,
Nor circle sober fifty with thy charms.
  Mother too fierce of dear desires!
Turn, turn to willing hearts your wanton fires.
  To Number Five direct your doves,
There spread round Murray all your blooming loves;   10
  Noble and young, who strikes the heart
With every sprightly, every decent part;
  Equal the injured to defend,
To charm the mistress, or to fix the friend.
  He, with a hundred arts refined,
Shall stretch thy conquests over half the kind:
  To him each rival shall submit,
Make but his riches equal to his wit.
  Then shall thy form the marble grace
(Thy Grecian from), and Chloe lend the face: 20
  His house, embosomed in the grove,
Sacred to social life and social love,

195

Shall glitter o'er the pendant green,
Where Thames reflects the visionary scene:
　　Thither the silver-sounding lyres
Shall call the smiling loves and young desires;
　　There every Grace and Muse shall throng,
Exalt the dance, or animate the song;
　　There youths and nymphs, in consort gay,
Shall hail the rising, close the parting day.　　　　30
　　With me, alas! those joys are o'er;
For me the vernal garlands bloom no more.
　　Adieu! fond hope of mutual fire,
The still-believing, still-renewed desire;
　　Adieu! the heart-expanding bowl,
And all the kind deceivers of the soul!
　　But why? ah tell me, ah too dear!
Steals down my cheek the involuntary tear?
　　Why words so flowing, thoughts so free,
Stop, or turn nonsense, at one glance of thee?　　　40
　　Thee, dressed in fancy's airy beam,
Absent I follow through the extended dream;
　　Now, now I seize, I clasp thy charms,
And now you burst (ah cruel!) from my arms,
　　And swiftly shoot along the Mall,
　　Or softly glide by the canal,
　　Now shown by Cynthia's silver ray,
And now on rolling waters snatched away.

Composed c. 1736　　First published 1737

THE DUNCIAD IN FOUR BOOKS

from *Book the First*

Argument

The proposition, the invocation, and the inscription.
Then the original of the great empire of Dullness, and
cause of the continuance thereof. The college of the goddess in the city, with her private academy for poets in

196

particular; the governors of it, and the four cardinal virtues. Then the poem hastes into the midst of things, presenting her on the evening of a Lord Mayor's day, revolving the long succession of her sons, and the glories past and to come. She fixes her eyes on Bays to be the instrument of that great event which is the subject of the poem. He is described pensive among his books, giving up the cause, and apprehending the period of her empire: after debating whether to betake himself to the church, or to gaming, or to party-writing, he raises an altar of proper books, and (making first his solemn prayer and declaration) purposes thereon to sacrifice all his unsuccessful writings. As the pile is kindled, the goddess, beholding the flame from her seat, flies and puts it out by casting upon it the poem of Thulé. She forthwith reveals herself to him, transports him to her temple, unfolds her arts, and initiates him into her mysteries; then announcing the death of Eusden, the Poet Laureate, anoints him, carries him to court, and proclaims him successor.

The mighty mother, and her son, who brings
The Smithfield muses to the ear of kings,
I sing. Say you, her instruments, the great!
Called to this work by Dullness, Jove, and Fate;
You by whose care, in vain decried, and curst,
Still Dunce the second reigns like Dunce the first;
Say, how the goddess bade Britannia sleep,
And poured her spirit o'er the land and deep.

    In eldest time, ere mortals writ or read,
Ere Pallas issued from the Thunderer's head,
Dullness o'er all possessed her ancient right,
Daughter of Chaos and eternal Night:
Fate in their dotage this fair idiot gave,
Gross as her sire, and as her mother grave,
Laborious, heavy, busy, bold, and blind,
She ruled, in native anarchy, the mind.
    Still her old empire to restore she tries,
For, born a goddess, Dullness never dies.

. . .

Close to those walls where Folly holds her throne,
And laughs to think Monro would take her down,   20
Where o'er the gates, by his famed father's hand,
Great Cibber's brazen, brainless brothers stand;
One cell there is, concealed from vulgar eye,
The cave of Poverty and Poetry.
Keen, hollow winds howl through the bleak recess,
Emblem of music caused by emptiness.
Hence bards, like Proteus long in vain tied down,
Escape in monsters, and amaze the town.
Hence miscellanies spring, the weekly boast
Of Curll's chaste press, and Lintot's rubric post: 30
Hence hymning Tyburn's elegiac lines,
Hence journals, medleys, merc'ries, magazines;
Sepulchral lies, our holy walls to grace,
And new-year odes, and all the Grub Street race.
   In clouded majesty here Dullness shone;
Four guardian virtues, round, support her throne:
Fierce champion Fortitude, that knows no fears
Of hisses, blows, or want, or loss of ears:
Calm Temperance, whose blessings those partake
Who hunger and who thirst for scribbling sake: 40
Prudence, whose glass presents the approaching jail:
Poetic Justice, with her lifted scale,
Where, in nice balance, truth with gold she weighs,
And solid pudding against empty praise.
   Here she beholds the chaos dark and deep,
Where nameless somethings in their causes sleep,
Till genial Jacob, or a warm third day,
Call forth each mass, a poem, or a play:
How hints, like spawn, scarce quick in embryo lie,
How new-born nonsense first is taught to cry,   50
Maggots half-formed in rhyme exactly meet,
And learn to crawl upon poetic feet.
Here one poor word an hundred clenches makes,
And ductile Dullness new meanders takes;
There motley images her fancy strike,
Figures ill-paired, and similes unlike.
She sees a mob of metaphors advance,

Pleased with the madness of the mazy dance!
How tragedy and comedy embrace;
How farce and epic get a jumbled race;   60
How time himself stands still at her command,
Realms shift their place, and ocean turns to land.
Here gay description Egypt glads with showers,
Or gives to Zembla fruits, to Barca flowers;
Glittering with ice here hoary hills are seen,
There painted valleys of eternal green.
In cold December fragrant chaplets blow,
And heavy harvests nod beneath the snow.
    All these, and more, the cloud-compelling queen
Beholds through fogs, that magnify the scene.   70
She, tinselled o'er in robes of varying hues,
With self-applause her wild creation views;
Sees momentary monsters rise and fall,
And with her own fool's-colours gilds them all.

In each she marks her image full expressed,
But chief in Bays's monster-breeding breast;
Bays, formed by Nature stage and town to bless,
And act, and be, a coxcomb with success.
Dullness with transport eyes the lively dunce,
Remembering she herself was Pertness once.   80
Now (shame to fortune!) an ill run at play
Blanked his bold visage, and a thin third day:
Swearing and supperless the hero sat,
Blasphemed his gods, the dice, and damned his fate.
Then gnawed his pen, then dashed it on the ground,
Sinking from thought to thought, a vast profound!
Plunged for his sense, but found no bottom there,
Yet wrote and floundered on, in mere despair.
Round him much embryo, much abortion lay,
Much future ode, and abdicated play;   90
Nonsense precipitate, like running lead,
That slipped through cracks and zig-zags of the head;
All that on folly frenzy could beget,
Fruits of dull heat, and sooterkins of wit.
Next, o'er his books his eyes began to roll,

199

In pleasing memory of all he stole,
How here he sipped, how there he plundered snug,
And sucked all o'er, like an industrious bug....

A Gothic library! of Greece and Rome
Well purged, and worthy Settle, Banks, and Broome.   100
  But, high above, more solid learning shone,
The classics of an age that heard of none;...
  Of these, twelve volumes, twelve of amplest size,
Redeemed from tapers and defrauded pies,
Inspired he seizes; these an altar raise;
An hecatomb of pure unsullied lays
That altar crowns; a folio common-place
Founds the whole pile, of all his works the base;
Quartos, octavos, shape the lessening pyre;
A twisted birthday ode completes the spire.   110
  Then he: 'Great tamer of all human art!
First in my care, and ever at my heart;
Dullness! whose good old cause I yet defend,
With whom my muse began, with whom shall end;...
O! ever gracious to perplexed mankind,
Still spread a healing mist before the mind;
And, lest we err by wit's wild dancing light,
Secure us kindly in our native night.
Or, if to wit a coxcomb make pretence,
Guard the sure barrier between that and sense;   120
Or quite unravel all the reasoning thread,
And hang some curious cobweb in its stead!...
Some demon stole my pen (forgive the offence)
And once betrayed me into common sense:
Else all my prose and verse were much the same;
This, prose on stilts; that, poetry fallen lame....
  O born in sin, and forth in folly brought!
Works damned, or to be damned! (your father's fault)
Go, purified by flames ascend the sky,
My better and more Christian progeny!   130
Unstained, untouched, and yet in maiden sheets;
While all your smutty sisters walk the streets'....
  With that, a tear (portentous sign of grace!)

200

Stole from the master of the seven-fold face;
And thrice he lifted high the birthday brand,
And thrice he dropt it from his quivering hand;
Then lights the structure, with averted eyes:
The rolling smokes involve the sacrifice.

Roused by the light, old Dullness heaved the head,
Then snatched a sheet of Thulé from her bed;   140
Sudden she flies, and whelms it o'er the pyre;
Down sink the flames, and with a hiss expire.
   Her ample presence fills up all the place;
A veil of fogs dilates her awful face:
Great in her charms! as when on shrieves and mayors
She looks, and breathes herself into their airs.
She bids him wait her to her sacred dome:
Well pleased he entered, and confessed his home.

Here to her chosen all her works she shows;
Prose swelled to verse, verse loitering into prose: 150
How random thoughts now meaning chance to find,
Now leave all memory of sense behind;
How prologues into prefaces decay,
And these to notes are frittered quite away....
And lo! her bird (a monster of a fowl,
Something betwixt a Heideggre and owl)
Perched on his crown. 'All hail! and hail again,
My son: the promised land expects thy reign.
Know, Eusden thirsts no more for sack or praise;
He sleeps among the dull of ancient days; . . .   160
Thou, Cibber! thou, his laurel shalt support,
Folly, my son, has still a friend at court.
Lift up your gates, ye princes, see him come!
Sound, sound, ye viols; be the cat-call dumb!
Bring, bring the madding bay, the drunken vine;
The creeping, dirty, courtly ivy join . . . .
O! when shall rise a monarch all our own,
And I, a nursing-mother, rock the throne;
'Twixt prince and people close the curtain draw,
Shade him from light, and cover him from law;   170

201

Fatten the courtier, starve the learned band,
And suckle armies, and dry-nurse the land:
Till senates nod to lullabies divine,
And all be sleep, as at an ode of thine.'
    She ceased. Then swells the chapel-royal throat:
'God save King Cibber!' mounts in every note.

from *Book the Second*

And now the queen, to glad her sons, proclaims,
By herald hawkers, high heroic games.
They summon all her race: an endless band
Pours forth, and leaves unpeopled half the land,
A motley mixture! in long wigs, in bags,
In silks, in crapes, in garters, and in rags,
From drawing-rooms, from colleges, from garrets,
On horse, on foot, in hacks, and gilded chariots:
All who true dunces in her cause appeared,
And all who knew those dunces to reward.   10
    Amid that area wide they took their stand,
Where the tall May-pole once o'er-looked the Strand.
But now (so Anne and piety ordain)
A church collects the saints of Drury Lane.
    With authors, stationers obeyed the call,
(The field of glory is a field for all).
Glory, and gain, the industrious tribe provoke;
And gentle Dullness ever loves a joke.
A poet's form she placed before their eyes,
And bade the nimblest racer seize the prize;   20
No meagre, muse-rid mope, adust and thin,
In a dun night-gown of his own loose skin;
But such a bulk as no twelve bards could raise,
Twelve starveling bards of these degenerate days.
All as a partridge plump, full-fed, and fair,
She formed this image of well-bodied air;
With pert flat eyes she windowed well its head:
A brain of feathers, and a heart of lead;
And empty words she gave, and sounding strain,
But senseless, lifeless! idol void and vain!   30

202

Never was dashed out, at one lucky hit,
A fool, so just a copy of a wit;
So like, that critics said, and courtiers swore,
A wit it was, and called the phantom More.
　　All gaze with ardour: some a poet's name,
Others a sword-knot and laced suit inflame.
But lofty Lintot in the circle rose:
'This prize is mine; who tempt it are my foes;
With me began this genius, and shall end.'
He spoke: and who with Lintot shall contend?　　　40
　　Fear held them mute. Alone, untaught to fear,
Stood dauntless Curll, 'Behold that rival here!
The race by vigour, not by vaunts is won;
So take the hindmost, hell,' (he said) and run.
Swift as a bard the bailiff leaves behind,
He left huge Lintot and outstripped the wind.
As when a dab-chick waddles through the copse
On feet and wings, and flies, and wades, and hops:
So lab'ring on, with shoulders, hands, and head,
Wide as a wind-mill all his figure spread,　　　50
With arms expanded Bernard rows his state,
And left-legged Jacob seems to emulate.
Full in the middle way there stood a lake,
Which Curll's Corinna chanced that morn to make:
(Such was her wont, at early dawn to drop
Her evening cates before his neighbour's shop,)
Here fortuned Curll to slide; loud shout the band,
And 'Bernard! Bernard!' rings through all the Strand.
Obscene with filth the miscreant lies bewrayed,
Fallen in the plash his wickedness had laid:　　　60
Then first (if poets aught of truth declare)
The caitiff vaticide conceived a prayer.
　　'Hear, Jove! whose name my bards and I adore,
As much at least as any god's, or more;
And him and his if more devotion warms,
Down with the Bible, up with the Pope's arms.'
　　A place there is, betwixt earth, air, and seas,
Where, from ambrosia, Jove retires for ease.
There in his seat two spacious vents appear,

On this he sits, to that he leans his ear,   70
And hears the various vows of fond mankind;
Some beg an eastern, some a western wind:
All vain petitions, mounting to the sky,
With reams abundant this abode supply:
Amused he reads, and then returns the bills
Signed with that ichor which from gods distils.

 In office here fair Cloacina stands,
And ministers to Jove with purest hands.
Forth from the heap she picked her votary's prayer,
And placed it next him, a distinction rare!   80
Oft had the goddess heard her servant's call,
From her black grottoes near the temple-wall,
Listening delighted to the jest unclean
Of link-boys vile, and watermen obscene;
Where as he fished her nether realms for wit,
She oft had favoured him, and favours yet.
Renewed by ordure's sympathetic force,
As oiled with magic juices for the course,
Vigorous he rises; from the effluvia strong
Imbibes new life, and scours and stinks along;   90
Re-passes Lintot, vindicates the race,
Nor heeds the brown dishonours of his face.

 And now the victor stretched his eager hand,
Where the tall Nothing stood, or seemed to stand;
A shapeless shade, it melted from his sight,
Like forms in clouds, or visions of the night.
To seize his papers, Curll, was next thy care;
His papers light fly diverse, tossed in air;
Songs, sonnets, epigrams the winds uplift,
And whisk them back to Evans, Young, and Swift.   100
The embroidered suit at least he deemed his prey;
That suit an unpaid tailor snatched away,
No rag, no scrap, of all the beau, or wit,
That once so fluttered, and that once so writ.

Revision of 1728 version c. 1741   First published 1743

204

from *Book the Fourth*

Yet, yet a moment, one dim ray of light
Indulge, dread Chaos, and eternal Night!
Of darkness visible so much be lent,
As half to show, half veil, the deep intent.
Ye powers! whose mysteries restored I sing,
To whom time bears me on his rapid wing,
Suspend a while your force inertly strong,
Then take at once the poet and the song.

    Now flamed the dog-star's unpropitious ray,
Smote every brain, and withered every bay;   10
Sick was the sun, the owl forsook his bower,
The moon-struck prophet felt the madding hour:
Then rose the seed of Chaos, and of Night,
To blot out order, and extinguish light,
Of dull and venal a new world to mould,
And bring Saturnian days of lead and gold.

    She mounts the throne: her head a cloud concealed,
In broad effulgence all below revealed;
('Tis thus aspiring Dullness ever shines)
Soft on her lap her laureate son reclines.   20

    Beneath her footstool, Science groans in chains,
And Wit dreads exile, penalties, and pains,
There foamed rebellious Logic, gagged and bound,
There, stripped, fair Rhetoric languished on the ground;
His blunted arms by Sophistry are borne,
And shameless Billingsgate her robes adorn.
Morality, by her false guardians drawn,
(Chicane in furs, and Casuistry in lawn,)
Gasps, as they straiten at each end the cord,
And dies when Dullness gives her Page the word.   30

    And now had Fame's posterior trumpet blown,
And all the nations summoned to the throne.
The young, the old, who feel her inward sway,
One instinct seizes, and transports away.
None need a guide, by sure attraction led,
And strong impulsive gravity of head;

None want a place, for all their centre found,
Hung to the goddess and cohered around.
Not closer, orb in orb, conglobed are seen
The buzzing bees about their dusky queen.   40
   The gathering number as it moves along,
Involves a vast involuntary throng,
Who gently drawn, and struggling less and less,
Roll in her vortex, and her power confess.
Not those alone who passive own her laws,
But who, weak rebels, more advance her cause.
Whate'er of dunce in college or in town
Sneers at another in toupee or gown;
Whate'er of mongrel no one class admits,
A wit with dunces, and a dunce with wits.   50

   When Dullness, smiling – 'Thus revive the wits!
But murder first, and mince them all to bits;
As erst Medea (cruel so to save!)
A new edition of old Aeson gave;
Let standard authors, only thus, like trophies borne,
Appear more glorious as more hacked and torn.
And you, my critics! in the chequered shade,
Admire new light through holes yourselves have made.'

Now crowds on crowds around the goddess press,
Each eager to present their first address.   60
Dunce scorning dunce beholds the next advance,
But fop shows fop superior complaisance.
When lo! a spectre rose, whose index-hand
Held forth the virtue of the dreadful wand;
His beavered brow a birchen garland wears,
Dropping with infant's blood, and mother's tears.
O'er every vein a shuddering horror runs;
Eton and Winton shake through all their sons.
All flesh is humbled, Westminster's bold race
Shrink, and confess the genius of the place: 70
The pale boy-senator yet tingling stands,
And holds his breeches close with both his hands.
   Then thus: 'Since man from beast by words is known,

206

Words are man's province, words we teach alone.
When reason doubtful, like the Samian letter,
Points him two ways; the narrower is the better.
Placed at the door of learning, youth to guide,
We never suffer it to stand too wide.
To ask, to guess, to know, as they commence,
As fancy opens the quick springs of sense,   80
We ply the memory, we load the brain,
Bind rebel wit, and double chain on chain;
Confine the thought, to exercise the breath;
And keep them in the pale of words till death.'

   Prompt at the call, around the goddess roll
Broad hats, and hoods, and caps, a sable shoal:
Thick and more thick the black blockade extends,
A hundred head of Aristotle's friends.

Before them marched that awful Aristarch;
Ploughed was his front with many a deep remark: 90
His hat, which never vailed to human pride,
Walker with reverence took and laid aside.
Low bowed the rest: he, kingly, did but nod;
So upright Quakers please both man and God.
'Mistress! dismiss that rabble from your throne:
Avaunt – is Aristarchus yet unknown?
Thy mighty scholiast, whose unwearied pains
Made Horace dull, and humbled Milton's strains.
Turn what they will to verse, their toil is vain,
Critics like me shall make it prose again   100
In ancient sense if any needs will deal,
Be sure I give them fragments, not a meal;
What Gellius or Stobaeus hashed before,
Or chewed by blind old scholiasts o'er and o'er.
The critic eye, that microscope of wit,
Sees hairs and pores, examines bit by bit:
How parts relate to parts, or they to whole,
The body's harmony, the beaming soul,
Are things which Kuster, Burman, Wasse shall see
When man's whole frame is obvious to a flea.   110

Ah, think not, mistress! more true dullness lies
In folly's cap, than wisdom's grave disguise.
Like buoys that never sink into the flood,
On learning's surface we but lie and nod.
Thine is the genuine head of many a house,
And much divinity without a νοῦς.'

Then thick as locusts blackening all the ground,
A tribe, with weeds and shells fantastic crowned,
Each with some wondrous gift approached the power,
A nest, a toad, a fungus, or a flower.   120
But far the foremost, two, with earnest zeal
And aspect ardent to the throne appeal.
   The first thus opened: 'Hear thy suppliant's call,
Great queen, and common mother of us all!
Fair from its humble bed I reared this flower,
Suckled, and cheered, with air, and sun, and shower,
Soft on the paper ruff its leaves I spread,
Bright with the gilded button tipped its head;
Then throned in glass, and named it Caroline.
Each maid cried, charming! and each youth, divine!   130
Did Nature's pencil ever blend such rays,
Such varied light in one promiscuous blaze?
Now prostrate! dead! behold that Caroline:
No maid cries, charming! and no youth, divine!
And lo, the wretch! whose vile, whose insect lust
Laid this gay daughter of the spring in dust.
Oh, punish him, or to the Elysian shades
Dismiss my soul, where no carnation fades!'
He ceased, and wept. With innocence of mien,
The accused stood forth, and thus addressed the queen: 140
   'Of all the enamelled race, whose silvery wing
Waves to the tepid zephyrs of the spring,
Or swims along the fluid atmosphere,
Once brightest shined this child of heat and air.
I saw, and started from its vernal bower
The rising game, and chased from flower to flower.
It fled, I followed; now in hope, now pain;

208

It stopt, I stopt; it moved, I moved again.
At last it fixed, 'twas on what plant it pleased,
And where it fixed, the beauteous bird I seized: 150
Rose or carnation was below my care;
I meddle, goddess! only in my sphere.
I tell the naked fact without disguise,
And, to excuse it, need but show the prize;
Whose spoils this paper offers to your eye,
Fair even in death! this peerless butterfly.'
    'My sons!' (she answered) 'both have done your parts:
Live happy both, and long promote our arts.'

    Next, bidding all draw near on bended knees,
The queen confers her titles and degrees.   160
Her children first of more distinguished sort,
Who study Shakespeare at the Inns of Court,
Impale a glow-worm, or vertù profess,
Shine in the dignity of F.R.S. . . .
The last, not least in honour or applause,
Isis and Cam made doctors of her laws.
    Then, blessing all, 'Go, children of my care!
To practice now from theory repair.
All my commands are easy, short, and full:
My sons! be proud, be selfish, and be dull.   170
Guard my prerogative, assert my throne:
This nod confirms each privilege your own.'

    More she had spoke, but yawned – All Nature nods:
What mortal can resist the yawn of gods?
Churches and chapels instantly it reached;
(St James's first, for leaden Gilbert preached)
Then catched the schools; the hall scarce kept awake;
The convocation gaped, but could not speak:
Lost was the nation's sense, nor could be found,
While the long solemn unison went round: 180
Wide, and more wide, it spread o'er all the realm;
Even Palinurus nodded at the helm:
The vapour mild o'er each committee crept;

209

Unfinished treaties in each office slept;
And chiefless armies dozed out the campaign;
And navies yawned for orders on the main.
    O Muse! relate, (for you can tell alone
Wits have short memories, and dunces none,)
Relate, who first, who last resigned to rest;
Whose heads she partly, whose completely, blest;   190
What charms could faction, what ambition lull,
The venal quiet, and entrance the dull;
Till drowned was sense, and shame, and right, and wrong –
O sing, and hush the nations with thy song!

    In vain, in vain – the all-composing hour
Resistless falls: the Muse obeys the power.
She comes! she comes! the sable throne behold
Of Night primeval and of Chaos old!
Before her, fancy's gilded clouds decay,
And all its varying rainbows die away.   200
Wit shoots in vain its momentary fires,
The meteor drops, and in a flash expires.
As one by one, at dread Medea's strain,
The sickening stars fade off the ethereal plain;
As Argus' eyes by Hermes' wand opprest,
Closed one by one to everlasting rest;
Thus at her felt approach, and secret might,
Art after art goes out, and all is night,
See skulking truth to her old cavern fled,
Mountains of casuistry heaped o'er her head!   210
Philosophy, that leaned on Heaven before,
Shrinks to her second cause, and is no more.
Physic of metaphysic begs defence,
And metaphysic calls for aid on sense!
See mystery to mathematics fly!
In vain! they gaze, turn giddy, rave, and die.
Religion blushing veils her sacred fires,
And unawares morality expires.
Nor public flame, nor private, dares to shine,
Nor human spark is left, nor glimpse divine!   220
Lo! thy dread empire, Chaos! is restored;

210

Light dies before thy uncreating word;
Thy hand, great Anarch! lets the curtain fall,
And universal darkness buries all.

Composed c. 1741   First published 1743

Critical commentary

GENERAL CONSIDERATIONS IN JUDGING POPE

The best commentary upon the poems of Pope is to be found in Dr Johnson's *Life of Pope*; this is the ideal starting point for the student of Pope and it is the one work to which the reader of Pope will constantly return. Modern scholarship has filled in the details of Pope's life and the social background to his poems, but no other account of the life and writings can rival Johnson's for its critical authority. The reader may often be stimulated to dissent, but is invariably brought to what time has proved to be central issues of the poetry. What was said of *An Essay on Criticism* by Johnson may with equal propriety be applied to his own *Life of Pope*: it is

> a work which displays such extent of comprehension, such nicety of distinction, such acquaintance with mankind, and such knowledge both of ancient and modern learning, as are not often attained by the maturest age and longest experience.[1]

The *Life* was written in the maturity of Johnson's experience and came out in 1781 by which time Pope had been dead for almost forty years and a critical debate about his poems had long been engaged. Johnson was of course fully aware of this debate and in particular of the critical assessment of Joseph Warton in *An Essay on the Writings and Genius of Pope*, the first volume of which had appeared in 1756. The second volume

213

was not published until after the *Life* in 1782 (probably because of the hostile reception accorded to the first) but although the first part treated only the early poetry up to and including *Eloisa to Abelard*, in the dedicatory letter and in the final remarks on *Eloisa*, Warton's general view is made very clear. His criticism is of interest not merely in establishing the context of Johnson's more valuable *Life* but also for its own sake as it raises acutely for the first time questions about Pope's poetry that have been raised time and again since.

Warton genuinely admires Pope but finds the species of poetry in which he excelled to be an inferior kind. In the dedicatory epistle he distinguishes between a man of sense, a man of wit, and a true poet. The true poet who writes 'pure poetry' is distinguished by a 'creative and glowing imagination'. This is his translation of a phrase used by Horace (*'acer spiritus et vis'*) in a well-known passage from one of his satires (I, iv, 38–62) in which he disclaims the name of poetry for his *'sermones'* or conversations as he called his satires and ethical epistles. Horace had here devised a test for poetry: take from the verses their metrical regularity and transpose the order of the words (presumably to the regular order of prose). If the original passage is truly poetical, it will be possible to discern the essential lineaments of the poet, *'disjecti membra poetae'*, even in this disfigurement. Using Horace as his authority, Warton proceeds to try the test on the opening fourteen lines of Pope's third *Moral Essay*, the 'Epistle to Cobham', and finds the result most excellent sense but as unpoetical as the verses of Horace who recommends the trial. The essential poetry of Homer or Milton, he argues, cannot be so reduced to the tamest of prose. He then comes to his central question, and proceeds to the verdict of Voltaire on Boileau to characterize Pope:

> The sublime and the pathetic are the two chief nerves of all genuine poesy. What is there very sublime or very pathetic in Pope? . . . 'Incapable, perhaps, of the sublime which lifts the soul, and of the feeling which softens it, but made to enlighten those upon whom nature bestowed the one and the other, diligent, exacting, precise, pure, harmonious, he becomes finally the poet of reason.'[2]

214

In English the three great poets of the sublime and the pathetic are Spenser, Shakespeare, and Milton. The attitudes in the dedication are given practical expression in comment on the poems in the *Essay* itself and lead to the conclusion of its final paragraph:

This epistle [*Eloisa to Abelard*] is, on the whole, one of the most highly finished and certainly the most interesting, of the pieces of our author: and, together with *The Elegy to the Memory of an Unfortunate Lady*, is the only instance of the pathetic Pope has given us. I think one may venture to remark, that the reputation of Pope, as a poet, among posterity, will be principally owing to his *Windsor Forest*, his *Rape of the Lock* and his *Eloisa to Abelard*; whilst the facts and characters alluded to and exposed, in his later writings, will be forgotten and unknown, and their poignancy and propriety little relished. For wit and satire are transitory and perishable, but nature and passion are eternal.[3]

In the course of time Warton modified his position or at least the expression of it. Transcribing in the second volume a passage from *An Essay on Man* he feels himself 'almost tempted to retract and assertion at the beginning of this work that there is nothing transcendently sublime in Pope'. In comment on *The Moral Essays*, he is highly appreciative of the poetic quality of individual passages. Nevertheless in a judicious summing-up he remained true to his earlier position:

it will appear that the largest portion of them is of the didactic, moral and satiric kind; and consequently, not of the most poetic species of poetry; whence it is manifest that good sense and judgement were his characteristical excellencies, rather than fancy and invention; not that the author of the *Rape of the Lock* and *Eloisa*, can be thought to want imagination, but because his imagination was not his predominant talent, because he indulged it not and because he gave not so many proofs of this talent as of the other . . . . Whatever poetical enthusiasm he actually possessed, he withheld and stifled . . . . Surely it is no narrow and niggardly

215

encomium to say he is the great poet of reason, the first of ethical authors in verse?[4]

The final thought with which he leaves the reader is that Pope never wrote anything 'in a strain so truly sublime as "The Bard" of Gray' (a poem that had been severely castigated by Johnson in his *Life of Gray*[5]).

In applying the Horatian test to Pope, Warton could be said to be working within the mainstream of the ancient classical inheritance in which literature is classified into kinds or genres where the greatest prestige is attached to those with lofty subjects and elevated styles, notably epic tragedy and the Pindaric ode. Warton did not allow that Pope excelled in any of these kinds since he discounted the Homer translation on the grounds that it was not original. He does not give it a mention in either volume of the *Essay*. But in his criticism of Pope he is also reflecting and to some extent foreshadowing radical changes of taste and sensibility that began in the middle and continued through the later years of the eighteenth century. He looks favourably upon a developing new school of poetry based not so much like that of Dryden and Pope upon re-creation of the classics as upon cultivation of 'original genius'. The terms in which he praises *The Rape of the Lock* make it clear what he means by original genius:

> It is in this composition that Pope principally appears a poet; in which he has displayed more imagination than in all his other works taken together. It should however be remembered, that he was not the FIRST and former creator of those beautiful machines, the sylphs, on which his claim to imagination is chiefly founded. He found them existing ready to his hand; but has, indeed, employed them with singular judgement and artifice.[6]

Warton does not therefore deny Pope the name of poet altogether (this was to come later with Matthew Arnold[7]) as he had virtually denied the name of poet to Donne and Swift in his dedicatory epistle, but through the Horatian test he implies that Pope works for the most part in genres essentially unpoetic and is more a man of sense and wit than a true poet. Nevertheless the questions he asked – How are we to rank Pope among the

216

poets? Can there be a hierarchy of subjects and kinds? Did Pope suppress his imaginative side? Did he make an inferior choice in concentrating upon the moral, the didactic and the satiric? Is satire a lower and transient form? – these questions about Pope have been much debated and raise in their turn fundamental questions about the nature of poetry itself.

What then is Johnson's estimate of Pope? He agrees with Warton that good sense is a characteristic excellence though he transcends him in his definition of it:

> Of his intellectual character, the constituent and fundamental principle was good sense, a prompt and intuitive perception of consonance and propriety . . . . But good sense alone is a sedate and quiescent quality ... Pope likewise had genius.[8]

Genius Johnson describes as a combination of qualities each of which he defines with trenchant precision and each of which he locates in particular works, having first suggested that they are well adjusted to each other in Pope generally:

> Pope had, in proportions very nicely adjusted to each other, all the qualities that constitute genius. He had *Invention*, by which new trains of events are formed, and new scenes of imagery displayed, as in *The Rape of the Lock*, and by which extrinsic and adventitious embellishments and illustrations are connected with a known subject, as in the *Essay on Criticism*. He had *Imagination*, which strongly impresses on the writer's mind, and enables him to convey to the reader, the various forms of nature, incidents of life, and energies of passion, as in his *Eloisa, Windsor Forest* and the *Ethic Epistles*. He had *Judgement* which selects from life or nature what the present purpose requires, and by separating the essence of things from its concomitants, often makes the representation more powerful than the reality: and he had colours of language always before him, ready to decorate his matter with every grace of elegant expression, as when he accommodates his diction to the wonderful multiplicity of Homer's sentiments and descriptions.[9]

The distinction between invention and imagination improves upon Warton, and he asserts directly what Warton's comments on the ethical epistles (published after the *Life*) often illustrate, indirectly, that imagination has as much play in these works as in 'Eloisa' and 'Windsor Forest'. Judgement in Johnson's account acts upon the imagination and no easy distinction is allowed between them. Johnson's greater discrimination in the use of terms makes his analysis much more convincing than Warton's. Given his comprehensive statement, it is not surprising that he will not countenance any narrow definition of poetry to exclude Pope:

> After all this, it is surely superfluous to answer the question that has once been asked, Whether Pope was a poet? otherwise than by asking in return, If Pope be not a poet, where is poetry to be found? To circumscribe poetry by a definition will only show the narrowness of the definer, though a definition which shall exclude Pope will not easily be made. Let us look around upon the present time, and back upon the past; let us inquire to whom the voice of mankind has decreed the wreath of poetry; let their productions be examined, and their claim stated, and the pretensions of Pope will be no more disputed. Had he given the world only his version, the name of poet must have been allowed him: if the writer of the *Iliad* were to class his successors, he would assign a very high place to his translator, without requiring any other evidence of his Genius.[10]

This assertion of Pope's claim to poetical genius, made at the conclusion of his account of the poetry, specifically draws attention to the Homer translation. Indeed he devoted more pages to what he calls 'that poetical wonder, the translation of the *Iliad*, a performance which no age or nation can pretend to equal'[11] than to any other single work. Ignored by Warton, 'the noblest version of poetry that the world has ever seen' was for Johnson at the centre of Pope's achievement.

THE CHARACTER OF POPE'S POETRY ILLUSTRATED IN THE TRANSLATION OF HOMER

Warton's Horatian test may be countered by a Homeric test of a slightly different kind. In his long account of the growth of the Homer translation, Johnson gives extracts from a manus-

218

cript containing earlier versions of several passages of the *Iliad*, one of which is the famous 'nightpiece' included in this selection.[12] Comparison of the earlier lines with the finished product can serve to illuminate both the poetical method and the character of Pope. The Trojan warriors have beaten back the Greeks to their fortifications before the ships and, as night falls, they light their camp-fires on the Trojan plain. At this point Homer introduces a five-line simile, the bare bones of which are accurately represented in this literal version by Richmond Lattimore:

> As when in the sky the stars about the moon's shining
> are seen in all their glory, when the air has fallen to stillness,
> and all the high places of the hills are clear, and the
>   shoulders out-jutting,
> and the deep ravines, as endless bright air spills from
>   the heavens
> and all the stars are seen, to make glad the heart of
>   the shepherd.

(VIII, 555–9)[13]

The literal version cannot of course suggest what Pope saw in the simile; for this we may first go to the appreciative prose description in the notes that accompany the version:

> This comparison is inferior to none in Homer. It is the most beautiful nightpiece that can be found in poetry. He presents you with a prospect of the heavens, the seas and the earth: the stars shine, the air is serene, the world enlightened and the moon mounted in glory.[14]

The seas are not actually mentioned by Homer and in the figurative emphasis Pope makes explicit what he took to be the implicit meaning, which he had translated in his version. Homer's scene has been imaginatively extended, embellished, and transformed. However, for immediate purposes it is the growth in his imaginative involvement that is to be remarked.

In the opening Pope's first thoughts centre upon stillness and shining, brightness and lustre:

> As when in stillness of the silent night,
> As when the moon in all her lustre bright.

The changes he made give a sharper idea of the moon shining in darkness. *Refulgent* is not simply a dignified Latinism, for it appropriately expresses the idea of reflection in the light of the moon:

> As when the moon, refulgent lamp of night,
> O'er heaven's clear azure sheds her silver light.
>   pure   spreads   sacred

In the second couplet his thoughts again turned first to the quality of the moonlight, to its trembling lustre and to the flood of golden colour it sheds:

> As still in air the trembling lustre stood,
> And o'er its golden border shoots a flood.

In the revision there is a radical change to quietness, solemnity, and deep serenity (the deep of course also refers to the sea):

> When no loose gale disturbs the deep serene,
> And no dim cloud o'ercasts the solemn scene.

At this stage we may note the change in epithet from 'silver' to 'sacred' in the second line of the opening couplet. As the idea of a sacred and solemn serenity took hold, it is underscored by the lulling smoothness induced by rhythmical changes and the removal of the unnecessary epithets 'loose' and 'dim':

> When not a breath disturbs the deep serene,
> And not a cloud o'ercasts the solemn scene.

'Not a breath' is a much more delicate touch than 'no loose gale'. In the third couplet the change is not so radical:

> Around her silver throne the planets glow,
> And stars unnumbered trembling beams bestow

becomes in the revision:

> Around her throne the vivid planets roll,
> And stars unnumbered gild the glowing pole.

Energy is heightened in the first line through the introduction of movement around a fixed point; the change has the effect of enhancing the dignity and centrality of the moon more effectively than the comparatively inert epithet 'silver'; 'vivid' improves upon 'glow' by sharpening the connection between the moon and the moonlit planets. (The fact that the planets do not revolve around the moon is immaterial; at night they may be imagined to do so.) In the second line 'gild the glowing pole' gives the mind and ear something more distinct than the phrase it replaces, harking back to the sharp clarity in the 'clear azure' (here 'pure' is judiciously rejected in favour of 'clear' on the grounds of both sense and sound). In the fourth couplet Pope's expression is made neater and more pointed:

> Clear gleams of light o'er the dark trees are seen,
> > o'er the dark trees a yellow sheds,
> And tip with silver all the mountain heads.
> > > forest

In the revision:

> O'er the dark trees a yellower green they shed,
> > gleam
> > verdure
> And tip with silver every mountain's head.

In the first line the simple antithesis of 'clear' and 'dark' is improved upon with the addition of the more daring 'yellower verdure' to express the paradoxical quality of moonlight, but the phrase is less bold and more subtle than 'yellower green' since verdure more obviously includes vegetation as well as colour. In the fifth couplet the improvement is radical:

> The valleys open, and the forests rise,
> All nature stands revealed before our eyes

becomes

> The vales appear, the rocks in prospect rise,
> A flood of glory bursts from all the skies.

The opening up of the scene as the moonlight spreads is finely suggested in 'the rocks in prospect rise'. We may note here the change of 'sheds' to 'spreads' in the first line of the simile; in the final version of the whole there is a gradual spreading of the light, brought to a dramatic climax here with the 'flood of glory', recalling a phrase rejected in the second couplet, 'shoots a flood'. A final change to 'Then shine the vales' improves further by drawing attention to the time sequence and by giving emphasis to the increasing light in 'shine'.

In the completed version, movement and colour advance in delicate stages. The light 'spreads' in the first couplet; in the second movement is suspended, in the third it is advanced with the 'vivid' planets and the starlight that 'gilds' the 'glowing' pole; in the fourth there is more colour with the comparative 'yellower' and the silver light on the mountains, but the movement is still delicate with the verbs 'shed' and 'tip'; finally the valleys 'shine' and then comes the strongest burst in the 'flood of glory'.

In the final couplet of the simile there is also radical change:

> The conscious shepherd, joyful at the sight,
> Eyes the blue vault, and numbers every light.

becomes:

> The conscious swains, rejoicing in the sight,
>   shepherds, gazing with delight,
> Eye the blue vault, and bless the vivid light.
>   glorious
>   useful

Here the modern reader may perhaps regret this change in the first line, but must be grateful that Pope amended the infelicity of the second. The final thought, 'useful', extends the significance of Pope's emphasis in the simile upon the 'vivid' and the 'glorious'. That the shepherds should 'bless the useful light' makes explicit the spiritual meaning with which he invests the scene.

Finally it may be noted that Pope did not abandon the first thoughts, images, and words that the simile had prompted. When he goes on to describe the effect of the fires, the reflected light 'glimmers', 'gleams', and 'trembles', and the fires 'shoot a shady lustre'; but as he imagined the whole scene more powerfully and more precisely he separated the gradually evolving clarity in the natural scene of the simile from the flickering evanescent half-light in the human sphere to which it is related:

So many flames before *proud* Ilion blaze,
And lighten glimmering Xanthus with their rays.
The long reflections of the distant fires
Gleam on the walls, and tremble on the spires.
A thousand piles the *dusky horrors* gild.
And shoot a shady lustre o'er the field.

In what is italicized (all additions to Homer) Pope artfully
evokes behind the present scene the future doom of flaming
Troy. The *dusky horrors* cast by the piles (the fires) are no mere
poetical cliché. There is a poignant contrast, most delicately
suggested, between the peace, serenity, and order of this night
and the trembling terror of that future night, and between the
exultant mood of the Trojan troops fresh from their triumph
and eagerly expectant in their shining armour:

The troops exulting sat in order round . . .
And ardent warriors wait the rising morn

and what awaits them when proud Ilion falls. The embellish-
ment of Homer is not gratuitous artifice but the product of the
poet's imaginative involvement with the great moral and psy-
chological drama of the *Iliad* vividly present in every line he
translates.

Johnson offers these specimens for every one who 'delights
to trace the mind from the rudeness of its first conceptions to
the elegance of the last' and so that the reader of Pope's *Iliad*
may see 'by what gradations it advanced to correctness'. This
latter is a cold word which when applied to eighteenth-century
poetry has not usually helped its reputation subsequently. But
we may recall that Pope, who is always held to be the most
'correct' of poets, ridiculed the 'correctly cold' in *An Essay on
Criticism* (ll. 239–52), and in these lines, though there is certainly a masterly polishing up in matters of metre, sound, and
diction, what is striking is that there is a gradually evolving
conception of the whole as the poet sorts out precisely what
picture and feeling he wishes to conjure up and as he finds the
best words to express them. It is, as Johnson suggests, conceptions that change not merely the surface as Pope's imaginative engagement with the raw material of Homer deepens. The

method of composition that may be deduced here shows at work all the faculties that in Johnson's analysis constitute Pope's genius, in particular what he has to say about judgement, imagination, and colours of language. If Pope's method does not quite seem to be Wordsworth's 'spontaneous overflow of powerful feelings',[15] we may again have recourse to Johnsonian wisdom and experience, for the following account was doubtless how he himself composed:

> Of composition there are different methods . . . . It is related of Virgil, that his custom was to pour out a great number of verses in the morning, and pass the day in retrenching exuberances and correcting inaccuracies. The method of Pope, as may be collected from his translation, was to write his first thoughts in his first words, and gradually to amplify, decorate, rectify and refine them.[16]

The nightpiece was much admired in the eighteenth century but much attacked in the next on the grounds of artificial diction and lack of realism. An interesting 'Romantic' defence is offered by Byron who praised it, not as it might have been praised in the eighteenth century on the basis of its splendid diction, but on the grounds that, in Arnold's words, 'it gives us the emotion of seeing things in their truth and beauty', for, having visited the site of Troy, he believed it to be agreeable to fact as he had experienced it:

> it is no translation, I know, but it is not such a false description as asserted. I have read it on the spot; there is a burst and a glow about the night in the Troad, which makes 'the planets vivid' and the 'pole glowing'. The moon is – at least the sky is, clearness itself; and I know no more appropriate expression for the expansion of such a heaven o'er the scene . . . than that of a 'flood of glory'.[17]

The manuscript lines given by Johnson enable us to catch a glimpse of the workings of Pope's imaginative processes. He enlarged further upon the poetical character of Pope's Homer by remarking upon Pope's greatest help in the arduous undertaking which he found in the versions of Dryden. As the debt extends beyond Homer to the whole of his poetry, embracing

224

diction and versification, further discussion of the Homer and its allusive character can serve to illuminate general characteristics of Pope's poetry. In the relation to Dryden, an interaction of some complexity is broached. In the *Aeneid*, Virgil translated, adapted, and embellished many particular passages from his Homeric originals. Pope often incorporates through Dryden's Virgil many of these embellishments into his own Homer. For example, to express the failing powers of Turnus in his final combat with Aeneas, Virgil had adapted a simile used by Homer in the final chase between Hector and Achilles. When Pope came to Homer's simile, he recalled Dryden's version of Virgil and embellished his own translation accordingly (words common to Dryden and Pope and not in Homer are given in italics):

> As in a dream a man is not able to follow one who runs
> from him, nor can the runner escape, nor the other pursue
> him,
> so he could not run him down in his speed, nor the other
> get clear.
>
> Homer, Iliad, XXII, 199–201 (Lattimore)

> And as, when heavy sleep has closed the sight,
> The sickly *fancy* labours in the night;
> We *seem* to run; and, destitute of force
> Our *sinking limbs forsake* us in the course:
> *In vain* we heave for breath; *in vain* we cry;
> The nerves, unbraced, their usual strength deny.
>
> Dryden, Aeneis, XII, 1312–17

> So oft Achilles turns him to the plain:
> He eyes the city, but he eyes *in vain*.
> As men in slumbers *seem* with speedy pace,
> One to pursue, and one to lead the chase,
> Their *sinking limbs* the *fancied* course *forsake*,
> Nor this can fly, nor that can overtake.
>
> Pope, Iliad, XXII, 257–62

Here a whole passage has been re-seen through Virgil mediated by Dryden. But in the translation at large the process is also less particular. Virgil's language, generally speaking, is more ornate than Homer's, and Pope, in creating an English poem, drew upon Dryden's heroic diction because Virgilian Latinate elegance was closer to the aspirations of his age than the simpler style of the original Greek.

Pope was steeped in Dryden and it was not only his Virgil that entered his imagination as he translated Homer. To give added point to Achilles' rejection of Lycaon's plea for mercy, he incorporates a whole line (acknowledged in quotation marks) from Dryden's Lucretius:

'And thou, dost thou bewail mortality?'

(XXI, 118)

evoking by this allusion the philosopher's arguments against the fear of death in an emotional context and at a point in the action where, since Achilles is beyond reason and Lycaon desperately wants to live, the words acquire a remarkable new resonance.

In translating, therefore, Pope did not imagine that he was reproducing Homer; he sought rather to create in English a poem that might be worthy of his original, and to this end, he did not scruple to use every means at his disposal to enrich his language, so that Johnson can conclude 'he cultivated our language with such diligence and art that he left in his Homer a treasure of poetical elegances to posterity'. To adopt Johnsonian phrases, in the nightpiece he *colours* Homer's *images* and in Achilles' speech to Lycaon he *points* Homer's *sentiments*.

A final example from the *Iliad* may serve to suggest why Pope felt this colouring and pointing to be necessary. It is a moment when Apollo thinks better of coming into conflict with his fellow gods to support a mortal cause. What Pope saw in the moment which may not be so apparent in the literal version is again evident in the note that follows his translation:

> Shaker of the earth, you would have me be as one without prudence
> if I am to fight even you for the sake of insignificant
> mortals, who are as leaves are, and now flourish and grow warm
> with life, and feed on what the ground gives, but then again

226

fade away and are dead. Therefore let us with all speed
give up this quarrel and let the mortals fight their own
battles.

Homer, Iliad, XXI, 462–7 (Lattimore)

Apollo thus: To combat for mankind
Ill suits the wisdom of celestial mind:
For what is man? Calamitous by birth,
They owe their life and nourishment to earth;
Like yearly leaves, that now, *with beauty crowned*,
Smile on the sun; now, wither on the ground:
To their own hands commit the *frantic scene*
Nor mix immortals in a cause so mean.

Pope, Iliad, XXI, 535–42

The poet is very happy in interspersing his poem with moral
sentences; in this place he steals away his reader from war
and horror, and gives him a beautiful admonition of his own
frailty.

The note concludes with the citation of a similar sentiment in
Ecclesiastes XIV, 18. The dramatic rhetorical question *For what
is man?* points the sentiment, but is in itself simply recalling the
urgency of the Psalmist. In the italicized phrases, the difference
between the divine and human nature is made more colourful
and pointed, but the passage is not as ornate as the nightpiece;
to use a phrase from Pope's own description of Homer's style
in his preface, it retains 'a graceful and dignified simplicity'.[18] If
we turn from this to the 'bald and sordid' simplicity of the lines
when literally rendered, it will be apparent that, even if the
translator elects not to go the way of Pope, something must be
done, for in the words of John Denham, a pioneer of creative
translation in the previous century:

poetry is of so subtle a spirit, that, in pouring out of one
language into another, it will all evaporate; and if a new
spirit be not added in the transfusion, there will be nothing
but a *caput mortuum*.[19]

Johnson believed that in his Homer Pope had wonderfully
enriched English poetry and his final point of admiration is for
its sweet melody. 'His version may be said to have tuned the

227

English tongue.' This may be the point at which to cite his judicious account of Pope's versification:

> Poetical expression includes sound as well as meaning. 'Music', says Dryden, 'is inarticulate poetry'; among the excellencies of Pope, therefore, must be mentioned the melody of his metre. By perusing the works of Dryden, he discovered the most perfect fabric of English verse, and habituated himself to that only which he found the best; in consequence of which restraint, his poetry has been censured as too uniformly musical, and as glutting the ear with unvaried sweetness. I suspect this objection to be the cant of those who judge by principles rather than perception; and who would even themselves have less pleasure in his works, if he had tried to relieve attention by studied discords or affected to break his lines and vary his pauses.[20]

Finally Johnson admits to failings in the version when it is judged not as an English poem but as a translation of Homer. He does not deny that there is some truth in the charge that it does not represent Homer's characteristic manner 'as it wants his awful *simplicity*, his *artless* grandeur, his *unaffected* majesty'. Though eminently rapid, clear, and noble, Pope's Homer is not, of course, *simple*. Johnson believed that the passage of two thousand years had put this simplicity beyond the achievement of a modern poet, and defends Pope on the grounds that a translator must make concessions to the age in which he lives.[21]

Comment on the *Odyssey* is complicated by the circumstances of its composition for Pope had two collaborators who between them translated twelve books, though it appears that their work was submitted to Pope for revision. (What is included in this selection is wholly translated by Pope.) In his postscript he is concerned to stress the very different poetical characters of the two works, the *Odyssey* being political and moral, abounding in narrative and fable, and written in a plain and sometimes familiar style. The low subject-matter in many of the scenes involving the suitors in the palace of Ulysses, particularly in the second half of the poem when the hero is disguised as a beggar, caused the translator some difficulty so that signs of strain are evident. Yet in the fabulous world of

228

Ulysses' adventures, Pope is thoroughly at ease; in the episodes involving the Cyclops and Circe the narrative moves with lucid ease in a style that rightly does not aspire to the elevated pitch of the *Iliad*, but is suitably graceful and varied. In *An Essay on Pope's Odyssey* of 1726 Joseph Spence offers a fine appreciation of the moment when Circe is surprised and discovered (X, 380–95):

> What starts, what terror and amazement? What passionate breaks are there in these lines? How solemn is the beginning? How emphatical the account of the action, and how lively the surprise and confusion of the enchantress, upon finding the inefficacy of her charms? Nature here appears in every word that she says . . . . The extraordinary beauty I mean, is that *insight* which the poet gives his readers into Circe's mind . . . . Everyone may perceive the tumult, and the successive enlightenings of her mind. We are led into a full view of the shifting of her thoughts; and behold the various openings of them in her soul.[22]

The Homer translation is a major poetic achievement, unjustly neglected on the grounds that it is not 'original', and any assessment of Pope's output and career that ignores it will be deficient. For most readers in the eighteenth century the answer to Warton's question 'What is there very sublime or very pathetic in Pope?' was the translation of Homer. Here in the melody of its verse and the brilliant variety of its colourful language we can enjoy the fruits of a creative and glowing imagination happily engaged in the heroic task of making in English a poem worthy of its noble original.

INDIVIDUAL POEMS

Pope had published extracts from Homer including the Sarpedon episode among his first pieces in 1709. He was therefore well exercised in the heroic before the occasion that prompted what is universally acknowledged to have been a triumph, *The Rape of the Lock*, much admired in all periods as the perfection of the mock-heroic in English. His poetic talent is shown to its best advantage in the imaginative creation of the divine machi-

he didn't create them
they were already created See Pg 216

nery (especially in the beautiful description of the sylphs at canto II, 55ff) and in the judicious intermixture of the machinery with the action. These delicate and insubstantial beings reflect perfectly the character of the world over which they preside; in them the divine machinery of epic is delightfully miniaturized in order portentously to magnify the trivial characters and events of the poem.

The early allusion to Virgil's fourth *Georgic*, the most notable example of the mock-heroic surviving from antiquity, in a direct quotation from Dryden's translation, 'slight is the subject' (*Georgics*, IV, 8), is a signal that he approaches his own subject in a similar spirit of light-hearted regard, for Virgil's elevated language has the dual effect of raising a slight subject in the imagination (he delights in his bees) and through the witty juxtaposition of the human and the insect worlds of deflating the heroic pretensions of men. In *The Rape of the Lock* two worlds that are both familiar but normally distinct, the polite and the heroic, are united in Pope's imagination so that they are both made new and seen in a new perspective. This ingenious, subtle, and sometimes paradoxical effect is of a radically different order from simple epic travesty:

> I sing the man (read it who list)
> A Trojan true as ever pist.[23]

In Belinda's exclamation

> Happy! ah ten times happy had I been,
> If Hampton Court these eyes had never seen!
>
> (canto IV, 149–50)

if we catch the allusion to the famous last words of Dido, 'Happy ah too happy had I been, if only the Trojan ships had not touched our shores' (*Aeneid*, IV, 657–8), it is not Dido and Virgil who are mocked. It is not necessary to recognize the allusion to appreciate the sense of the lines where the irony lies in the truth of the exclamation beyond the exclaimer's perception, but when recognized it serves, like the epic magnification in general, to put Belinda's distress into its proper perspective by juxtaposing the trivial and the truly serious, in this case the tragic. At the same time Pope's playful wit delights in the happy combination of dissimilar images. The effect of the wit can be subtle and various. It seems to be purely comic when the Baron swears a great oath (canto IV, 133–8) that reminds us of the oath of Achilles at the opening of the *Iliad* or when the bodkin's ancestry (canto V, 89–96) is described in terms reminiscent of Agamemnon's sceptre or when Jove weighs the men's wits against the ladies' hairs in his scales (canto V, 71–4) as he had weighed the fates of Achilles and Hector and Aeneas and Turnus in Homer and Virgil. Both the characters of the poem and to a lesser extent the solemnities of epic are being mocked here. On the other hand when the characters fight like Homer's gods, there is a shift to apparent seriousness in the simile:

> So when bold Homer makes the gods engage,
> And heavenly breasts with human passions rage.
>
> (canto V, 45–52)

But underlying the seriousness is the comedy of the Olympian gods whose passionate actions because they are not subject to mortality are touched with absurdity. In the epic allusions therefore the serious and the comic combine in varying proportions. They are most finely balanced in the speech of Clarissa added later in response to criticism that the poem lacked a moral, and closely modelled upon the heroic speech of Sarpedon. When it is recognized as a translation of heroic idealism into an idealism appropriate to polite society, the effect is, of course, finely comic but, since age, disease, and death are transcendent facts of nature that affect man no less in the polite than the heroic society, the comedy is complicated by a serious elegiac undertone, apparent too elsewhere, notably in the witty evocation of the power of time at the close of the third canto. Pope is writing about society people whose thoughts and actions are out of touch with the facts of nature and time, so that with appropriate decorum Clarissa's speech is ignored.

The subtle variety achieved by Pope in his epic allusion is seen too in the many tonal shifts and in the manipulation of artistic effects within the couplet form. At the opening of the third canto, for example, comes the majestic description of Hampton Court in two smoothly flowing couplets. The ele-

231

vated note is sustained in the fifth line to be punctured in the sixth by a zeugma and neat antithesis as statesmen foredoom the *fall*

Of foreign tyrants, and of nymphs at home.

The vocabulary remains elevated, if ironically so in the case of the nymphs. (The split line is a favourite device; compare, for example,

To stain her honour/or her new brocade.

(canto II, 107))

A second and more famous zeugma follows in which great Anna *takes* both counsel and tea, and this time the bathetic effect of the zeugma and the antithesis is reinforced by contrasting rhyme words, the powerful solemnity of 'obey' against the humdrum 'tea'. But the bathos has further to go yet as the scene becomes more animated. In the description of the various talk is another favourite device in Pope, the juxtaposition of opposites (here the portentous and the less than portentous) not in a split line but in a split couplet:

One speaks the glory of the British Queen,
And one describes a charming Indian screen

(a famous example in which this device is used in a rising climax occurs at the opening of the fourth canto). From the high poetry of the opening we now sink to 'chat' and the commonest of language to describe the commonest of activities:

Singing, laughing, ogling, and all that.

Again the rhyme words give appropriate emphasis to the sense. The linguistic range of the poem is remarkable; it is a poem of many voices, the silliest being that of the effete fop Sir Plume in whose utterance Pope delightfully captures the clipped manner of the English aristocratic buffoon. The next lines describing noontide revert to the upper register to be followed by a couplet of more cutting satire as the poet suggests the truly dire effects springing from trivial causes:

The hungry judges soon the sentence sign,
And wretches hang that jurymen may dine.

232

Such moments as these, however, are rare in the poem as a whole for Pope views the objects of his satire with genial good humour and detached amusement. He has himself followed the advice of Clarissa and maintained good sense in the face of absurdity. The gallant tribute to Belinda's beauty as she sails down the Thames at the opening of the second canto and the famous dressing-table scene at the close of the first convey an image of beauty incompatible with sharp satirical intent. As he decks the goddess with the glittering spoil, the artist is half in love with the image of his own creation and, although we are only too conscious of the pride and vanity of Belinda's self-regard, nature is indeed dressed to advantage and new wonders truly called forth. To appreciate this, we need only compare Pope's later description of Sappho 'at her *greasy* task' in the 'Epistle to a Lady' (l. 25) or examine one of the sources of his description in Dryden's translation of part of Juvenal's sixth satire on the subject of women:

> She duly, once a month, renews her face;
> Meantime, it lies in daub, and hid in grease:
> Those are the husband's nights; she craves her due,
> He takes fat kisses, and is stuck in glue.
> But, to the loved adulterer when she steers,
> Fresh from the bath, in brightness she appears:
> For him the rich Arabia sweats her gum,
> And precious oil from distant Indies come,
> How haggardly soe'er she looks at home
> The eclipse then vanishes; and all her face
> Is opened, and restored to every grace.

(ll. 593–603)

A further contrast is provided by Swift in 'The lady's dressing room' (1730):

> Now listen while he next produces
> The various combs for various uses,
> Filled up with dirt so closely fixt
> No brush could force a way betwixt . . .
> Here gallypots and vials placed,
> Some filled with washes, some with paste,

Some with pomatams paints and slops
And ointments good for scabby chops.

(ll. 19–22, 33–6)

The advice of Clarissa had been good-humouredly and grace-
fully given in the 'Epistle to Miss Blount with the works of
Voiture' and in the 'Epistle to Miss Blount, on her leaving the
town, after the coronation', Zephalinda is surely a literary
younger sister of Belinda. In the witty contrasting parallel
between her plight in the country where the only male company is the bluff country squire and the plight of the poet who
would dearly wish to escape the vexation of the town is an
elegant comedy of manners, a delicate blend of irony, sympathy, gallantry, and amusement in 'social' verse that looks
beyond social values. 'Windsor Forest' is a poem of patriotic
idealism celebrating the peace of Utrecht in 1710; the natural
landscape in which the poet sees 'order in variety' reflecting the
greater order and variety of the cosmos is admired not because
it is wild, unspoilt, or apart from man, but as it has been
shaped by improving human culture into an harmonious order.
The poem is inspired by the *Georgics* in which Virgil celebrates
the fruitful cultivation of nature made possible by the Augustan
peace. Similarly elevated in its design is the heroic epistle *Eloisa
to Abelard* inspired by the *Heroides* of Ovid, a series of verse
letters in which the heroine, usually abandoned or forlorn,
expresses feelings of intense passion addressed to her unattain-
able lover. Pope's subject is drawn from Christian history
rather than pagan myth, and in it the conflict between two
kinds of love, love for God and love for Abelard, is passion-
ately and tenderly treated. The dialectical form of the couplet is
an ideal medium for the exploration and expression of conflict-
ing emotions. The description of the Gothic setting is justly
famous. The 'Elegy to the memory of an unfortunate lady', an
unusually obscure poem for Pope, is similarly renowned for its
tender pathos. Together with *An Essay on Criticism* with its
strong affirmation of a critical ideal, all these poems of Pope's
early career show a sensitive and aspiring idealism allied to a
strong intellect given expression in a wide variety of forms.

After he had translated Homer, Pope, who had in Johnson's

234

description a mind 'active, ambitious and adventurous, always investigating always aspiring', conceived the ambitious plan of writing 'a system of ethics in the Horatian way',[24] of which *An Essay on Man* and *The Moral Essays* were to be a part. He gave up the grand plan, but his output in poetry was now almost exclusively devoted to the didactic, the moral, and the satiric, as he seems to acknowledge himself when reviewing his career first in *An Essay on Man* (IV, 391–3) and then in the 'Epistle to Dr Arbuthnot' (ll. 147–50; 340–1).

What is engaging in philosophical poems is the appeal of the poetry as in the opening of *An Essay on Man*. With highly appropriate figurative emphasis, Pope awakens his noble lord to their philosophical enterprise as to an exciting day out on the grouse moor where, away from 'meaner things', they (and we) can

Expatiate free o'er all this scene of man.

The figure is extended in the dynamic verbs, 'Together let us beat', 'Try, explore, eye, shoot, catch'. The scene of man is variously figured as a 'maze', a 'wild', and a 'garden', which in their various contradictory associations of the hidden plan, beauty amidst disorder, and tempting fruit even where nature is ordered and dressed to advantage, suggest complexity, variety, and paradox. The irresistible middle way between those who 'blindly creep' and those who 'sightless soar' may be said to be philosophical and also suggests the pitch of Pope's style which manages to be familiar without being low and to be elevated without losing sight of the general reader. The paragraph ends with a confident intention to 'vindicate the ways of God to man', echoing Milton (*Paradise Lost*, I, 26), but the hint of absurdity in the second couplet and the leaning to satire at the end suggest a radically unMiltonic temper and perspective. Pope's theodicy is conceived and written very much in the terms of his age without reference to the story of Adam and Eve, and indeed without any mention of the divine revelation of truth through Christ at all. Yet in the famous opening of the second epistle, 'Know then thyself', it is from the standpoint of a humanism firmly rooted in the biblical conception of man as half-beast half-angel that he brings to bear a traditional

235

perspective upon the new science of his day. Pope is sometimes thought of as the poet of the Enlightenment, a view that might be encouraged by his famous epitaph upon Isaac Newton, even if we see wit in it:

Nature and Nature's laws lay hid in night;
God said, 'Let Newton be!', and all was light.

Certainly Pope was not one of those for whom new philosophy cast all in doubt. Nevertheless he viewed progress with a sceptical if not jaundiced eye (note the use of the prism in *An Essay on Criticism* (l. 311) and the microscope in *The Dunciad* (IV, 233)). Man is

A being *darkly* wise and *rudely* great.

The emphasis in these oxymoronic couplings falls heavily upon the qualifying adverbs impressing the idea of limitation. And the passage as a whole in which the paradoxical 'middle state' is created imaginatively by the balancing of opposites in and between lines in the condensed dialectic of the Augustan couplet, should be evidence enough that, however much he believed the universe itself to be an expression of divine reason, Pope's view of man was far too complex to allow any easy uncritical faith in the fruits of human reason. Though the success of the whole poem is debatable, few would doubt the brilliance of its parts.

In *The Moral Essays* Pope turned more explicitly to satire, and this is perhaps the point at which to consider his satirical intent, method, and practice. In the 'Epistle to Augustus', in which like Horace before him he aims to assert the civic utility of poetry, he traces the origin of satire to innocent jesting at country festivals; when holiday licence turned malicious, legal restraint became necessary, turning most poets to flattery but the more discriminating were able to distinguish between liberty and licence:

Hence satire rose that just the medium hit,
And heals with morals what it hurts with wit.

(ll. 261–2)

In this justification of satire Pope is at one with Horace in asserting an ideal, a moral balance between hurting and healing

236

in which wit is not indulged in to delight itself but is subject to restraint and serves a moral purpose. In pursuit of such an ideal medium, Pope developed the moral essay, a blend of satire and panegyric, in which the positive healing element is fully explicit as it often is in the satires and epistles of Horace. Both poets characteristically conduct a moral dialogue, usually with a specific addressee, and through the addressee with the reader. Poet, addressee, and reader are all implicated in a set of civilized values that are defined, asserted, and represented in the style and conduct of the poem.

The portrait of Chloe from the 'Epistle to a lady' (ll. 157–80) may serve as an example. After some of the more obvious targets have been attacked, the addressee (Martha Blount) interjects:

'Yet Chloe sure was formed without a spot?'

to which the poet replies:

Nature in her then erred not, but forgot.

In this portrait is explicitly played out a conflict that underlies Pope's social satire generally, the opposition between the social being and the spontaneous natural self. The use of 'formed' is not incidental, indicating the social conditioning of which women in the highly formalized society of his day were the principal victims. Addressing Martha in the 'Epistle to Miss Blount with the works of Voiture', he had written:

Too much your sex is by their forms confined,
Severe to all but most to womankind.

(ll. 31–2)

In the later epistle Martha extends her question and Pope extends his reply:

'With every pleasing, every prudent part,
Say, what can Chloe want?' – She wants a heart.

The two voices continue as the poet takes over from Martha (his own fictional convenience in the epistle anyway). Here is the voice supporting the thesis that Chloe is virtuous:

She speaks, behaves, and acts just as she ought . . .
So very reasonable, so unmoved . . .

> Observes how much a chintz exceeds mohair!
> Forbid it, Heaven, a favour or a debt
> She e'er should cancel . . .
> Safe is your secret still in Chloe's ear;
> Of all her dears she never slandered one . . .
> Chloe is prudent.

There is quite a catalogue of virtue here – in fact all the virtues conventionally associated with high society in the eighteenth century: prudence, decorum, propriety, reasonableness, un-flappable calm, discriminating taste, discretion, control, dignity – but in the brilliant dialectic of the couplet the antithetical reply insisting that her virtue is a denial of nature turns all her qualities into the essential limitation of mere social form. The wit may be said to be present in the ridiculing dialectic of the satire, but in the larger sense of wit meaning the imagination and what it creates we may applaud the wit of Pope in painting his portrait with such appropriateness in the colouring and such precise clarity of outline. There are just enough details – and the props are all there for a purpose and not unduly obtrusive – to place the society lady in her world: the Indian chest (finely rhyming with breast), the chintz and mohair, and the footman. Finally, in phrases like 'Forbid it, Heaven' or 'Of all her dears', the poet catches her very accent. This portrait of an elegant society lady is itself elegant and polished and as such embodies the virtues of the age in which it was painted. But elegance and polish are not enough. The values of the age are turned against itself. The moral point made through and controlling the wit could not be clearer. But for further clarity, the positive moral content of the poem is embodied in the winsome portrait of Martha herself whose virtues of good sense, good taste, and true feeling are wittily praised at the close of the poem.

On satire and Warton's objection to it, it may be useful here to offer the judgement of Byron:

> There may or may not be, in fact, different 'orders' of poetry, but a poet is always judged according to his execu-tion, not according to his branch of the art.[25]

On Pope's satire on women, a contrast may be suggested with Juvenal's notorious sixth satire on the subject of women, a long declamatory tirade which is deliberately indiscriminate and extreme (for he has not a good word for any member of the sex) and in which, whatever moral point may be implicit in the particular parts, the whole force of the satire lies in the wit.

The 'Epistle to Burlington' about taste and the use of riches is conceived and written within a similar moral framework. Praise of the noble lord at the opening and the close provides the occasion for a declaration of a central thesis:

> Tis use alone that sanctifies expense,
> And splendour borrows all her rays from sense.

(ll. 179–80)

As he asserts the civic utility of poetry in the 'Epistle to Augustus', so here the visual arts are to serve greater human ends than to express pride and vanity or even merely to gratify the aesthetic impulse. The patriotic idealism of 'Windsor Forest' which had celebrated imperial peace in the political order is transmuted in Pope's maturity into a vision of an ideal order in which artistic endeavours like those of Burlington serve the cause of civilization by imposing man's dominion over nature. But if this artistic dominion is to be exercised wisely, it must itself be the expression of good sense, a prerequisite even of taste, which will ensure that the improvement of art works with and not against the grain of nature. In the monstrous grandeur of Timon's villa

> The suffering eye inverted Nature sees.

(l. 119)

The dismal regularity of the gardens, finely suggested in the rhythm and arrangement of the couplet here:

> Grove nods at grove, each alley has a brother
> And half the platform just reflects the other

(ll. 117–18)

betrays the aesthetic ideal of 'Windsor Forest' where order in variety, as well as expressing the stylistic ideal Pope developed in his use of the couplet and in the structuring of his poems, reflects a greater *concordia discors* in nature herself. Needless to say, the life lived in the interior of this stupendous pile is an inversion of the truly civilized and the antithesis of good sense.

239

To defend himself against attacks made upon his satire in *The Moral Essays*, Pope turned directly to his Roman predecessor in *The Imitations of Horace*: 'An answer from Horace was both more full and of more dignity than any I could have made in my own person.' The poems were printed alongside the Latin, so that readers might appreciate the parallels. In the defence of satire wittily made by Horace in dialogue with the lawyer Trebatius (Satire II, i) and wittily adapted by Pope addressing Fortescue, an old friend but supporter of the government which Pope opposed, the poet represents himself as a doughty champion of virtue against vice: satire is distinguished from libel and thus the dignity and probity of this time-honoured form are vigorously asserted. As his contemporaries soon noted, Pope, in his imitation, is sharper and more particular in his attack than his Latin original. Though particular references are much more difficult to decipher in Horace than in Pope, it seems that despite asserting the intention to do so, Horace in fact does not very often attack recognizable living individuals. Pope's greater particularization is not, however, the whole *raison d'être* of the satire; it is merely part of the more general imaginative process whereby the modern freely adapts to his own circumstances and purposes the sentiments and images of his ancient original. For example, in humorous self-defence, Horace argues that while each man has his pleasure, his delight is to follow in the footsteps of the old Roman satirist Lucilius, making verses and entrusting his secrets to his books so that his whole life is open to view, and he further associates his satirical independence jokingly with his ancestry, coming as he does from the borders of Apulia or Lucania, he does not know which, both frontier states that had stubbornly held out against the might of Rome in time past (ll. 29–39). Pope's adaptation of the first part is more pointedly defensive, and in the second, instead of trying a comparable joke about his own origins (this might have been difficult to parallel), from the hint of ambiguity in Horace's ancestry (Lucanian or Apulian) he goes his own way to the famous lines in which he lays claim to moderation and discretion, being all things to all men, sentiments quite different from the implication of independent ferocity in Horace, but perfectly adapted to the requirements of

240

his own defence in 1733 (ll. 55–70). And when Horace later points out that the great and the good were not afraid to unwind in the presence of the satirist (his phrase '*discincti ludere*' (l. 73), to play disrobed, is a wrestling metaphor suggesting bouts of verbal wit) while their simple dish of herbs was on the boil, Pope changes the imagery to suit the refinement and dignity of life at Twickenham in the famous couplet:

> There St John mingles with my friendly bowl
> The feast of reason and the flow of soul.

(ll. 127–8)

However much he may vary the sentiments and images of Horace, and change his manner and tone, Pope remains loyal to the living essence of Horatian philosophy. In a celebrated passage in *The Art of Poetry* Horace claimed to be fulfilling the function of a whetstone in sharpening awareness of the poet's office and duty. Wisdom is the fount of good writing, and the Socratic writings can furnish the poet's material (ll. 304–10). In his satires and epistles Horace is characteristically Socratic, challenging the reader to philosophic self-examination and to fruitful thought about the true goods of life. Horace, like Socrates, has no formal system to impart – he reserves an eclectic's independence – and in his quest for self-knowledge his irony works upon himself. In pursuit of equanimity and philosophic calm, *otium*, he sets himself against all that in the business of urban living denies this, *negotium*, cultivating an independent reliance upon inner resources. Though his withdrawal often takes the form of active praise of the simpler country life he could lead away from Rome on his Sabine farm, he is neither reclusive nor ascetic, and speaks as *vir urbanus*, a man of the world, yet not inured to the world's values. The famous injunction *nil admirari* (Epistle I, vi, 1)

> Not to admire is all the art I know,
> To make men happy and to keep them so

(Pope's translation)

is at root a call to reject the allure of riches, position, and power, the pursuit of which brings anxiety and restlessness. In Epistle I, i (imitated by Pope and included here) he dedicates

241

himself late in life to the task of achieving wisdom, but recognizes in himself all the changeability and restlessness that he can satirize in more obvious forms in others. It is a poem in which the quest is made to seem no less urgent in spite of the implied recognition in the end that the goal may never be reached. The vital start is to orientate existence towards the desired end. In adapting Horace, Pope intensifies both the urgency of withdrawal from false goals (of which poetry may be one) in favour of 'Life's instant business' (l. 42) and the contrasting evils of the world from which he withdraws:

> While with the silent growth of ten per cent,
> In dirt and darkness, hundreds stink content.

(ll. 132–3)

Equally striking is the powerful confession of his own error at the end:

> . . . each opinion with the next at strife,
> One ebb and flow of follies all my life.

(ll. 167–8)

The fruits of Pope's self-knowledge achieved by way of Horatian self-questioning are not paralleled anywhere else in his works. In the intensity of his re-creation, we can see that Pope's affinity with Horace is not really a matter of temperament, manner, or style, but goes deeper to the philosophical core of the poems.

Pope's satire was the product and cause of much controversy. His first reaction to attack was *The Dunciad* of 1728. Thereafter, though many of his portraits were composites drawn from a variety of sources, he was increasingly drawn into personal satire in a crusade of defence and counter-attack that occupied most of the last years of his life. His defence through Horace provoked one of his victims, Lady Mary Wortley Montagu ('Sappho'), in conjunction with Lord Hervey (later 'Sporus') to reply that his satire was nothing better than warped malignancy, the impotent hatred of a misanthropic soul imprisoned in a deformed body:

> Who but must laugh, this bully when he sees
> A little insect shivering at a breeze.[26]

242

Some admirers of his earlier poetry felt that he was now cultivating the least attractive of the Muses. Others thought satire unchristian. One of his close friends, Arbuthnot, feared for his safety and urged him not to be so combative. In his prose reply, Pope defends the use of particular example: the great end of satire is reformation of character, which can only be accomplished if evil men are named. In the verse *An Epistle to Dr Arbuthnot*, he acknowledges a weakness in this theory:

> 'Satire or sense, alas! can Sporus feel,
> Who breaks a butterfly upon a wheel?'
> Yet let me flap this bug with gilded wings.

> (ll. 307–9)

The victim will not be affected, but Pope will continue anyway, and goes on to paint the most darkly passionate of all his satirical portraits in which the human being, the gilded courtier and would-be wit, is imaginatively transformed through the use of animal imagery and Satanic association and by the concentrated application of Pope's favourite rhetorical figure into something that is the reverse of what it seems to be: 'one vile antithesis'. We may admire the art with Byron:

> Now is there a line in all the passage without the most forceful imagery (for his purpose)? Look at the variety, at the poetry, of the passage – at the imagination, there is hardly a line from which a painting might not be made and *is*.[27]

Or the thought that an actual figure is submerged in the portrait may make us uneasy, provoking the natural question: was Pope fair? Johnson, who admired the elegance, spirit, and dignity of Pope's vindication of his own character at the close of the epistle, nevertheless concluded: 'The meanest passage is the satire on Sporus.'[28]

While admiring the persuasive arts of Pope in the epistle, many have been prompted by its often strident tone to wonder what relation the self-dramatization there of the talented and forbearing poet innocently beset by fools and malignant critics bears to the facts of the case. It is one thing to ask whether the image of the poet is persuasive and credible, another to ask whether it is entirely honest and true. If we desire an answer to the second question, we must go beyond the poem, to the life of

Pope and the the history of the times in which he lived. In his *Life*, Johnson, while admiring Pope's art and applauding his genius, does not gloss over what he considered to be defects in his character, pointing to a tendency in Pope to deception of himself and of others, to affectation, snobbery, and aggression in dispute. He admired *The Dunciad* as 'the best specimen that has yet appeared of personal satire ludicrously pompous' but was not convinced that its design was moral, feeling that it owed its origin in part to a petulance and malignancy in Pope.[29]

Pope himself asserted the integrity of his intentions:

> Ask you what provocation I have had?
> The strong antipathy of good to bad.
>
> 'Epilogue to the satires', Dialogue II, 197–8

It would be churlish not to recognize a ruling passion here. But was he always undeceived? What of the morals of the moralist? In judging his particular character we may bear in mind his own general account of the elusive paradox of human character, when judging and when judged, in the first *Moral Essay*, the 'Epistle to Cobham':

> Know, God and Nature only are the same:
> In Man, the judgement shoots at flying game;
> A bird of passage! gone as soon as found,
> Now in the moon, perhaps, now underground.
>
> (ll. 154–7)

As judges, the poet argues, we are prevented from seeing the object clearly because our vision is coloured by our own passions and imagination:

> All manners take a tincture from our own;
> Or come discoloured through our passions shown.
> Or fancy's beam enlarges, multiplies,
> Contracts, inverts, and gives ten thousand dyes.
>
> (ll. 25–8)

We often do not know our own motives:

> Oft in the passions' wild rotation tossed
> Our spring of action to ourselves is lost.
>
> (ll. 41–2)

244

Even the best lives are deceptive:

> Unthought-of frailties cheat us in the wise.

(l. 128)

This is part of the more general puzzle involving radical human inconsistency wherein

> The rogue and fool by fits is fair and wise,
> And even the best, by fits, what they despise...
> (*An Essay on Man,* II, 233–4)

We owe it to the author of these lines not to take a simple view.

The relation between morals, which we think of as a matter of conscious intention, and wit, which originates in the unconscious, is nowhere more complex than in *The Dunciad*, in which the hint afforded by Dryden's *MacFlecknoe* is developed and magnified to portentous effect. If it is the office of the satirist to unsettle and to shock, Pope succeeded here as nowhere else and the work continues to be controversial. Some contemporaries felt it to have been beneath the dignity of the great poet, and Johnson criticized the grossness of its images. Others felt that in the duncies Pope had succeeded in lionizing and immortalizing countless insignificant figures who otherwise would have been erased by time, and called into question his judgement, his good sense, and his sense of proportion in so doing. The exaggeration and distortion which are so much a part of the satire offended those who took it primarily as a joke and those who recognized in the joke a serious critique of the cultural life of his day. Yet no other work of Pope has exerted such a fascination subsequently, and the difficulty and the paradoxical effect of its intense witty seriousness (particularly in the fourth book) have had great appeal in an age brought up on *The Waste Land* and *Ulysses*. Of its subject Johnson remarked:

> Dullness or deformity are not culpable in themselves but may be very justly reproached when they pretend to the honour of wit or the influence of beauty.[30]

The particular named duncies have had few defenders, except perhaps Richard Bentley 'Aristarchus', who 'made Horace dull and humbled Milton's strains' (IV, 212), the formidable classical

245

scholar and Master of Trinity.[31] Here is Bentley's comment on a striking phrase of Milton (admired by Pope since he used it at *Dunciad*, IV, 3) taken from his edition of *Paradise Lost*:

No light but rather darkness visible
Served only to discover sights of woe.

(ll. 64–5)

Darkness visible and *darkness palpable* are in due place very good expressions; but the next line makes visible here a flat contradiction. Darkness visible will not serve to discover sights of woe through it, but to cover and hide them. Nothing is visible to the eye, but so far as it is opaque, and not seen through; not by transmitting the rays, but by reflecting them back. To come up to the author's idea we may thus say

No light but rather a transpicuous gloom.

Who can doubt that the author of this deserves to be remembered in the roll-call of the dull? If we ask, by what authority did Pope judge, then the answer must be, by the authority of his prodigious creative talent, a talent in which he had a just confidence since his poetry continues to be read.

NOTES

1 Samuel Johnson, *Lives of the English Poets*, in two volumes, Everyman's Library, London and New York: Dent, 1925, vol. 2, p. 149. All references to Johnson are to the Everyman edition which exists in many reprints. Comments on individual poems are to be found in two places in the *Life of Pope*, in the chronological review of the works given as Johnson recounts the life, and in a second assessment of the works without reference to the life from p. 215 onwards.

2 *Pope: The Critical Heritage*, edited by John Barnard, London and Boston: Routledge & Kegan Paul, 1973, paperback, 1985, pp. 381–2. The whole of the dedication is included here and a generous selection from the *Essay* itself, pp. 379–407. The citation from Voltaire is in French.

3 ibid., p. 407.

4 ibid., p. 520. The selection from volume two covers pp.

508–20. The comment on *An Essay on Man* cited above comes at p. 513.

5 Johnson, *Life of Gray*, Everyman edition, vol. 2, pp. 390–1.

6 *The Critical Heritage*, p. 399.

7 'Dryden and Pope are not classics of our poetry, they are classics of our prose', from his introduction to *The English Poets*, edited by T. H. Ward (1880), in *Alexander Pope: A Critical Anthology*, edited by F. W. Bateson and N. A. Joukovsky, Harmondsworth: Penguin, 1971, pp. 249–52.

8 Johnson on Pope's intellectual character, *Life*, p. 211.

9 ibid., p. 228.

10 ibid., p. 230.

11 Johnson on Pope's Homer, *Life*, pp. 156–76, pp. 222–5. The quotations are on p. 161 and p. 222.

12 On pp. 108–9. See Johnson, *Life*, pp. 166–7.

13 *The Iliad of Homer*, translated by Richmond Lattimore, London: University of Chicago Press, 1951.

14 Pope's notes, printed below the translation, are to be found in the Twickenham edition of Pope, volumes VII–X.

15 In his preface to *Lyrical Ballads* (1800).

16 Johnson, *Life*, p. 212.

17 From a letter to Leigh Hunt of 1815, cited in Upali Amarasinghe, *Dryden and Pope in the Early Nineteenth Century*, Cambridge: Cambridge University Press, 1962, pp. 206–7. See also pp. 104–5 for the verdicts of Southey and Wordsworth, and Bateson and Joukovsky, p. 189, for the verdict of Coleridge.

18 Twickenham edition of Pope, vol. VII, p. 18.

19 From the preface to his translation of the second book of Virgil's *Aeneid: The Destruction of Troy* (1656).

20 Johnson, *Life*, p. 229.

21 ibid., pp. 223–4.

22 *The Critical Heritage*, pp. 185–8.

23 Charles Cotton, *Scarronides, or Virgil Travestie* (1664).

24 Pope's own phrase in a letter to Swift, 28 November 1729; see *The Correspondence of Alexander Pope*, edited by George Sherburn, in five volumes, Oxford: Clarendon Press, vol. 3, p. 81.

25 From a letter to John Murray, 1821; see Bateson and Joukovsky, pp. 203–4.

26 An adaptation of Pope's lines on Timon in the 'Epistle to Burlington' (107–8). The whole poem is printed in *The Critical Heritage*, pp. 269–72.

27 From a letter to John Murray, 1821; see Bateson and Joukovsky, pp. 207–8.

28 Johnson, *Life*, p. 228.

29 ibid., p. 225.

30 ibid., p. 225.

31 See the note on p. 303. Bentley had said of Pope's Homer: 'it is a pretty poem, Mr Pope, but you must not call it Homer'.

Select Bibliography

THE LIFE AND BACKGROUND

Greene, Donald (1970) *The Age of Exuberance. Backgrounds to Eighteenth-Century English Literature*, New York: Random House. A lively introduction.

Mack, Maynard (1985) *Alexander Pope: A Life*, New Haven and London: Yale University Press. Voluminously informative.

Malins, Edward (1966) *English Landscaping and Literature 1660–1840*, London: Oxford University Press. Includes a chapter on 'Kent, Pope, Burlington and friends' in which Pope's contribution to the subject is clearly presented in its wider context.

Osborn, James M. (ed.) (1966) *Anecdotes, Observations and Characters of Books and Men by Joseph Spence*, 2 vols, Oxford: Clarendon Press. Includes reports of Spence's own conversations with Pope.

Sherburn, George (1934) *The Early Career of Alexander Pope*, Oxford: Clarendon Press. Includes a useful account of early biographers.

EDITIONS OF POPE

See also the note on the text following the introduction.

Butt, John (ed.) (1960) *Letters of Alexander Pope*, London: Oxford University Press, The World's Classics. A manageable selection of the most attractive letters for the general reader.

249

Goldgar, Bertrand A. (ed.) (1965) *Literary Criticism of Alexander Pope*, Lincoln, Nebr.: University of Nebraska Press. A useful collection of Pope's own pronouncements under the headings 'general theory', 'pastoral', 'epic', 'drama'.

Hammond, Paul (1987) *Selected Prose of Alexander Pope*, Cambridge: Cambridge University Press. The critical prose and a selection of letters in one volume.

Mack, Maynard (ed.) (1969) *The Twickenham Edition of the Poems of Alexander Pope*, volume XI, general editor John Butt, in ten volumes (1938–1968) London and New Haven: Methuen; with index (volume XI, 1969). Contains bibliographical information, introductory material, and commentary upon the poems.

Rosslyn, Felicity (ed.) (1985) *Pope's Iliad. A Selection with Commentary*, Bristol: Bristol Classical Press. This affordable paperback includes a generous selection of Pope's own notes accompanying the text.

CRITICISM

Amarasinghe, Upali (1962) *Dryden and Pope in the Early Nineteenth Century*, Cambridge: Cambridge University Press. A study of the complexities of the Romantic reaction to the Augustans and the controversy over Pope's poems that engaged the leading figures of the time.

Barnard, John (ed.) (1973) *Pope: The Critical Heritage*, London and Boston, Mass.: Routledge & Kegan Paul; paperback, 1985). A most useful selection of texts detailing the critical response to the poems during Pope's life-time and thereafter throughout the eighteenth century.

Bateson, F. W. and Joukovsky, N. A. (eds) (1971) *Alexander Pope: A Critical Anthology*, Harmondsworth: Penguin. Another most useful anthology of extracts from critical texts divided into three sections, the first part representing contemporaneous criticism and the eighteenth century, the second the continuing debate in the nineteenth and early twentieth centuries, and the third modern views including those of Empson, Leavis, and the American New Critics.

Brower, Reuben A. (1959) *Alexander Pope: The Poetry of Al-*

lusion, Oxford: Clarendon Press; paperback, 1968. A lively and wide-ranging book written for the general reader relating Pope's poems to the classical tradition.

Hammond, Brean S. (1986) *Pope*, Harvester New Readings, Brighton: Harvester Press. A discussion of Pope in the light of modern critical theory.

Mason, H. A. (1972) *To Homer Through Pope: An Introduction to Homer's Iliad and Pope's translation*, London: Chatto & Windus; reissued (1986) Bristol: Bristol Classical Press. Not merely a specialist account, a book that raises central questions about Homer and Pope, and about translation.

Notes

ODE ON SOLITUDE

Pope said that he wrote this poem when he was not yet 12
years old. The first copy dates from 1709 and the poem was
subsequently revised. The present version incorporates those
revisions.

2 *paternal acres*   inherited land.

from BOETIUS, DE CONS. PHILOS.

A translation of the sixth-century Roman philosopher Boethius,
On the Consolation of Philosophy, III, 1, tentatively dated not
later than 1710.

2 *ambient main*   surrounding sea.

ADRIANI MORIENTIS AD ANIMAM

(Literally, 'To the soul of the dying Hadrian') Hadrian was
Roman emperor AD 117–38. First alluded to in the *Spectator* no. 532 of 10 November 1712 where Pope discusses the
original. The editor of the journal, Richard Steele, requested
him to write 'an ode as of a cheerful dying spirit', which resulted in 'The dying Christian to his soul' See G. Sherburn,

The Correspondence of Alexander Pope, vol. I, pp. 149–50 and pp. 159–60. The poems were first printed in 1730, the second having been substantially rewritten when it was next printed in 1736.

THE DYING CHRISTIAN TO HIS SOUL

See previous entry.

TO HENRY CROMWELL, 19 OCTOBER 1709
[WITH ARGUS]

See Sherburn, vol. I, pp. 73–4. Henry Cromwell was an older friend of Pope who encouraged him to undertake the Homer translation.

4   *Montaigne* Michel de (1533–92). Pope was an early admirer of his *Essays*, famous for their questioning self-knowledge and recognition of the limitation of human reason. They are written in an informal and urbane style.

22   *Toby* There is a dog in the Book of Tobias in the Old Testament Apocrypha.

25   *Argus* means swift in Greek. The passage occurs in *Odyssey*, XVII (ll. 344–99 in Pope's version). The present poem is a summary. The text is from the original letter including an alexandrine (l. 10) subsequently amended by the removal of 'alone' and a triplet subsequently altered with the removal of l. 13.

TO HENRY CROMWELL, 25 NOVEMBER 1710
[ON VERSIFICATION]

See Sherburn, vol. I, pp. 105–8.

2   *numbers* versification.

28   *alexandrines* a line with two extra syllables and therefore six feet as opposed to the usual five. See *An Essay on Criticism* (ll. 337–83) for Pope's exemplification of what he considered to be faults in versification.

35	*Waller* Edmund Waller (1606–87) often regarded as a precursor of the Augustans in his management of the heroic couplet.
47	*coulante* flowing.
50	*Style of Sound* Pope quotes from the Latin of the Renaissance writer Marcus Hieronymus Vida before singling out 'Alexander's feast' as an example in English. See also *An Essay on Criticism* (ll. 374–83) for a poetic tribute to Dryden.

AN ESSAY ON CRITICISM

Pope's manuscript bears the words 'written in the year 1709'. Following the table of contents that first appeared in the *Works* of 1736, the *Essay* is sometimes printed in three parts, the second of which commences at line 201 where Pope considers the obstacles hindering true judgement, and the third at line 560 where he discourses upon the morals that true critics ought to show.

34	*Maevius* a bad poet referred to in the poems of Horace.
43	*equivocal* equivocal generation: 'the (supposed) production of plants and animals without parents: spontaneous generation' (*OED*).
86	*The winged courser* Pegasus, associated with the Muses and poetry, cp. line 150.
88	*Those rules* see *Introduction*, p. 17, for discussion of the rules.
94	*Parnassus* a mountain in central Greece sacred to Apollo and the Muses.
108	*'pothecaries* chemists frequently criticized for usurping the role of the doctor. Dr Samuel Garth's mock epic *The Dispensary* was an attack on the apothecaries.
120	*fable* plot.
129	*Mantuan* Virgil, Publius Vergilius Maro, was born at Mantua in 70 BC.
130	*young Maro* In his first attempt at epic Virgil is

reputed to have started upon an historical poem before reverting to myth in the *Aeneid* which, loosely based upon the *Odyssey* (I–VI) and the *Iliad* (VII–XII), imitates Homer's form, beginning '*in medias res*', and abandons the linear order of an historical narrative.

138   *Stagyrite* Aristotle (384–322 BC) was born at Stageira in northern Greece.

181   *bays* the leaves of the laurel sacred to Apollo, god of poetry.

186   *paean* an ancient hymn of praise.

216   *Pierian* The Muses were sometimes called the Pierides, as haunting Pieria, a district in northern Thessaly.

225   *Alps* Johnson in the *Life of Pope* (p. 218) praises this as one of the finest similes in English.

247   *some well-proportioned dome* St Peter's basilica in Rome.

267   *La Mancha's knight* Don Quixote, hero of Cervantes' romance: the episode here mentioned is from a continuation by another hand.

270   *Dennis* John Dennis (1657–1734), critic and playwright who subsequently attacked the *Essay* and *The Rape of the Lock*.

272   *Aristotle's rules* see *Introduction*, p. 18.

289   *conceit* a far-fetched image.

321   *regal purple* the traditional colour of kingly robes.

328   *Fungoso* a character in Ben Jonson's *Every Man out of his Humour* of whom Jonson wrote: 'one that has revelled in his time, and follows the fashion afar off, like a spy. He makes it the whole bent of his endeavours to wring sufficient means from his wretched father, to put him in the courtier's cut at which he earnestly aims, but so unluckily that he still lights short a suit.'

345   *open vowels* There are three sets of open vowels (hiatus) in this line.

346   *expletives* words that fill out as 'do' here.

347   *ten low words* a wholly monosyllabic line in which the rhythm imitates the sense.

356   *Alexandrine* a line with an extra foot making six (the next line is an example).

361   *Denham . . . Waller* Sir John Denham (1615–69) and Edmund Waller (1606–87) often called precursors of the major Augustans because of their similar classical interests and their use of the heroic couplet.

366   *Zephyr* a light spring breeze.

370   *Ajax* Homer's hero who wields a mighty stone at *Iliad*, XII, 453–60 (Pope's translation).

372   *Camilla* Virgil's heroine renowned for her fleetness of foot. See Dryden's *Aeneis*, VII, 1100–3.

374   *Timotheus* a Theban lyricist who in Dryden's poem 'Alexander's feast' plays before Alexander the Great 'the son of Lybian Jove'. See the letter to Cromwell on versification for further comment.

419   *hackney* 'doing or ready to do work, or hire, hireling' (*OED*).

444   *Scotists and Thomists* the followers of John Duns Scotus (medieval theologian of the thirteenth century) in conflict with those of Thomas Aquinas, who lived slightly earlier. Renaissance humanists reacted against the subtle disputation of the scholastic theologians. Dunce is derived from Scotus's name.

445   *Duck-lane* site of second-hand bookshops.

463   *Blackmores and . . . Milbourns* feeble poets and critics who had attacked Dryden.

465   *Zoilus* hyper-critic of Homer.

468   *Sol* the sun, one of the many images of light in the *Essay*.

513   *Crowns* or garlands were awarded to distinguished soldiers when generals celebrated a Roman triumph.

529   *flagitious times* profligate or vicious times.

536   *easy monarch* Charles II, king from 1660–85. His association with prostitutes was notorious and his mistresses were many. The court took its tone from the monarch.

538   *Jilts* kept mistresses.

541   *mask* worn by women in the Restoration theatre.

544   *foreign reign* that of the Dutchman William of Orange from 1688–1702.

545   *Socinus* Laelius Socinus (1525–62). Socinians rejected the doctrine of the divinity of Christ.

257

552   *Titans* giants who rebelled against the rule of Olympian Zeus, here representing deistic writers who were often thought of as atheists.

553   *licensed blasphemies* When the licensing act of 1663 was not renewed in 1695, there was no restriction on publishing.

585   *Appius* Dennis whose tragedy *Appius and Virginia* was performed in 1709.

591   *without learning* Degrees were sometimes awarded to the privileged without examinations.

603   *jades* worthless nags; applied to horses and also women.

617   *Dryden . . . Durfey* the *Fables* (1700), perhaps Dryden's greatest poetic achievement; Durfey's *Tales* (1704 and 1706), of little merit.

619   *Garth* Sir Samuel Garth (1661–1719) whose mock epic *The Dispensary* (1699) had attracted envious comment.

623   *Paul's church* St Paul's Cathedral, a place where much business was transacted; booksellers had stalls nearby.

648   *Maeonian* Homer. Maeonia is a region in Asia Minor, reputedly his birthplace.

662   *phlegm* lack of ardour, as in phlegmatic.

665   *Dionysius* of Halicarnassus, a Greek rhetorician living in the age of Augustus. In his *Composition of Words* he writes appreciatively of Homer's style.

667   *Petronius* a Roman writing in Nero's reign, famous for his *Satyricon*.

669   Quintilian rhetorician of *c.* AD 35–100.

675   *Longinus* a Greek rhetorician of the second century AD, thought to be the author of the treatise *On the Sublime*.

684   *eagles* on the standards of the Roman armies and therefore symbols of Roman power.

692   *monks . . . Goths* Pope follows the humanists of the Renaissance who in reviving the learning of classical antiquity dismissed out of hand the dark ages (initiated by the Goths who contributed to the overthrow of

258

the Roman empire) and the medieval inheritance (here associated with monkish ignorance).

693   *Erasmus*   Desiderius Erasmus of Rotterdam (1466–1536) who sought to unite the best of pagan culture with Christianity in an ideal of lettered piety. His humanism made him an opponent of scholasticism and church abuses satirized in his *Praise of Folly* and *Colloquies*, subsequently put on the index of prohibited books by the Catholic church. He supported reform, but a natural inclination to moderation and concord precluded full support for Luther. Pope again praises his 'honest mean' in the Horatian imitation addressed 'To Mr Fortescue', line 66.

697   *Leo*   Leo X, Pope from 1513–21, also believed in the Erasmian ideal, and was a great patron of the arts.

704   *Raphael . . . Vida*   Raphael, the famous painter 1483–1520. Vida of Cremona wrote an *Art of Poetry* in Latin much admired in the Renaissance and eighteenth century, because like Horace in the *Art of Poetry* and Pope here Vida embodied in the beauty of his verse the critical precepts he advocated. He therefore merits the laurel wreath accorded in ancient times to the poet and the wreath of ivy bestowed upon the critic. Pope may be echoing Dryden in his fine poem 'To the memory of Mr Oldham':

Thy brows with ivy and with laurels bound.

709   *Latium*   the ancient name for the region in Italy in which Rome was founded, here meaning modern Italy.

714   *Boileau*   Nicolas Boileau (1636–1711), French poet and critic identifying much, like Pope, with Horace.

723   *the Muse* refers to an 'Essay on poetry' by John Sheffield, Duke of Buckingham (1648–1721) from which the next line is a quotation.

725   *Roscommon*   Wentworth Dillon, Earl of Roscommon (1633–85), who translated Horace's *Art of Poetry* and wrote 'An essay upon translated verse' (1684).

729   *Walsh*   William Walsh (1663–1708), a friend to

whom Pope submitted his early work for comment and who put Pope on the road to 'correctness'.

EPISTLE TO MISS BLOUNT WITH THE WORKS OF VOITURE

The epistle was first printed in 1712 addressed simply 'to a young lady'. Pope altered the title in 1735 in a compliment to Martha Blount, a long-standing friend. Vincent de Voiture (1598–1648) was a French poet and writer of elegant letters, some of which had been translated into English by Dryden and Dennis in 1696 and reprinted in 1700. The opening lines of the poem describe the qualities admired in Voiture, which Pope aims to emulate in his own verse letter.

1   *Loves and Graces* the personifications suggest the classical Graces and the cupids of baroque art. Compare line 19.

22   *serious comedy* obeying the rules and reforming our vices, as in the case of the comedies of Ben Jonson, for example.

49   *Pamela* It seems unlikely that any particular individual is being referred to here.

53   *front boxes* In the theatre men sat in the side boxes, women in the front boxes facing the stage and in full view of the men.

        the Ring the fashionable driving circuit in Hyde Park.

58   *Hymen* Roman god of marriage.

61   *Good humour* Compare Clarissa's speech in *The Rape of the Lock*, V, 30 and the final line of the 'Epistle to a Lady'.

69   *Voiture's early care* Mademoiselle Paulet who is featured in his letters.

70   *Monthausier* The Duchess de Montausier also features in the letters.

73   *Elysian coast* Elysium, the classical paradise whither go the souls of the blest in Hades, the underworld.

76   *Rambouillet* the maiden name of the duchess alluded to above.

from WINDSOR FOREST

The poem was first written in 1704 and substantially revised in the year 1713 when it was published just before the formal ratification of the treaty of Utrecht between Britain and France which secured peace in Europe. The extracts are as follows: 1–42, 85–118, 235–76, 427–end.

5   *Granville* George Granville, Lord Lansdowne to whom the poem was dedicated. He was himself a poet and author of the verse 'Essay upon unnatural flights in poetry'.

31   *our oaks* the British navy.

37   *Pan ... Pomona* the nature god in Greek myth, often associated with the spring, and the Roman goddess of fruitfulness associated with the autumn.

39   *Ceres* the Roman goddess of agriculture and fertility.

42   *a Stuart* It was published in the last year of Queen Anne's reign.

50   *golden years* referring both to the harvest, and to the golden age of peace, virtue, and plenty celebrated in pastoral poetry.

77   *this bright court* of Queen Anne. Virgil had similarly praised the life of civilized and philosophic retirement in the second of his *Georgics*, poems in praise of country life.

99   *Scipio* Scipio Africanus after his victories over Hannibal in the second Punic War withdrew from public life and retired to his country estate.

100   *Atticus* Titus Pomponius called Atticus because he withdrew from Rome to Athens (in Attica) taking up a life of study in preference to politics.
        Trumbull Sir William Trumbull (1639–1716), an early friend of Pope who retired from public life in 1698.

101   *Ye sacred Nine* the nine Muses. Following Virgil, Pope pays tribute to his poetic predecessors.

106   *Cooper's Hill* both an actual hill bordering on the forest and a topographical poem by John Denham of

1642 containing the celebrated lines on the Thames which in their arrangement and sense represent an ideal to which the Augustans aspired in their use of the couplet:

> Though deep, yet clear; though gentle, yet not dull;
> Strong without rage and without o'erflowing full.

(191–2)

113   *Denham*   Sir John (1615–69). Pope had already saluted the strength of his versification in *An Essay on Criticism*, line 361. 'Cooper's Hill' was doubtless one of the main inspirations in English of 'Windsor Forest'.

114   *Cowley*   Abraham Cowley (1618–67) who had written many poems in praise of retirement, and whose muse Pope had imitated among his first poetic efforts.

119   *My humble Muse*   Like Virgil before him Pope puts a modest estimate on pastoral and georgic poetry; more ambitious muses attempt heroic themes.

[ON SICKNESS]

Printed in the *Guardian*, no. 132, Wednesday 12 August 1713.

9   *Waller*   from 'Of the last verses of the book', ll. 13–14.

53   *the Wisdom of Solomon*   one of the books of the Old Testament Apocrypha.

THE RAPE OF THE LOCK

In the wake of the family acrimony that followed the jest of Lord Petre in cutting off a lock of Miss Arabella Fermor's hair, it was suggested to Pope by a friend of all concerned, John Caryll, that he should 'write a poem to make a jest of it, and laugh them together again'. The first edition in two cantos was published in 1712. Subsequently in 1714 Pope expanded the poem adding the divine machinery, and in 1717 the speech of Clarissa in canto V in response to criticism that the poem lacked a moral. The accompanying letter to Arabella Fermor has acquired the status of a dedication.

To Mrs Arabella Fermor

20   *Rosicrucian* 'a supposed society or order reputedly founded by one Christian Rosenkreuz in 1484, but first mentioned in 1614, whose members were said to claim various forms of secret and magic knowledge, as the transmutation of metals, the prolongation of life, and power over the elements and elemental spirits.' (*OED*)

Canto I

5   *Slight is the subject*   see *Critical commentary*, p. 230.
7   *Say what strange motive*   At the opening of the *Aeneid* Virgil bids his muse say what are the causes of Juno's anger, then asks whether such rage can dwell in heavenly minds (I, 11).
     goddess   the muse traditionally addressed by the epic poet.
13   *Sol*   the sun.
17   *the slipper knocked the ground*   the usual way to summon a servant.
18   *pressed watch*   a repeater.
23   *birth-night beau*   a young man dressed in the finery worn at court to celebrate royal birthdays.
44   *box ... Ring*   a box in the theatre. The Ring (also called the tour or circus) was a fashionable route to drive along in Hyde Park.
45   *equipage* 'a carriage and horses with attendant footmen' (*OED*).
46   *chair*   a sedan chair.
55   *chariots*   Carriages were so called.
56   *ombre*   a fashionable card game; compare bridge

today; see III, 27ff, below. This couplet recalls Virgil's description of the classical underworld as translated by Dryden (*Aeneis*, VI, 890–1):

> The love of horses which they had, alive,
> And care of chariots, after death survive.

59   *termagant*   scold.
60   *Salamander*   a kind of lizard, once thought to be able to live in fire.
73   *spark*   an elegant fashionable young man.
85   *garters, stars, and coronets*   worn by the nobility.
89   *bidden blush*   achieved by means of rouge.
94   *impertinence*   a trifle.
96   *treat*   an entertainment of food and drink.
101   *sword-knot*   a ribbon tied to the hilt of a sword.
115   *Shock*   refers to a breed of dog; a lap-dog.
121   *And now, unveiled*   For discussion of this passage see *Critical commentary*, p. 233.
125   *glass*   the mirror.
144   *keener lightnings*   induced by belladonna.
148   *Betty*   a generic name for a maid.

Canto II

25   *springes*   snares for catching small game.
35   *Phoebus*   epithet of Apollo, the sun god.
45   *granted half his prayer*   an epic motif. Compare Virgil in Dryden's translation:

> Apollo heard and granting half his prayer
> Shuffled in winds the rest, and tossed in empty air.

(XI, 1195)

64   *glittering textures*   gossamers formerly supposed to be the product of sunburnt dew, not spiders.
84   *painted bow*   rainbow.
97   *wash*   a medical or cosmetic lotion.
100   *flounce*   'an ornamental appendage to the skirt of a lady's dress' (*OED*).

264

105	*Diana's law* Diana was the goddess of chastity.
113	*drops* diamond ear-rings.
119	*seven-fold fence* Shields in epic are invariably sevenfold.
128	*bodkin* needle or hairpin.
129	*pomatums* ointments.
131	*styptics* astringents which stop bleeding.
132	*rivelled* shrivelled.
133	*Ixion* punished by Zeus for making advances to his wife Hera by being fixed to an eternally revolving wheel in Tartarus.

Canto III

1	*Close by those meads* For discussion of the opening see *Critical commentary*, p. 231.
12	*visit* a formal call.
27	*ombre* a game with three players and a pack of forty cards. The player taking the most tricks wins. Belinda wins the first four, and then the Baron the next four, so that the final trick decides the game.
30	*sacred nine* each player has nine cards.
33	*Matador* one of three cards of high value including the ace of spades and ace of clubs and one other ace depending upon what were trumps.
42	*halberts* a combination of spear and battle-axe.
44	*velvet plain* describing the green cloth-covered card table but reminiscent of the Trojan plain.
46	*Let Spades be trumps* Compare the divine fiat in Genesis, 'Let there be light.'
49	*Spadillio* the ace of spades. Belinda, perhaps imprudently, plays her winning cards first.
51	*Manillio* the two of spades, the second-highest card.
53	*Basto* the ace of clubs.
61	*Pam* the knave of clubs, which in the game of Lu (or Loo) was the chief trump.
67	*Amazon* the queen of spades.
92	*Codille* The winner was said to have given codille to the loser.

106	*berries* coffee berries, first roasted then ground.
107	*shining altars of Japan* lacquered tables.
110	*China's earth* porcelain cups.
122	*Scylla* daughter of Nisus. His safety and that of his kingdom depended upon a lock of hair which Scylla stole to betray him to his enemy Minos with whom she had fallen in love. She was punished for her impiety by being turned into a bird.
147	*forfex* scissors.
165	*Atalantis* refers to a novel by Mary Manley notorious for its libels which had led to her arrest.
167	*visits* made in the evening when the lady was escorted by servants bearing lights.

Canto IV

8	*manteau* a loose upper garment worn by women.
13	*Umbriel* the Latin *umbra* means shadow.
16	*Cave of Spleen* Compare Ovid's Cave of Envy in the *Metamorphoses*, II, 760ff and see *Introduction*, p. 19. Spleen was a fashionable complaint of high society associated with melancholia and moroseness.
18	*vapour* The spleen was also called the vapours, supposedly induced by a misty climate.
20	*east* a wind favourable to spleen.
24	*Megrim* headache.
40–6	*phantoms* Hallucinations were symptoms of the spleen. Here Pope satirizes scenic effects in contemporary opera and pantomime.
51	*pipkin* a small earthen boiler.
	Homer's tripod an allusion to *Iliad*, XVIII, 440–8 in Pope's version.
56	*spleenwort* a kind of fern with medicinal properties supposed to cure the spleen, reminiscent here of the Golden Bough carried by Aeneas as his passport through Hades.
62	*physic* medicine.
64	*in a pet* in a fit of ill humour.
69	*citron waters* brandy flavoured with citron or lemon rind.

266

71	*airy horns* horns, a conventional image suggesting adultery; airy because they are imaginary here.
82	*Ulysses* Homer's hero who in *Odyssey*, X is given a bag enclosing the storm winds which his companions foolishly unleash with dire effects.
109	*toast* a lady whose beauty was honoured with raised glasses in company.
114	*Exposed through crystal* displayed under glass as in a finger ring.
117	*Hyde Park Circus* See note on I, 44.
118	*Bow* St Mary le Bow is in Cheapside, the site of business and commerce and therefore no place for a person of fashion.
124	*nice conduct* fine management.
	clouded cane a variegated walking-stick.
133	*But by this lock* recalls the oath of Achilles, 'Now by this sceptre', at *Iliad*, I, 309 in Pope's version.
156	*bohea* a blend of tea.
161	*omens* common in epic; omens foreshadow Dido's death.
164	*Poll* the pet parrot.

Canto V

5	*the Trojan* Aeneas whom Dido begged not to leave her for Italy. When Aeneas left she committed suicide.
6	*Anna* Dido's sister.
9	*Say* in parody of Sarpedon's speech, see p. 110.
14	*side-box* In the theatre men sat in the side boxes, women in the front boxes.
20	*small-pox* Lord Petre (the Baron) died of smallpox in 1713 after the first edition of the poem. This speech was added in 1717 to 'open more clearly the moral of the poem' (Pope).
24	*paint* put on make-up.
40	*whalebones* to stiffen the petticoat.
45	*So when bold Homer* Pope's *Iliad*, XX, 91ff. Pallas is another name for Athene; Mars is the god of war; Latona is the mother of Apollo; Hermes is the

messenger of the gods; Jove's weapon is the thunderbolt; Neptune is god of the sea and causes earthquakes; the pale ghosts inhabit Hades which is under the earth.

53   *sconce* a pendent candlestick.

60   *metaphor, and . . . song* in mockery of the exaggerated language of love songs. Dapperwit is a character in Wycherly's *Love in a Wood* and Sir Fopling a character in Etherege's *The Man of Mode*.

64   *'Those eyes are made so killing'* from an opera called *Camilla* performed in 1706.

65   *Maeander* a winding river in Asia Minor.

71   *golden scales* in parody of epic; see, for example, the reference in the Sarpedon episode (line 263, p. 116) and Dryden's *Aeneis*, XII, 1054:

> Jove sets the beam; in either scale he lays
> The champions' fate, and each exactly weighs.
> On their side, life and lucky chance ascends;
> Loaded with death, that other scale descends.

78   *on his foe to die* The verb die can refer to sexual orgasm. See IV, 54 and 175–6 for further bawdy innuendo.

88   *bodkin* a hairpin or clasp. Its history recalls in parody that of Agamemnon's sceptre. See Pope's *Iliad*, II, 129–36.

105   *Othello* The handkerchief is a crucial element in the plot; a serious example of dire effects springing from amorous causes.

122   *tomes of casuistry* minutely reasoned philosophy.

125   *Rome's great founder* Romulus who ascended to heaven during an eclipse. He then appeared to Proculus in a vision ordering the Romans to sacrifice to him as to a god.

129   *Berenice's locks* the wife of Ptolemy III who pledged to make a votive offering of her hair if her husband returned victorious from war. The offering was subsequently stolen and thought to have been made into a constellation by Zeus.

136	*Rosamonda's lake* a pond in St James's Park.
137	*Partridge* the absurd John Partridge, a contemporary astrologer who repeatedly predicted the deaths of the Pope and the king of France (a rival kingdom) without success.
138	*Galileo's eyes* the telescope.

EPISTLE TO MISS BLOUNT, ON HER LEAVING THE TOWN, AFTER THE CORONATION

The coronation is that of George I in 1714. Zephalinda is a name used by Teresa Blount, and her sister Martha is spoken of as Parthenissa elsewhere.

4	*spark* a fashionable young man.
7	*Zephalinda* The name suggests youth and beauty, from zephyr, a spring wind.
11	*plain-work* simple sewing as opposed to intricate embroidery involving purling stitches. The stale poetical cliché 'purling brooks' is enlivened by the pun.
15	*bohea* a blend of tea.
24	*whisk . . . sack* the entertainment and the drink of the less sophisticated.
26	*buss* 'an enthusiastic kiss; "we buss our wantons, but our wives we kiss"' (Herrick) (*OED*).
38	*flirt* literally means a sudden movement of the fan.
47	*Gay* John Gay, who wrote *The Beggar's Opera*, a close friend of Pope.
48	*chairs* sedan chairs.

ELOISA TO ABELARD

4	*Vestal* a virgin priestess of the Roman goddess Vesta, by transference a nun.
7	*Abelard* an historical figure, Pierre Abélard (1079-1142), a French theologian. Eloisa (Héloïse) was one of

his pupils. She has just come upon a letter talking of their love written by Abelard to a third person.

20   *horrid*   bristling.

64   *lambent*   radiant.

99   *sudden horrors*   Eloisa is thinking of the castration of Abelard ordered by her father to end the affair.

110   *bade the world farewell*   in entering the nunnery.

133   *You raised these hallowed walls*   Abelard founded the nunnery.

177   *the spouse*   The nun is regarded as the bride of Christ; see also line 219.

212   *Obedient slumbers*   taken from 'Of a religious house' by Richard Crashaw (*c.* 1612–49).

220   *hymeneals*   wedding songs.

343   *May one kind grave*   They were interred in adjoining monuments.

ELEGY TO THE MEMORY OF AN UNFORTUNATE LADY

The identity of the lady and the reasons that brought her to her misfortune remain mysterious.

8   *a Roman's part*   suicide.

9   *reversion*   a legal term relating to the restitution of property after a fixed period.

35   *ball*   the world.

41   *Furies*   deities who avenge familial wrongs in Greek myth.

59   *Loves*   representations of weeping Cupids on funeral monuments.

THE ILIAD OF HOMER

The translation of Homer: the *Iliad* was published in six volumes between 1715 and 1720. Pope provided notes which were intended as a running commentary and printed below the text in all editions in his lifetime. The notes referred to here can be looked up in the Twickenham edition of Pope's Homer in the appropriate book under the line reference added in brackets.

The titles at the head of each extract, unless otherwise stated, are those given by Pope himself to the books from which the extracts have been taken.

from *the preface*

50   The line of Homeric Greek is *Iliad*, II, 780.

59   *vivida vis animi*   from the Latin of Lucretius meaning the lively force of the mind.

67   *Lucan and Statius*   writers of Latin epic coming after Virgil.

89–90   *the 'soul of poetry'*   Aristotle, *Poetics*, VI, 19.

105–6   *'Everything in it has manners'*   Aristotle, *Poetics*, XXIV, 13–14.

122   *Longinus*   the Greek rhetorician referred to in *An Essay on Criticism* (ll. 675–80) to whom was attributed the treatise *Peri Hypsous, On the Sublime*, in which Homer is frequently cited to illustrate the sublime in conception and style. Pope wrote a mock treatise satirizing bad poets called the *Peri Bathous, Or Martinus Scriblerus His Treatise of the Art of Sinking in Poetry* (1727).

156   *'living words'*   Aristotle, *Rhetoric*, III, xi.

226   *[Virgil's Jupiter] laying plans for empires*   See his dignified speech at *Aeneid*, I, 257–96.

from *the second book of the Iliad*

The speech is by Agamemnon, leader of the Greek expedition against Troy and brother of Menelaus whose wife Helen had been abducted by the Trojan Paris from Sparta, thus occasioning the war. In the ninth year of the siege of Troy, the Greeks are weary and have been showing an inclination to return. Lines 452–69 and 520–71 of the complete version.

23   *the blue-eyed virgin*   Minerva, daughter of Jupiter, a warrior goddess and ardent supporter of the Greek cause.

33	*As on some mountain* Pope comments on the fertility of Homer's imagination and invention apparent in the five similes in this passage, all different, illustrating splendour, movement, number, ardour, and the discipline of the troops (line 534).
41	*Caÿster* a river in Lydia, south of Troy.
46	*Scamander* the river that flows through the Trojan plain.
68	*Neptune* brother of Jupiter and god of the sea.
	Mars the god of war.

from *the eighth book of the Iliad*

After a day's success in battle, the Trojan troops await the dawn. Lines 685–708 of the completed version. For discussion of this passage see *Critical commentary*, pp. 218–24.

| 15 | *Ilion* another name for Troy. |
| 16 | *Xanthus* a river on the Trojan plain. |

from *the twelfth and sixteenth books of the Iliad*

'The episode of Sarpedon': Pope published this episode (of which the representation here is a substantial extract) in *Poetical Miscellanies* in 1709. The title, the argument, and the prose connecting the two parts are from this edition, except that Pope has the plural *Iliads* commonly used for the whole poem in the Renaissance and beyond. The text is the later (slightly revised) version of 1717. The extracts are XII, 345–410 and 509–62, and XVI, 512–626 and 773–836 from the complete version.

| 1 | *Hector* is the oldest son of Priam king of Troy and the Trojans' chief defender. His death at the hands of Achilles is the climax of the poem. Here the Trojans are trying to storm a defensive wall that the Greeks have built around their ships. |
| 27 | *Why boast we* Pope's note on Sarpedon's speech points to its generosity and nobleness: it includes |

'justice, in that he scorns to enjoy what he does not merit; gratitude, because he would endeavour to recompense his obligations to his subjects; and magnanimity, in that he despises death, and thinks of nothing but glory' (line 371). The speech is adapted to the polite world in *The Rape of the Lock*, V, 9–34.

61   *Teucer* an expert bowman who generally stood alongside his half-brother Ajax son of Telamon in order to use the latter's large shield as cover.

        the Ajaces Ajax the son of Telamon, and Ajax the son of Oileus, stout defenders both.

130   *Patroclus* Achilles' great comrade in arms. As a result of the quarrel with Agamemnon at the opening of the poem Achilles has withdrawn from the fighting. In his absence the Trojans gain success; the leading Greeks are wounded and Hector breaks through the wall threatening to set fire to the Greek ships. The angry Achilles still refuses to rescue the Greeks but relents to the extent of allowing Patroclus to act on his behalf, wearing his armour. Patroclus has some success, killing Sarpedon in this episode, until he himself falls victim to Hector in the pivotal action of the poem. Achilles then returns to avenge his friend.

140   *Phrygian* referring to the region around Troy, here used for Trojan.

166   *the cloud-compeller* Jupiter (Jove) who as god of the upper air controls storms, rain, and thunder, and so compels the clouds.

182   *Pedasus* The other two horses of Achilles were immortal (one of them even speaks in the poem) having been given to his father Peleus by Neptune as a wedding present. The third trace-horse is loosely harnessed beside a pair to take the place of either of them in case of need. Automedon, Achilles' charioteer, cuts the traces to free the chariot.

214   *Glaucus, be bold* Pope comments on the noble sentiments of Sarpedon's dying speech: 'being sensible of approaching death, without any transports of rage, or desire of revenge, he calls to his friend to take care to

preserve his body and arms from becoming a prey to the enemy: and this he says without any regard to himself, but out of most tender concern for his friend's reputation, who must for ever become infamous, if he fails in this point of honour and duty' (line 605).

263   *The scales of Jove*   Compare *The Rape of the Lock*, V, 17.

278   *ambrosial*   means immortal in Greek.

286   *mount Ida*   behind Troy.

from *the eighteenth book of the Iliad*

Patroclus has now been killed by Hector. News has come to Achilles. In the customary fashion Hector had stripped his defeated opponent of his armour to take as his rightful spoils. Since Patroclus was wearing Achilles' armour, Thetis, the goddess-mother of Achilles, requests Vulcan, the god of fire and divine craftsman, to make a replacement set. Lines 365–416 and 537–712 of the complete version.

14   *Myrmidons*   the followers of Achilles.

15   *In what vain promise*   Pope comments: 'The lamentation of Achilles over the body of Patroclus is exquisitely touched: it is sorrow in the extreme, but the sorrow of Achilles. It is nobly ushered in by that simile of the lion, an idea which is fully answered in the savage and bloody conclusion of this speech' (line 379).

16   *Menoetius*   the father of Patroclus who lived in Opuntia.

67   *the immense and solid shield*   Pope notes that Homer's intention was 'to draw the picture of the whole world in the compass of this shield' for in it we see 'all the occupations and the ambitions and all the diversions of mankind' (concluding note to Book XVIII).

80   *the Bear*   never sets and is ever in opposition to Orion the hunter on the far horizon.

86   *hymeneal*   Hymen is the god of marriage.

115   *Pallas* another name for Minerva, daughter of Jupiter.

144   *hind* workman, labourer.

178   *Linus* perhaps a personification of the spring or the summer.

199   *Daedalean art* Daedalus was employed by King Minos at Cnossus to build the labyrinth, a maze in which the Minotaur was imprisoned. Ariadne was the daughter of Minos who helped Theseus to escape from the labyrinth by means of a thread after he had killed the monstrous Minotaur.

201   *simar* scarf.

218   *ocean* in Homer it encircles the world, and is therefore appropriately placed on the border of the shield.

222   *cuirass* breastplate.

227   *Olympus* dwelling place of the immortal gods, a mountain in Greece.

from *the nineteenth book of the Iliad*

The title is taken from Pope's argument. Lines 1–24 and 378–471 in the complete version.

1   *Aurora* the dawn goddess.

27   *Boreas* the north wind.

45   *cuishes* armour protecting the thighs. Pope comments: 'There is a wonderful pomp in this description of Achilles arming himself; every reader without being pointed to it, will see the extreme grandeur of all these images; but what is particular, is, in what a noble scale they rise one above another, and how the hero is set still in a stronger point of light than before; till he is at last in a manner covered over with glories; he is at first likened to the moonlight, then to the flames of a beacon, then to a comet, and lastly to the sun itself' (line 398).

69   *Pelion* a mountain in Thessaly in northern Greece, near the home of Achilles.

70	*Chiron* the wise centaur, half-man half-horse, who taught the young Achilles.

70   *Chiron*   the wise centaur, half-man half-horse, who taught the young Achilles.

83   *Phoebus*   means shining in Greek; another name for Apollo the sun god.

111   *the Furies*   the powers that punish violations of divine laws. It is not the destiny of horses, even if immortal as here, to speak.

115   *I know my Fates*   Achilles had earlier been given a choice of two fates: a long undistinguished life if he returned home or eternal fame and an early death if he remained at Troy. In continuing to fight, Achilles is bidding for glory in the certain knowledge of imminent death. He died by an arrow shot by Paris which pierced his heel.

from *the twenty-first book of the Iliad*

Lines 1–43, 50–95, 103–52, and 231–447 in the complete version. Pope remarks on the fertility of Homer's imagination and invention in contriving a battle of 'an entirely new and surprising kind . . . diversified with a vast variety of imagery and description . . . . There is no book of the poem which has more force of imagination . . . after the description of an inundation there follows a very beautiful contrast in that of the drought: the part of Achilles is admirably sustained' (introductory note).

7   *Saturnia*   Juno, daughter of Saturn, and wife of Jupiter.

21   *tamarisks*   graceful evergreen shrubs.

35   *twelve chosen youths*   Pope notes the 'ferocious and vindictive spirit of his hero' (line 35) even allowing for the different customs of antiquity which, unlike some of his contemporaries, he does not excuse or sentimentalize.

42   *Priam*   the old king of Troy; he had fifty sons.

50   *His well-known face*   Pope comments: 'Homer has a wonderful art and judgement in contriving such incidents as set the characteristic qualities of his

heroes in the highest point of light. There is hardly any in the whole *Iliad* more proper to move pity than this circumstance of Lycaon; or to raise terror, than this view of Achilles. It is also the finest picture of them both imaginable . . . . I believe everyone perceives the beauty of this passage and allows that poetry (at least in Homer) is truly a speaking picture' (line 56).

78   *Thy well-known captive* Pope comments: 'It is impossible for anything to be better imagined than these two speeches; that of Lycaon is moving and compassionate, that of Achilles haughty and dreadful' (line 84).

81   *gifts of Ceres* bread. Ceres is the goddess of agriculture.

102   *what boots it* what use is it?

105   *'And thou, dost thou bewail mortality?'* See *Critical commentary*, p. 226.

108   *The day shall come* Pope comments: 'There is an air of greatness in the conclusion of the speech that strikes me very much: he speaks very unconcernedly of his own death, and upbraids his enemy for asking life so earnestly, a life that was of so much less importance than his own' (line 121).

157   *godhead of the silver bow* Apollo, the archer god.

162   *Hyperion's fall* the sun god. Jove had promised the Trojans success until sunset on the previous day when Hector had killed Patroclus.

172   *Now bursting on his head* Pope comments: 'There is a great beauty in the versification of this whole passage in Homer: some of the verses run hoarse, full and sonorous, like the torrent they describe; others by their broken cadences, and sudden stops, image the difficulty, labour and interruption of the hero's march against it. The fall of the elm, the tearing up of the bank, the rushing of the branches in the water, are all put into such words, that almost every letter corresponds in its sound, and echoes to the sense, of each particular' (line 263). The lines in Pope that

277

imitate these effects in Homer are remarkably
varied.

198   *So when a peasant* Pope comments: 'This changing
of the character is very beautiful: no poet ever knew
like Homer to pass from the vehement and the
nervous to the gentle and agreeable; such transitions
when properly made give a singular pleasure, as
when in music a master passes from the rough to the
tender' (line 289).

228   *By Phoebus' darts* Later literature records that
Achilles was killed by an arrow from the Trojan Paris
which pierced his heel, his one point of vulnerability.
Thetis had dipped her infant son in the waters of Styx
(in Hades) to make him invulnerable but evidently
forgot about the heel by which she held him.

230   *Oh! had I died* Pope comments: 'Nothing is more
agreeable than this wish to the heroic character of
Achilles: glory is his prevailing passion; he grieves
not that he must die, but that he should die unlike a
man of honour' (line 321).

307   *ignipotent* literally, powerful through fire.

THE ODYSSEY OF HOMER

For his translation of the *Odyssey* published in six volumes
between 1723 and 1726, Pope used two collaborators, William
Broome and Elijah Fenton, who between them translated
twelve books which were then revised by Pope. The extract
here is wholly translated by Pope.

from *the tenth book of the Odyssey*

Newly released from his seven-year imprisonment on the
island of the goddess Calypso, Ulysses is shipwrecked as he
makes his way home to Ithaca from which he left nineteen
years earlier to fight in the Trojan War. He lands at Scheria, an
island inhabited by the Phaeacians, and is welcomed by Alcin-
ous, their king. In an after-dinner speech he tells the Phaeacians
the story of his wanderings after the fall of Troy. Lines 157–8,
163–80, 232–581 of the complete version.

278

1	*Aeaean* Circe, a minor deity, lives on Aeaea, the floating isle, a mythical place but identified with one of the Lipari islands north of Sicily.
60	*Pramnian wines* proverbial for their excellence.
99	*falchion* sword.
119	*Hermes* The messenger of the gods, his emblem is his wand.
154	*Moly* a mythical plant.
251	*dishonest* dishonourable.
304	*Cyclops* In the previous book Ulysses had narrated his adventure with the Cyclops, Polyphemus, a one-eyed giant who had imprisoned them in his cave and fed off Ulysses' men until the hero had been able to devise their escape. Eurylochus' understandable view is that Ulysses' curiosity had killed his companions.
370	*realms of darkness* Ulysses' next adventure is to visit Hades where dwell the spirits of the dead to meet the prophet Tiresias who will tell him his future.

from the PREFACE TO THE WORKS OF
SHAKESPEARE

4	*Egyptian strainers* The ancient lives of Homer record that he had travelled in Egypt and so imbibed the wisdom of Egyptian civilization.
60	*Gothic architecture* Compare *An Essay on Criticism* (lines 242–52) where Pope uses the classical figure of the well-proportioned dome (of St Peter's basilica in Rome) to express the effect of beauty.

TO MRS M.B. ON HER BIRTHDAY

Written for Martha Blount, to whom he dedicated the 'Epistle to a lady', for her birthday, 15 June 1723, and subsequently revised.

EPITAPH. ON MRS CORBETT, WHO DIED
OF A CANCER IN HER BREAST

In St Margaret's, Westminster.

EPITAPH. ON MR ELIJAH FENTON.
AT EASTHAMSTEAD IN BERKS, 1730

He had been one of Pope's collaborators in the translation of the *Odyssey*.

EPITAPH. ON MR GAY. IN WESTMINSTER ABBEY, 1732

One of Pope's closest friends.

from AN ESSAY ON MAN

The titles of each epistle were added by Pope to the edition of the poem that appeared in his *Works* of 1735.

from *the first epistle*

The extracts are lines 1–16, 77–90, 189–206, and 267–80.

1   *St John* Henry St John, Viscount Bolingbroke (1678–1751), a leader of the Tories and a political philosopher whose thought influenced Pope. For discussion of this extract, see *Critical commentary*, p. 235.

16   *the ways of God to man* an echo of Milton's intention to 'assert eternal providence and justify the ways of God to men' (*Paradise Lost*, I, 25–6). Pope's variation 'vindicate' sets the tone of the *Essay*.

30   *bubble* The South Sea bubble burst in 1720.

41   *effluvia* streams of invisible particles by which it was believed that odours communicated themselves to the brain.

44   *music of the spheres* the ancient belief that in their rotation the heavenly bodies make music.

60   *seraph* an angel of the highest order, from the Hebrew 'to burn'.

from *the second epistle*

The extracts are lines 1–42 and 53–66.

5	*Sceptic* one who doubts the possibility of any knowledge.
6	*Stoic's pride* The Stoic takes pride in the capacity of human reason to subdue the passions and to rise above the accidents of fortune.
20	*weigh air* These lines (20–3) refer to actual experiments and discoveries being made in Pope's time by Boyle, Halley, Newton, and others.
23	*empyreal sphere* the outermost sphere of the universe, abode of God and of Plato's forms or ideas (the first good, etc.).
25	*his followers* the neo-Platonists.
34	*Newton* Isaac Newton (1642–1729), President of the Royal Society and the greatest natural scientist of his day, famous for his laws of motion and his work on the principle of gravity.

from *the third epistle*

The extracts are lines 7–26, 169–98, and 283–302.

55	*Relumed* made clear or bright again.

from *the fourth epistle*

The extract is from line 373 to the end.

1	*my friend* Bolingbroke: compare the 'Imitation of Horace' addressed to him, line 177.

EPISTLE TO A LADY. OF THE CHARACTERS OF WOMEN

(1735) In volume two of the *Works* of the same year it was grouped with 'To Cobham', 'To Bathurst' and 'To Burlington' as the second of the 'Ethic Epistles, the Second Book'. In the revision of his works that Pope was working on at the end of his life, these became the *Epistles to Several Persons*. In the posthumous edition of Warburton the four epistles are first called *The Moral Essays*. The characters of Chloe, Philomede,

281

and Atossa were added after the first edition. The lady of the title is Pope's long-standing friend Martha Blount.

7	*Arcadia's countess* referring to *The Countesse of Pembrokes Arcadia* (1590) by Sir Philip Sidney. The countess was painted as a shepherdess by J. van der Vaart.
8	*Pastora* a pastoral heroine as above.
9	*Fannia* a Roman name possibly recalling a famous adulteress who saved the life of the Roman general Marius.
10	*Leda* seduced by Zeus in the form of a swan.
12	*Magdalen* Mary Magdalene the repentant sinner.
13	*Cecilia* patron saint of music.
16	*romantic* extravagant.
18	*trick her off* sketch her.
20	*Cynthia* goddess of the moon, associated with change.
21	*Rufa* redhead.
22	*spark* a beau.
23	*Locke* John Locke, the philosopher.
24	*Sappho* the Greek poetess, referring to Lady Mary Wortley Montagu whose dirty clothes were often remarked upon. See 'To Bolingbroke', line 164.
26	*mask* a masked ball, a masquerade.
29	*Silia* The name suggests silence.
31	*nice* punctilious. Calista is the penitent heroine of *The Fair Penitent* by Nicolas Rowe.
32	*Simplicius* a commentator upon the Stoic Epictetus.
37	*Papillia* Latin for butterfly.
43	*nice* discriminating.
45	*Calypso* the nymph who detained Ulysses on his return from Troy.
53	*Narcissa* The name suggests vanity.
54	*wash* a lotion for the hair or the skin.
57	*trim* dress.
63	*Taylor Holy Living and Holy Dying* (1650–1), a popular devotional work by Jeremy Taylor.
64	*citron* brandy flavoured with lemon peel.
	Chartres a notorious rake.

70	*punk* prostitute.
71	*frank* free.
78	*Tall-boy* a handsome young lover in popular comedy.
	Charles a common name for a footman as is Betty for a maid.
79	*Helluo* Latin for glutton.
80	*hautgout* anything with a strong scent.
87	*Flavia* a Roman name, probably an imaginary figure here. *→ by stabbing → by poison.*
92	*Lucretia . . . Rosamonda* two suicides.
101	*Simo* a Roman name, perhaps chosen because it recalls the Latin word *simia* meaning an ape.
110	*ratafie* cherry brandy.
115	*Atossa* usually identified as the Duchess of Buckinghamshire (1682–1743), illegitimate daughter of James II. The name suggests whirlwind.
139–40	*bust . . . temple* memorial monuments.
155	*equal* unvaried or unshaded. Pope keeps up the painting metaphor.
157	*Chloe* identified as Henrietta Howard, Countess of Suffolk (1681–1767). *See Critical Commentary* pp. 237–8.
182	*queen* Caroline, wife of George II.
184	*ball* the orb, symbol of power.
193	*Queensberry* The Duchess of Queensberry was renowned for her beauty.
198	*Mahomet* the name of the Turkish servant of George I.
	Parson Hale Stephen Hales, friend of Pope.
207	*ruling passions* in the 'Epistle to Cobham. Of the knowledge and characters of men', ll. 174ff, Pope had given examples of the ruling passions of men.
210	*sway* domination.
239	*hags* witches; who hold annual meetings called sabbaths.
240	*night* the time for formal visits.
249	*friend* the addressee, Martha Blount.
251	*Ring* the fashionable driving circuit in Hyde Park.
257	*temper* a good disposition, equanimity.

266	*tickets* lottery tickets.
	codille See the note on *The Rape of the Lock*, III, 92.
267	*vapours* See *The Rape of the Lock*, IV, 18.
268	*China* both the kingdom and a vase or teacup.
285	*Phoebus* Apollo, here as god of prophecy.
286	*simple prayer* presumably for beauty and riches.
289	*the generous god* Phoebus, here as god of poetry and the sun by which gold generates in the earth.
292	*good humour* Compare *The Rape of the Lock*, V, 30 and the earlier 'Epistle to Miss Blount with the works of Voiture', l. 61.

EPISTLE TO BURLINGTON

(1731) 'Occasioned by his Publishing Palladio's Designs of the Baths, Arches, Theatres etc. of Ancient Rome' (from the title-page of the first edition). Pope also gave it the half-title 'Of taste' which subsequently became 'Of false taste'. In the *Works* of 1735 it is associated with the 'Epistle to Bathurst' with the common heading 'Of the use of riches'. Although written before the other three, in Pope's arrangement it was the fourth of these ethic epistles or moral essays. Richard Boyle, Earl of Burlington (1695–1753), was largely responsible for introducing the Palladian style into English building, a severer, more classical style than the existing baroque or rococo. Burlington House in Piccadilly and the earl's villa, Chiswick House, were based upon the designs of the Italian architect Andrea Palladio (1518–80).

7	*Topham* the first of a series of collectors mentioned here by Pope. The collection of Hans Sloane became the nucleus of the British Museum.
13	*Virro* perhaps from *virr* – force, energy, vigour; here misdirected.
15	*Sir Visto* A visto is a view seen at the end of an avenue of clipped trees, chosen doubtless to echo Virro. In neither case can any particular individual be identified.
18	*Ripley* Thomas Ripley, architect and protégé of Walpole.

20	*Bubo* George Bubb Doddington completed East-bury in Dorset.

20   *Bubo*   George Bubb Doddington completed East-bury in Dorset.

25   *noble rules*   Burlington had published Palladio's designs in 1730.

33   *pilaster*   a square pillar projecting from a wall.

34   *rustic*   'characterized by a surface artificially roughen-ed or left rough-hewn' (*OED*).

36   *Venetian door*   'a door or window so called from being much practised at Venice by Palladio and others' (Pope). The door probably incorporated panes of glass for Palladio exploited opportunities for light and airiness afforded by the Mediterranean sun. *Starve* in line 38 is used in the sense of starve for cold. Slavish imitators reproduce these features inappro-priately in colder northern climes.

38   *starve*   See previous entry.

39   *brother peer*   Allen, Lord Bathurst, see line 178.

44   *the seven*   referring to the seven liberal arts that were the traditional university subjects.

46   *Jones*   Inigo Jones (1573–1652), the famous English architect and designer working in a classical style.

        Le Nôtre   André Le Nôtre (1613–1700) designer of the formal gardens at Versailles. Pope was an early champion of the informality that came to be associated with the great landscape gardeners of the eighteenth century. He put his ideas into practice in his own garden at Twickenham.

57   *genius*   guardian spirit.

70   *Stowe*   the house and gardens of Richard Temple, Viscount Cobham, in Buckinghamshire.

72   *Nero's terraces*   raised garden walks now in ruins in Rome.

73   *parterre*   'a level space in a garden occupied by an ornamental arrangement of flower-beds of various shapes and sizes' (*OED*).

78   *Dr Clarke*   a philosopher of unorthodox religious views whose bust, put there by Queen Caroline, was out of place in the hermitage in Richmond Park.

80   *quincunx*   five trees, one at the centre of a square formed by the rest.

espaliers trellis-work for the support of trees or shrubs.

94   *Dryads* in Greek myth the spirits that inhabit trees.

98   *alley* a walk in a garden generally bordered with trees or bushes; an avenue.

99   *Timon* like Villario and Sabinus, an imaginary character, though many of the details were drawn from contemporary examples. Pope's enemies identified the villa with Cannons, the country seat of the Duke of Chandos, who had earlier been a patron of Pope. The poet denied this, and it is acknowledged to be a composite portrait.

104   *Brobdignag* land of the giants in Swift's *Gulliver's Travels* (1726).

117   *Grove nods at grove* See *Critical commentary*, p. 239.

118   *platform* a raised terrace.

123   *Amphitrite* a sea goddess.

126   *Nilus' dusty urn* Nilus, the river god, whose urn is incongruously dry instead of being the source of a fountain.

127   *majestic mien* a grand facial expression and demeanour.

136   *Aldus ... Du Sueil* Aldo Manutio (1449–1515), the famous Venetian printer of the classics, and the Abbé du Sueil, an early eighteenth-century binder.

138   *they are wood* refers to the practice of filling the upper shelves of libraries in great houses with painted wooden books.

139   *Locke* John Locke (1632–1704), the recent philosopher of enlightened and tolerant views.

146   *Verrio or Laguerre* Antonio Verrio painted ceilings at Windsor and Hampton Court, and Louis Laguerre at Blenheim.

154   *Tritons* water outlets in the shape of the classical sea god, Triton.

156   *hecatomb* a solemn sacrifice of a hundred beasts.

160   *Sancho's dread doctor* In *Don Quixote* by Cervantes, the hungry Sancho is prevented from eating by a

doctor who sends successive dishes away on the grounds that they are unhealthy, with the tap of his whalebone wand.

162   *God bless the king* the toast at the end of the meal.

176   *Ceres* the Roman goddess of agriculture and fertility.

194   *Vitruvius* M. Vitruvius Pollio of the Augustan age, author of a famous treatise on architecture.

204   *imperial works* a conscious echo of Dryden's translation of a famous passage in Virgil's *Aeneid* in which Rome's imperial destiny is articulated:

> These are imperial arts, and worthy thee.
>
> (VI, 1177)

In Virgil the imperial arts are the arts of government and the establishment of peace; in Pope it is the arts themselves which are to express and impress an imperial destiny of grandeur, refinement, and beauty.

TO DR ARBUTHNOT, 26 JULY 1734 [ON HIS SATIRE]

Sherburne, III, 417. Arbuthnot in his last illness had written: 'I make it my last request that you continue that noble disdain and abhorrence of vice which you seem naturally endued with, but still with a due regard to your safety, and study more to reform than chastise, though the one cannot be effected without the other.'

66   *Boileau* had written at the court of Louis XV.

75   *Nero* reigned from AD 54–68 and Domitian from AD 81–96. Both emperors terrorized their subjects. Aulus Persius (AD 34–62) covertly attacked Nero. Juvenal's dates are uncertain, but it is believed that his sharp satire of Domitian was written after his reign was over. Lucan (AD 39–65), author of an epic poem on Caesar and Pompey called the *Pharsalia*, was required to commit suicide after being implicated in the conspiracy of Piso against Nero.

(1735) Called by Warburton 'The prologue to the satires', it has traditionally been printed before *The Imitations of Horace* in editions of Pope, though this order breaks chronological sequence. It was evidently put together in a hurry because the doctor was dying. Many of its parts had already long been written. In a note to the first edition, Pope says: 'This epistle contains an apology for the author and his writings.'

Advertisement

4   *persons of rank and fortune* Lady Mary Wortley Montagu ('Sappho') in conjunction with Lord Hervey ('Lord Fanny' and here 'Sporus'). For their verses published in 1733 see *Pope: The Critical Heritage*, pp. 269–72.

1   *John* Pope's servant, John Serle.

3   *dog-star* Sirius appears in the season of the late summer heat. The associations are with madness and poetry readings in ancient Rome.

4   *Bedlam* Bethlehem hospital, the madhouse.
         Parnassus the mountain sacred to the Muses.

8   *grot* his grotto running underneath the road connecting the house to his garden.

10   *barge* Twickenham was situated by the Thames.

13   *Mint* a sanctuary for debtors, who were safe from arrest elsewhere too on Sundays.

18   *engross* copy a legal document.

23   *Arthur* Arthur Moore, MP. His son James Moore became a poet and dramatist.

25   *Cornus* a fictitious name derived from the Latin for horns, so meaning cuckold.

29   *drop or nostrum* medicine.

40   *nine years* the advice of Horace in his *Art of Poetry*, line 388.

41   *Drury Lane* associated with prostitutes and starving poets.

43   *Term* The publishing season coincided with the legal terms.

49	*Pitholeon* a foolish and pretentious poet in ancient times.
50	*place* sinecure.
53	*Curll* Edmund Curll (1675–1747), a disreputable and piratical publisher who might commission another libel.
54	*journal* become a party writer in politics or religion.
61	*house* theatre.
62	*Lintot* Bernard Lintot (1675–1736), Pope's publisher.
66	*go snacks* share the profits.
69	*Midas' ears* the ass's ears given to him by Apollo for preferring the music of Pan; he tried to hide his ears but was betrayed by his queen. Pope alludes to the king, the queen, and Walpole here.
85	*Codrus* a bad playwright.
86	*mighty crack* alluding to Addison's infelicitous translation of the Stoic's resolve in Horace's Odes, III, iii:

> Should the whole frame of nature round him
> break . . .
> He unconcerned would hear the mighty crack
> And stand secure amidst a falling world.

97	*Colley* Colley Cibber (1671–1757), poet laureate, later hero of *The Dunciad*.
98	*Henley* a preacher who once addressed a special sermon to butchers.
99	*Bavius* a bad Roman poet.
100	*Philips* Ambrose Philips, writer of pastorals, secretary to the Bishop of Armagh.
101	*Sappho* Pope's name for Lady Mary Wortley Montagu whose attack on Pope (together with Lord Hervey) precipitated the epistle.
103	*twice as tall* Pope was only 4 feet 6 inches.
111	*Grub Street* popular haunt of hack writers.
113	*Letters* that is, in a pirated version.
117	*Ammon's great son* Alexander the Great.
118	*Ovid's nose* Publius Ovidius Naso, the Augustan poet whose last name suggests nose (nasal).

122	*Maro* the familiar name of Virgil, the greatest Roman poet. As no contemporary representations of ancient poets survive the satire is doubly pointed.
128	*numbers* verses.
133	*art and care* Arbuthnot was Pope's doctor.
135	*Granville* George Granville, Lord Lansdowne, to whom Pope dedicated 'Windsor Forest'.
136	*Walsh* an early encourager; see *An Essay on Criticism*, ll. 729–44.
137	*Garth* Sir Samuel Garth, author of the mock-heroic poem *The Dispensary* (1699).
139	*courtly Talbot* Charles Talbot, Duke of Shrewsbury; all these writers had been friends of Dryden and had encouraged the young Pope.
140	*mitred Rochester* Francis Atterbury, Bishop of Rochester.
141	*St John* Henry St John, Viscount Bolingbroke.
146	*Burnets, Oldmixons, and Cookes* all minor writers who had attacked Pope.
149	*Fanny* Lord Hervey, also 'Sporus' at line 305.
151	*Gildon* Charles Gildon, a critic who attacked amongst other things *The Rape of the Lock* for its bawdiness and misuse of machinery.
153	*Dennis* John Dennis attacked *An Essay on Criticism* and *The Rape of the Lock*.
163	*laurel* the crown of true poets.
	ribalds buffoons.
164	*Bentley* Richard Bentley (1662–1742), textual critic: 'slashing' is a comment on his editorial activity. See *Critical commentary*, p. 245.
	Tibbalds Lewis Theobald, pronounced as spelt by Pope, scholar and dramatist, had pointed out the deficiencies of Pope as an editor of Shakespeare, and was made hero of *The Dunciad* for his pains. His own edition of Shakespeare came out in 1734.
177	*casting-weight* ballast.
179	*The bard* Ambrose Philips wrote derivative pastorals and a book of *Persian Tales*.
180	*half-a-crown* the fee of a prostitute.

190   *Tate*   Nahum Tate (1651–1715), a former poet laureate of limited ability.

192   *Addison*   Joseph Addison (1672–1719), the eminent arbiter of taste, a *Spectator* editor and author of *Cato*, a tragedy on the life of the Roman Republican Stoic, for which Pope wrote a prologue. They quarrelled over the translation of Homer when Addison promoted a rival (and inferior) version of the first book of the *Iliad* by a protégé, Thomas Tickell, in 1715. Pope's response was to compose the Atticus portrait finally published here. Atticus was a Roman man of letters, friend of Cicero and later Augustus. Atticus betrays the ideal of the true critic set out in *An Essay on Criticism*.

198   *the Turk*   the Sultan who, it was said, on succeeding to the throne executed his brothers to secure his position.

211   *Templars*   law students.

215   *stood rubric*   Publishers displayed title pages in red letters, 'rubric', on billboards. These posters were called claps.

222   *birthday song*   The poet laureate recited a birthday ode in the presence of the king. The poetry was feeble, and George II did not like poetry anyway.

225   *daggled*   dragged.

228   *orange*   commonly sold at theatres.

230   *Bufo*   Latin for toad, a creature that puffs itself up with air. The portrait is a composite of notable patrons, Bubb Doddington and the Earl of Halifax.
        Castalian state   poetry; Castalian refers to the spring on the twin-peaked mountain, Parnassus, the 'forked hill', sacred to the Muses.

234   *Horace and he*   as a modern Maecenas, the great patron of Virgil and Horace.

236   *Pindar*   famous Greek lyric poet of the fifth century BC. The line ridicules the taste for decorative busts of poets.

244   *in kind*   with verses of his own.

245   *Dryden*   the point being that the patron fails to

recognize the greatest poetic talent. Dryden had money difficulties for much of his life. At his death Halifax proposed to erect a monument to him in Westminister Abbey.

250   *Bavius*   May every bad poet be matched by a bad patron.

256   *Gay*   John Gay, friend of Pope whose epitaph was written by Pope (see p. 151) and whose patron was the Duke of Queensberry.

276   *Balbus*   Viscount Dupplin who had a reputation for small talk. Balbus in Latin means stutterer.

280   *Sir Will*   Sir William Yonge, politician and poetaster, held in general contempt.

299   *dean and silver bell*   a reference to the chapel described in Timon's villa ('Epistle to Burlington', lines 141–50). Gossip wrongly associated the villa with the Duke of Chandos's estate, Cannons.

305   *Sporus*   John, Lord Hervey, favourite courtier of Queen Caroline (here Eve) and Walpole who had quarrelled with Pope and attacked him in pamphlets and poems. A Roman historian records that the Emperor Nero had gone through a marriage ceremony with a eunuch called Sporus. Hervey was noted for the soft beauty of his features.

306   *ass's milk*   prescribed as a tonic for the delicate.

319   *at the ear of Eve*   See *Paradise Lost*, IV, 800, where Satan is 'squat like a toad, close at the ear of Eve' (here Queen Caroline).

       familiar   as in familiar spirit or demon, supposedly in the command of a witch (here the queen).

330   *Rabbins*   rabbis, interpreters of scripture.

331   *cherub's face*   a reference to Hervey's beauty and to the depiction of the tempting serpent with an attractive human face in paintings.

341   *stooped*   as a falcon is said to stoop to its prey. Appropriate here where Pope is talking of his change to satire.

353   *The libelled person*   attacks upon his deformity.

356   *The whisper*   of Lord Hervey, intimate confidant of the court.

363	*Japhet* Japhet Crook, a forger convicted in 1731. He was jailed and had his ears cut off.
365	*Knight of the post* one who lived by giving false evidence for money.
	[*knight*] *of the shire* an MP for one of the counties.
369	*Sappho* Lady Mary Wortley Montagu, a former friend now 'biting' Pope.
371	*distress* The satirist (Pope) wrote a prologue to a play performed for Dennis's benefit in 1733.
373	*Moore* who plagiarized from Pope.
375	*Welsted* Leonard Welsted, a long-standing enemy of Pope. It is not certain which particular lie Pope had in mind.
378	*Budgell* accused Pope of contributing to the *Grub-Street Journal*. He was said to have forged a will in his own favour.
380	*Curlls* the publisher (line 53) and Lord Hervey.
391	*Bestia* a Roman consul who was bribed by the enemy into making a dishonourable peace, perhaps referring here to the Duke of Marlborough.
398	*schoolman's subtle art* scholastic casuistry.
410	*a mother's breath* The lines were written in his mother's last illness. She had in fact died by the time that the epistle was published.
417	*queen* Arbuthnot had been the physician of Queen Anne.

THE FIRST SATIRE OF THE SECOND BOOK OF
HORACE IMITATED

(1733) Printed alongside the Latin original. It is sometimes referred to as 'To Mr Fortescue'. In the 'Advertisement' Pope wrote: 'The occasion of publishing these Imitations was the clamour raised on some of my Epistles. An answer from Horace was both more full, and of more dignity, than any I could have made in my own person.' For further discussion see *Critical commentary*, pp. 240–1.

3	*Peter* Peter Walter, MP, a wealthy moneylender to the aristocracy (see line 40).

4	*Chartres* the notorious rake mentioned in the 'Epistle to a lady' (line 64).
6	*Lord Fanny* Lord Hervey.
8	*Counsel* Fortescue was a Whig lawyer and friend of Walpole (as well as a friend of Pope). A lawyer (Trebatius) had been addressed in the original.
18	*Lettuce and cowslip wine* to induce sleep.
	Probatum est it is proven, a legal phrase.
19	*Celsus* the chief Roman writer on medicine.
20	*Hartshorn* ammonia.
21	*Caesar* ironically referring to George II.
22	*bays* the laureateship, held from 1730–57 by Colley Cibber.
23	*Sir Richard* Blackmore, author of several dull patriotic epics.
24	*Brunswick* George II belonged to the house of Brunswick.
27	*Budgell* author of a celebration of George II whose horse had been shot from under him at the battle of Oudenarde.
31	*Amelia* the third child of George II and Queen Caroline.
34	*twice a year* at new year and on the king's birthday. The king disliked poetry.
38	*quadrille* a fashionable card game slighted in the third moral essay.
42	*Timon . . . Balaam* Timon occurs in the 'Epistle to Burlington' (lines 99ff) and Balaam in the 'Epistle to Bathurst' (lines 399ff); both are composite portraits and therefore represented by Pope here as fictions.
44	*Bond . . . Harpax* a specific target and a general one. Harpax means robber.
46	*Scarsdale . . . Darty* a known drunkard and an epicure.
47	*Ridotta* a type of society lady, derived from the Italian for a musical assembly.
49	*F—* probably Stephen Fox, an MP.
	Hockley-hole a beargarden.
52	*Shippen* a leading Jacobite MP admired for his honourable loyalty to his cause.

> *Montaigne* the French essayist (1553–92) noted like
> Horace for candour and self-revelation.

66   *Erasmus* See note to *An Essay on Criticism*, line 693.

71   *hectors* bullies.

72   *supercargoes* officers concerned with the trade of
shipping vessels (often corrupt).
directors The directors of the South Sea Company,
for example, had been guilty of fraud.

73   *Save but our Army* a satirical thrust against the
maintenance of a standing army in time of peace.

75   *Fleury* the French cardinal whose policy, like
Walpole's, was peace.

81   *Delia* Mary Howard, Countess of Delorain, who
was supposed to have poisoned a rival in love.

82   *Page* Sir Francis Page, a hard judge.

83   *Sappho* Lady Mary Wortley Montagu. This couplet
provoked the attack which in turn led to the 'Epistle
to Dr Arbuthnot'.

88   *Pug* a Cornish boxer.

98   *whitened wall* in Bedlam, for example.

99   *the Mint* a sanctuary for debtors.

100   *Lee or Budgell* both poets who were insane for a
time.

103   *Plums* large sums of money.

104   *club their testers* pool their sixpences.

108   *star* the decoration for the knight of the garter.

116   *unpensioned* having no income from the state,
therefore independent.

127   *St John* Henry St John, Viscount Bolingbroke. See
the first note on the next poem.

129   *Iberian lines* the Earl of Peterborough who captured
Barcelona and Valencia in 1705–6.

130   *quincunx* five trees, one at the centre of a square
formed by the rest.

145   *Richard* Richard III in whose reign a poet was
executed for calling the king a hog.

153   *Sir Robert* Walpole, the prime minister, to whom
Pope was opposed and who took a keen interest in all
writing with any political content. The passage is
finely double-edged. The king *might* read (but

disliked poetry), bishops might write if they were honest and active in the campaign against vice, and Sir Robert would approve because he could not afford to ignore the truth.

THE FIRST EPISTLE OF THE FIRST BOOK OF HORACE IMITATED

(1738) Printed alongside the Latin original. Sometimes referred to as 'To Bolingbroke'. See *Critical commentary*, pp. 241–2.

1	*St John* Henry St John, Viscount Bolingbroke, who had been exiled in 1714 for support of the Jacobite cause. He returned to England with a pardon in 1723, and organized the Tory opposition to Walpole. He was a friend and encourager of Pope who praises him at the close of *An Essay on Man* (above, p. 157). Horace had addressed the original to Maecenas.
16	*Lord Mayor's horse* a slow horse for processions, appropriately contrasting to the winged Pegasus.
26	*Montaigne . . . Locke* the one an informal, the other a systematic, thinker.
27	*patriot* The opponents of Walpole called themselves patriots.
29	*Lyttelton* George Lyttelton, friend of Pope and outspoken opponent of Walpole.
31	*Aristippus* a Greek philosopher who held that pleasure is the chief good.
31	*St Paul* 'I am made all things to all men', I Corinthians IX, 22, and 'Let your moderation be known unto all men', Philippians IV, 5.
50	*lynx* Pope was near-sighted.
51	*Mead and Cheselden* two doctors who attended Pope.
60	*arrant'st puppy* most arrogant young man.
62	*punk* prostitute.
63	*bear* boorish person.
69	*either India* the West or the East Indies.
82	*low . . . high* low and high church preach the same doctrine.

83	*quill* the pen of a city clerk.
84	*notches sticks* refers to the method of notching tally sticks still used in the treasury and not yet replaced by written accounts.
85	*Barnard* MP for the City of London, an opponent of Walpole.
86	*wants* lacks.
88	*Bug* Henry de Grey, Duke of Kent, so called from his smell. The harness is the order of the garter.
	Dorimant a young fop in Etherege's *Man of Mode*.
89	*cit* a city fellow, often used pejoratively.
90	*D—l* not known, but evidently a worthless aristocrat in contrast to the worthy Barnard.
95	*screen* calling Walpole to mind because he had refused to hold a public enquiry into the directors of the South Sea Company.
100	*Cressy . . . Poitiers* two English victories in France in the fourteenth century.
103	*grace* gracefully or by the grace of God.
105	*eunuchs* Italian castrati who sang in opera.
112	*S—z* Augustus Schutz; keeper of the privy purse to George II.
114	*Reynard* the fox of folk-tale addressing the lion.
128	*farm the poor-box* embezzle donations made for the poor.
	the pews the rents taken for pews in church.
129	*assemblies* public ballrooms.
	stews brothels.
130	*bucks* young men seeking to inherit from childless couples.
133	*hundreds* of pounds.
138	*Sir Job* there is no known attribution for this figure.
148	*Flavio* an Italianate name perhaps chosen to suggest the Latin lover.
	stocking the bride threw her stockings among the wedding guests. Anyone hit was supposedly the next in line for marriage.
152	*Proteus* could transform himself into any shape he wished, hence Protean.

<dl>
<dd>Merlin is the wizard at the court of King Arthur.</dd>
</dl>

155   *news* newspaper.

156   *japanner* shoe polisher.

158   *chaise and one* a light carriage drawn by a single horse.

159   *sculler* oarsman.

162   *band* neckband.

164   *linen worthy Lady Mary* Lady Mary Wortley Montagu was notoriously slovenly.

165   *prelate's lawn* fine linen worn by bishops contrasted with the hair shirt of the penitent.

173   *Chancery* to the law courts (Chancery) for legal powers to act for a madman.

         Hale a doctor at Bedlam.

177   *guide, philosopher, and friend* Compare *An Essay on Man*, IV, 390.

181   *Great without title* Bolingbroke's name was erased from the roll of peers and he lost his estates in 1715.

184   *the Tower* He avoided the Tower, the place of punishment for treachery, by fleeing into exile. His fellow Tory, Oxford, was imprisoned there.

THE FIRST ODE OF THE FOURTH BOOK OF HORACE

['To Venus'] (1737)

6   *sober fifty* Pope was 49 when the poem was published.

10   *Murray* William Murray, later Lord Chief Justice, was 32 at the time. He lived at 5 King's Bench Walk, Temple, in London, on the banks of the Thames.

20   *Chloe* a classical name much used in romantic contexts.

47   *Cynthia* the moon. Diana the moon goddess was born on Mt Cynthus on the island of Delos.

THE DUNCIAD

The Dunciad was first published anonymously in 1728. Its hero was Lewis Theobald who had published in 1726 *Shakespeare*

Restored: or a Specimen of the Many Errors as well Committed as Unamended by Mr Pope in his late Edition of this Poet. Many of the other duncts had previously attacked Pope in print on poetical, religious, or moral grounds. An enlarged edition, still anonymous (Pope did not publicly acknowledge authorship until the poem was included in his *Works* of 1735) with notes partly explanatory and partly burlesque in mockery of modern pedantry (the extent to which these were a collaborative effort or Pope's own is uncertain), was published in 1729 with the joke title *The Dunciad Variorum*, in parody of variorum editions of established classics with notes by various editors and commentators. The original design entailed three books. In the first the hero is chosen by Dullness and crowned king in succession to a previous favourite recently dead, thus ensuring the continuity of her reign. There is a parodic inversion here, initiated by Dryden in *MacFlecknoe*, of the idea of cultural transmission associated with Virgil's *Aeneid*, a poem in which civilization is to be transferred through the chosen agent of fate (Aeneas) from Troy to Rome. In the second, games are held in honour of the goddess (in parody of the heroic games in honour of dead heroes in the *Iliad* and the *Aeneid*). In the third, the hero is transported in a vision to Elysium (paradise in the classical underworld) where the spirit of his predecessor shows him past and future triumphs of Dullness in which he will play a leading part (in parody of the vision of the glorious Roman future given to Aeneas in the underworld by the spirit of his father Anchises). In 1742 *The New Dunciad: As it was found in 1741* contains a fourth book in which the prophecies of the third are fulfilled. Pope then revised the poem replacing Theobald with a new hero, Colley Cibber, the poet laureate, in *The Dunciad in Four Books* of 1743. Extensive new notes were provided by a collaborator. The present selection is taken from the 1743 edition.

from *Book the First*

Lines 1–18, 29–84, 107–30, 145–8, 155–66, 173–80, 187–90, 225–30, 243–8, 257–66, 273–8, 289–94, 299–304 and 311–20. The dates of the original notes are given in brackets.

2   *Smithfield* 'Smithfield is the place where Bartho-
lomew Fair was kept, whose shows, machines and
dramatical entertainments formerly agreeable only to
the taste of the rabble were by the hero of this poem
and by others of equal genius brought to the threatres
of Covent Garden, Lincolns-inn-Fields and the Hay-
Market to be the reigning pleasures of the court and
town' (1729). 'The restoration of the reign of Chaos
and Night by the ministry of Dullness their daughter,
in the removal of her imperial seat from the city to
the polite world, as the action of the *Aeneid* is the
restoration of the empire of Troy by the removal of
the race from thence to Latium': Martinus Scriblerus,
'Of the poem' (an introductory essay, 1729). For
Martinus Scriblerus, see *Introduction*, p. 2.

10   *Pallas* Minerva, the goddess of wisdom, born from
the head of Jupiter who is called the Thunderer from
the thunderbolt, an emblem of his power.

20   *Monro* physician to Bethlehem hospital for the
insane, Bedlam.

21   *his famed father's hand* 'Mr Caius Gabriel Cibber,
father of the poet laureate. The two statues of the
lunatics over the gates of Bedlam hospital were done
by him and (as the son justly says of them) no ill
monuments to his fame as an artist' (1743).

27   *Proteus* in ancient myth a minor deity who could
change into whatever shape he pleased.

30   *Curll's chaste press* ironic; the bookseller was fined
for publishing obscene books. Edmund Curll and
Bernard Lintot were the leading publishers of Pope's
time, Curll being the more unscrupulous of the two.
He published a pirated edition of Pope's letters. They
feature prominently in the next book.
Lintot's rubric post Lintot was so fond of red-letter
title pages to the books he printed that the show-
boards and posts before his door were generally
bedaubed with them.

31   *Tyburn* 'It is an ancient custom for the malefactors
to sing a psalm at their execution at Tyburn; and no

less customary to print elegies on their deaths at the same time or before' (1729).

32   *merc'ries*   mercuries (Mercury was the messenger of the gods), newspapers.

33   *Sepulchral lies*   flattering epitaphs.

34   *new-year odes*   'Made by the poet laureate for the time being, to be sung at court on every New Year's day, the words of which are happily drowned in the voices and instruments. The New Year Odes of the hero of this work were of a cast distinguished from all that preceded him and made a conspicuous part of his character as a writer which doubtless induced our author to mention them here so particularly' (1743).
     Grub Street   an actual place from which emanated the *Grub-Street Journal*.

36   *Four guardian virtues*   The four cardinal virtues of the ancient world were fortitude, temperance, prudence, and justice.

47   *genial Jacob*   Jacob Tonson, a leading publisher. The proceedings of the third day of a play's run were usually given to the author.

53   *clenches*   puns.

60   *farce and epic*   violation of the decorum of genre.

64   *Zembla . . . Barca*   desert regions of cold and heat respectively. 'These six verses represent the incongruities in the descriptions of poets who heap together all glittering and gaudy images though incompatible in one season or in one scene' (1729).

69   *cloud-compelling*   an epithet of Jupiter in Homer.

76   *Bays*   leaves or sprigs of the bay or laurel tree woven into a garland to reward the poet, applied here to Cibber, the poet laureate. 'It is hoped that the poet hath done full justice to his hero's character which it were a great mistake to imagine was wholly sunk in stupidity: he is allowed to have supported it with a wonderful mixture of vivacity' (1743).

78   *act*   Cibber acted and was praised for his credibility in the part of a coxcomb (fool).

94   *sooterkin*   'an imaginary kind of afterbirth formerly

attributed to Dutch women; applied to a literary composition, of a supplementary or imperfect character' (*OED*).

100   *Settle, Banks, and Broome* Settle was a former laureate, the others were minor playwrights of time past.

101   *solid learning*   dull heavy books of a drab age.

104   *tapers and defrauded pies* the only other use such volumes might still serve.

106   *hecatomb*   a sacrifice.

        unsullied   that is, unreal.

110   *birthday ode*   the laureate was expected to do his duty on royal birthdays.

134   *seven-fold face*   suggesting either the sevenfold shield of epic (impenetrability) or the mobility of the actor.

140   *Thulé*   'an unfinished poem of that name of which one sheet was printed fifteen years ago by A. Ph. [Ambrose Philips] a northern author. It is an usual method of putting out a fire to cast wet sheets upon it. Some critics have been of the opinion that this sheet was of the nature of the *Asbestos* which cannot be consumed by fire: but I rather think it only an allegorical allusion to the coldness and heaviness of the writing' (1729).

156   *Heideggre*   a strange bird from Switzerland.

159   *Eusden*   a former laureate who died in 1730, Cibber's predecessor and equally dull.

        sack   wine that was part of the laureate's fee.

166   *ivy*   In ancient times the ivy crown is frequently associated with poets.

175   *chapel-royal*   'the voices and instruments used in the service of the chapel royal being also employed in the performance of the birthday and new year odes' (1743).

from *Book the Second*

Lines 17–120.

5	*bags*	bag wigs in which the hair was enclosed as in an ornamental bag.
6	*crape*	less expensive than silk.
	garters	suggesting knights of the garter.
8	*hacks*	hackney carriages, a common mode of transport.
13	*Anne*	Queen Anne in whose reign the church of St Mary Le Strand originated.
14	*the saints of Drury Lane*	irony; Drury Lane was frequented by prostitutes.
15	*stationers*	booksellers.
34	*More*	an insubstantial poet. The name suggests the Greek for folly.
47	*As when a dab-chick*	a grotesque version of a famous passage in Milton's *Paradise Lost* (II, 947–50) describing Satan's progress through Chaos:

> ... so eagerly the fiend
> O'er bog, o'er steep, through strait, rough, dense, or rare,
> With head, hands, wings, or feet, pursues his way,
> And swims, or sinks, or wades, or creeps, or flies.

54	*Corinna*	the name that the Roman love poet Ovid gave to his mistress.
57	*Here fortuned Curll to slide*	a grotesque parody of the heroic foot-race in which Ajax slips upon dung in the *Iliad* and Nisus (in Virgil's adaptation of Homer) slips on the blood and filth left behind from a sacrifice in the *Aeneid*.
59	*obscene with filth*	'Though this incident may seem too low and base for the dignity of an epic poem, the learned very well know it to be but a copy of Homer and Virgil; the very words ὄνθος [dung] and fimus [filth] are used by them, though our poet (in compliance with modern nicety) has remarkably enriched and coloured his language as well as raised his versification in these two episodes .... If we

consider that the exercises of his authors could with justice be no higher than *tickling, chattering, braying,* or *diving,* it was no easy matter to invent such games as were proportioned to the meaner degree of book-sellers. In Homer and Virgil, Ajax and Nisus, the persons drawn in this plight are heroes, whereas here they are such with whom it had been great impropriety to have joined any but vile ideas .... Nevertheless I have often heard our author own that this part of the poem was (as frequently happens) what cost him most trouble and pleased him least, but that he hoped 'twas excusable since levelled at such as understand no delicate satire' (1729).

62   *caitiff vaticide*   base murderer of poets.
66   *the Pope's arms*   the Bible is Curll's sign, the cross keys, as in the papal crown, Lintot's.
68   *ambrosia*   the solid food of the gods.
76   *ichor*   the blood of the gods.
77   *Cloacina*   the purifier, the Roman goddess of the common shores.
100   *Evans, Young, and Swift*   wits not dunces.

from *Book the Fourth*

Lines 1–30, 71–90, 119–26, 135–60, 189–92, 203–14, 229–44, 398–438, 565–70, 577–84 and 605–end.

9   *the dog-star*   See the 'Epistle to Dr Arbuthnot', line 3.
13   *the seed of Chaos*   Dullness.
14   *extinguish light*   the reverse of the action of God in 'Let there be light'. Dullness undoes creation.
15   *venal*   mercenary.
16   *Saturnian days of lead and gold*   In mythology the god Saturn is associated with the golden age of peace, innocence, and virtue. That age gave way to the silver, then to the bronze, and finally to the iron. Here a further degeneration is envisaged to a fifth age of lead (Saturn in alchemy is the technical term for lead) which will bring an ironic reversion to an age of

gold (the aspiration of the poets) in which mercenary values are supreme. A couplet of pregnant wit.

18   *all below revealed* Compare the ancient adage 'The higher you climb, the more you show your arse' (1743).

24   *Rhetoric* eloquence, much prized by Renaissance humanists aspiring to the Ciceronian ideal of the good man skilled in speaking.

28   *Chicane* fine linen here associated with a bishop's sleeve indicating corruption in the Church and state.

30   *Page* a hanging judge in Pope's day.

48   *in toupee* a fashionable dunce wearing the latest artificial hairpiece.

51   *revive the wits* republish distinguished writers but only after they have been bowdlerized.

53   *Medea* the sorceress who rejuvenated her father-in-law Aeson by boiling him in a cauldron of herbs.

63   *a spectre* Richard Busby, headmaster of Westminster School in the mid-seventeenth century.

64   *the wand* the cane, also suggested in 'birchen'.

65   *beavered* The beaver is a hat.

68   *Winton* Winchester school.

75   *Samian letter* the letter Y, used by Pythagoras of Samos as an emblem of the different roads of virtue and vice.

88   *Aristotle's friends* those who clung to Aristotle's natural philosophy ignoring the advances of Descartes and Newton.

89   *Aristarch* Aristarchus was the most famous textual critic of antiquity who had fearlessly emended the text of Homer. Under his name Pope is satirizing the foremost classical textual critic of his day, Richard Bentley, the Master of Trinity College, Cambridge. See *Critical commentary* pp. 245–6.

92   *Walker* the Vice-Master of Trinity and supporter of Bentley in his battle with the other Fellows of the college.

97   *scholiast* in antiquity one who writes marginal notes

around the manuscript text of an author, hence an annotator.

98   *Horace*   Bentley's edition of Horace was published in 1711 and his Milton in 1732. He was over-rationalistic in his approach to poetry. See *Critical commentary*, p. 246.

103   *Gellius or Stobaeus*   minor ancient grammarians.

109   *Kuster, Burman, Wasse*   three contemporary classical scholars in the mould of Bentley whose labours on the minutiae of the text were vitiated by a lack of any real poetical sense.

115   *house*   a college of Oxford or Cambridge.

116   *νοῦς*   the Greek word for mind or understanding.

127   *paper ruff*   used to protect prize blooms.

129   *Caroline*   'It is a compliment which the florists usually pay to princes and great persons to give their names to the most curious flowers of their raising: some have been very jealous of vindicating this honour but none more than that ambitious gardener at Hammersmith, who caused his favourite to be painted on his sign with this inscription: *This is My Queen Caroline*' (1743). Caroline, George II's queen.

150   *beauteous bird*   the butterfly.

163   *vertù*   excellence in the sense of virtue or perhaps in the collection of art objects as in virtuoso.

164   *F.R.S.*   Fellow of the Royal Society.

166   *Isis and Cam*   the rivers of Oxford and Cambridge.

176   *St James's*   the royal chapel of St James's Palace.
       Gilbert   later Archbishop of York.

177   *the hall*   Westminster Hall, the seat of government.

182   *Palinurus*   the helmsman of Aeneas who fell asleep and fell from his ship in the *Aeneid*. The reference is to Walpole.

192   *quiet, and entrance*   verbs here.

203   *Medea*   the powerful witch in ancient myth.

205   *Argus*   the monster with a hundred eyes slain by Hermes (Mercury).

212   *second cause*   nature; the first cause is God. The following lines suggest the abuses of human reason in confounding the sciences and rationalizing religion.